BIOLOGICAL RHYTHMS AND MENTAL DISORDERS

BIOLOGICAL RHYTHMS AND MENTAL DISORDERS

Edited by
DAVID J. KUPFER, M.D.
Western Psychiatric Institute and Clinic;
School of Medicine, University of Pittsburgh

TIMOTHY H. MONK, Ph.D.
Western Psychiatric Institute and Clinic;
School of Medicine, University of Pittsburgh

JACK D. BARCHAS, M.D.
Nancy Pritzker Laboratory of Behavioral Neurochemistry;
School of Medicine, Stanford University

THE GUILFORD PRESS
New York   London

© 1988 The Guilford Press

A Division of Guilford Publications, Inc.

72 Spring Street, New York, NY 10012

Printed in the United States of America

Last digit is print number: 9 8 7 6 5 4 3 2 1

Library of Congress Cataloging-in-Publication Data

Biological rhythms and mental disorders / editors, David J. Kupfer,
   Timothy H. Monk, Jack D. Barchas.
     p.   cm.
     Emanated from a conference held in Taos, N.M., March 30 – Apr. 2,
 1983, sponsored by the MacArthur Foundation Mental Health Research Network I:
 The Psychobiology of Depression and Other Affective Disorders.
    Includes bibliographies and index.
    ISBN 0-89862-746-X
     1. Depression, Mental—Pathophysiology—Congresses.   2. Affective
disorders—Psychopathology—Congresses.   3. Sleep disorders—
Congresses.   4. Biological rhythms—Congresses.   I. Kupfer, David
J., 1941 –   .   II. Monk, Timothy H., 1950 –   .   III. Barchas, Jack D., 1935 –
IV. MacArthur Foundation Mental Health Research Network I: The Psychobiology of
Depression and Other Affective Disorders.
    [DNLM: 1. Circadian Rhythm—congresses.   2. Depressive Disorders—
physiology—congresses.   3. Sleep—physiology—congresses.
4. Sleep Disorders—congresses.   WM 171 B6148 1983]
RC537.B496   1988
616.85′27071—dc19
DNLM/DLC
for Library of Congress   88-24598
                                    CIP

DEDICATION

This collection is special in that it contains chapters from two leading, well-respected chronobiologists who sadly are no longer with us. The untimely deaths of Gerard A. Groos and Dorothy T. Krieger have robbed the discipline of fine and gifted scientists.

Dr. Groos was a young scientist from the Netherlands who was working at the National Institute of Mental Health at the time that he was involved with the work that is included in this volume. A person of intelligence and fundamental decency who also was thoughtful and gentle, Dr. Groos was demonstrating a striking ability to see the totality of a research field and to relate basic research to clinical concerns.

Dr. Krieger was one of America's foremost research neuroendo-crinologists whose loss has resulted in a real void, for she had the capacity to be highly integrative while also being rigorous. Dr. Krieger's spark, intelligence, enjoyment of ideas, curiosity, willingness to learn and consider new approaches as well as her pleasure in the accomplishments of young people were a joy to those who knew her.

PREFACE

The purpose of this volume is to examine the emerging information that biological rhythms and sleep are related to behavioral processes. The volume developed from efforts of the MacArthur Foundation Network on the Psychobiology of Affective Disorders, which is concerned with consideration of a variety of biological and psychosocial approaches to the study of affective disorders. In that context, a series of conferences have been sponsored by the Network. Participants have included members of the Network, as well as scientists and scholars from various disciplines relevant to the concerns of the program. Since a significant portion of the information has not been presented elsewhere, or in the unified context of a monograph, preparation of the papers from the conference dealing with circadian rhythms was undertaken as it became clear that the materials could be helpful to the broader field of investigators.

Specific disturbances in ultradian and circadian rhythm are present in affective disorders. The aim of the conference from which the volume emanated was to allow each participant to bring his or her own personal views dealing with sleep and biological rhythms to the fore, discussing the particular issues that he or she held to be important, and relating those specific issues to the field of affective disorders. To help achieve this end, an effort was deliberately made to avoid the temptation to "carve up" the area between the participants, or to limit contributions in order to avoid overlap.

The structure that has been imposed on this volume is an arbitrary one, seeking only to find the order with which the chapters fit most easily together. The volume starts with consideration of issues related to sleep and then moves toward consideration of biological rhythms. Many of the sleep chapters have much to say about biological (particularly circadian) rhythms; many of the "biological rhythm" chapters have much to say about sleep.

The first four chapters use sleep as a central theme. The first two (Kupfer, et al. and Gillin, et al.) are primarily concerned with the relationship between certain stages of sleep — most notably Rapid Eye Movement (REM) and Slow Wave Sleep (SWS) — and the psychiatric disorder of depression. The findings discussed in these two chapters have demonstrated biological correlates for depression. Since these sleep parameters are inherently governed by the biological clock, attention is also paid to circadian rhythms, thus overlapping with certain of the later chapters.

The third and fourth chapters are concerned with mathematical models of the sleep process. Borbély's model is concerned with the timing of sleep, and its relation to other facets of the circadian system. Presented here is not only the model itself (which is rapidly becoming the accepted model of the human circadian system) but also an exposition of how it might be used to predict the sleep of the depressed. The chapter by McCarley and Massaquoi comprises a mathematically-based extension of the now famous McCarley and Hobson model of REM sleep which was based on the discharge activity of two populations of neurons. This model helps us by formalizing and quantifying the processes by which REM sleep abnormalities in depression might occur.

The next group of chapters are concerned with biological rhythms and their relation to depression. Groos offers an overview which provides many of the frameworks and questions with which this volume is concerned. The chapter describes core concepts and then relates them to clinical issues. The focus of Krieger deals with the pituitary adrenal axis, known to be altered by circadian processes, and observations that abnormalities of that axis have been described in some patients with severe endogenous depression.

Wehr considers circadian abnormalities that are associated with depression, a topic of intense research. This relationship between circadian dysfunction and depression clearly helps in our understanding of the sleep abnormalities described earlier in the volume and are one of the foundations of this monograph.

The discovery of the influence of bright light on the secretion of melatonin in the human has set the tone for much of the human circadian rhythms research conducted during this decade. In particular, attention has switched from the social time cues or zeitgebers, to the physical zeitgeber of daylight and darkness, and identification of "Seasonal Affective Disorder" which appears to respond positively to bright light therapy. These findings are discussed in the chapter by Lewy and Sack, which is followed by a chapter by Zucker giving detail concerning circannual rhythms, their relation to mood disorders and the chronobiology of animal circannual rhythms that may help in our understanding of them.

The final chapter is a detailed exposition by Wever of the vast wealth of findings that he and Aschoff have made in their human time isolation facility at Erling–Andechs over the last three decades. Those findings comprise the basic foundation on which our understanding of the human circadian system is grounded, and which will be equally crucial in determining how that system is disordered in the presence of depression.

David J. Kupfer
Timothy H. Monk
Jack D. Barchas

ACKNOWLEDGMENTS

This volume, exploring aspects of biological rhythms in relation to severe mental illness, is one of a series from the Psychobiology of Depression Network of the John D. and Catherine T. MacArthur Foundation. We are most appreciative for the support of the Foundation and its encouragement.

A number of individuals aided in the preparation of this volume. Edna Dorles served as Administrative Assistant for the Network in its earliest phases and was helpful in every aspect of the scholarly work of the Network, including the organization of the conference that led to this volume and the efforts that followed it. B.J. Panfil Kazmierczak was of enormous help in the preparation of the manuscript and its production; she made a substantial effort to produce a volume that was carefully edited and checked. Several persons, including Drs. James H. Eberwine, Laurence H. Tecott, Ines Zangger and Jacques F. Maddaluno helped with specific aspects, such as technical problems, corrections and translations. The index was graciously prepared by Frances M. Monk, and verified by Patricia Pierce Erickson. Finally, we would like to thank Seymour Weingarten and the staff of Guilford Press for their patience, thoughtfulness and consideration.

CONTRIBUTORS

Jack D. Barchas, M.D., Nancy Friend Pritzker Professor of Psychiatry and Behavioral Sciences and Director, Nancy Pritzker Laboratory of Behavioral Neurochemistry, Department of Psychiatry and Behavioral Sciences, School of Medicine, Stanford University

Alexander A. Borbély, M.D., Professor of Pharmacology, Pharmakologisches Institüt der Universitat Zürich, Switzerland

Ellen Frank, Ph.D., Assistant Professor of Psychiatry and Psychology, Western Psychiatric Institute and Clinic, Department of Psychiatry, School of Medicine, University of Pittsburgh

J. Christian Gillin, M.D., Professor of Psychiatry, Department of Psychiatry, School of Medicine, University of California, San Diego

Gerard A. Groos, M.D., Zoölogisch Laboratorium, Biologisch Centrum, Subfaculteit Biologie, Rijksuniversiteit Groningen, The Netherlands

David B. Jarrett, M.D., Ph.D., Assistant Professor of Psychiatry and Psychology, Western Psychiatric Institute and Clinic, Department of Psychiatry, School of Medicine, University of Pittsburgh

Dorothy T. Krieger, M.D., D.Sc., Division of Endocrinology, Department of Medicine, Mount Sinai Medical Center, New York City

David J. Kupfer, M.D., Professor and Chairman, Department of Psychiatry and Director of Research, Western Psychiatric Institute and Clinic, School of Medicine, University of Pittsburgh

Alfred J. Lewy, M.D., Ph.D., Professor of Psychiatry and Ophthalmology, Assistant Professor of Pharmacology, and Director, Sleep and Mood Disorders Laboratory, School of Medicine, University of Oregon

Steven C. Massaquoi, M.D., Neuroscience Laboratory, Department of Psychiatry, Harvard University School of Medicine

Robert W. McCarley, M.D., Neuroscience Laboratory, Department of Psychiatry, Harvard University School of Medicine

Wallace B. Mendelson, M.D., Unit on Sleep Studies, Biological Psychiatry Branch and Adult Psychiatry Branch, Intramural Research Program, National Institute of Mental Health

Timothy H. Monk, Ph.D., Associate Professor of Psychiatry, Department of Psychiatry, and Director, Human Chronobiology Research Program, Western Psychiatric Institute and Clinic, School of Medicine, University of Pittsburgh

Charles F. Reynolds III, M.D., Associate Professor of Psychiatry and Neurology, Western Psychiatric Institute and Clinic, Department of Psychiatry, School of Medicine, University of Pittsburgh

Robert L. Sack, M.D., Professor of Psychiatry, and Clinical Director, Sleep and Mood Disorders Laboratory, School of Medicine, University of Oregon

Michael E. Thase, M.D., Assistant Professor of Psychiatry, Western Psychiatric Institute and Clinic, Department of Psychiatry, School of Medicine, University of Pittsburgh

Thomas A. Wehr, M.D., Chief, Clinical Psychobiology Branch, Intramural Research Program, National Institute of Mental Health

Rütger A. Wever, M.D., Max–Planck–Institut für Psychiatrie Klinik, Außenstelle Andechs, Arbeitsgruppe Chronobiologie, West Germany

Irving Zucker, Ph.D., Professor, Department of Psychology, University of California, Berkeley

CONTENTS

BIOLOGICAL RHYTHMS AND MENTAL DISORDERS

1

INTERRELATIONSHIP OF ELECTROENCEPHALOGRAPHIC SLEEP CHRONOBIOLOGY AND DEPRESSION

David J. Kupfer
Ellen Frank
David B. Jarrett
Charles F. Reynolds III
Michael E. Thase

INTRODUCTION

Current knowledge of affective disorders leads to the conclusion that these disorders entail dysfunction in many systems and do not simply reflect alterations in mood. Since many of the core symptoms of affective disorder represent changes in regulatory systems, investigators have frequently searched for markers of vulnerability and explored the interdependencies among aspects of biological and psychological functioning. Such an approach has yielded promising findings with regard to electroencephalographic (EEG) sleep abnormalities.

In this chapter we intend to review the following areas with the overall intent of placing the data base available on sleep and affective disorders within the overall context of understanding ultradian, circadian, and sleep mechanisms in depression. First, the major methodological advances will be briefly discussed. After this methodological introduction, the key sleep characteristics in depression will be described. A brief overview of possible neurochemical sleep relationships in depression is followed by a more detailed recent data set developed to test one of the models proposed for sleep regulation (Borbély's Process S model; Borbély, 1987). Since the emphasis is on non–rapid–eye–movement (NREM) changes in depression, potential relationship with sleep–related hormones is outlined.

METHODOLOGICAL ADVANCES

From studies performed in sleep research settings in the 1970s and early 1980s, five major methodological advances have emerged, as shown in Table 1 below.

First, increased diagnostic precision, through the introduction of the Research Diagnostic Criteria (RDC) and the development of more operational criteria in all diagnostic categories (e.g., DSM-III and DSM-III R), particularly in affective disorders, has made it easier to select more homogeneous patient groups for research studies (Spitzer, Endicott and Robins, 1978).

Second, the importance of ruling out medical/neurological syndromes prior to the investigation of primary depression has become increasingly recognized. Indeed, several investigators have reported differences in the sleep of patients with primary depression versus depression associated with medical disease (e.g., Foster, et al., 1976; King, et al., 1981). In the latter, rate of production of REMs is typically diminished.

TABLE 1

METHODOLOGICAL ISSUES

---

1. Diagnostic precision (homogeneous samples).

2. Distinction of primary depression from medical/ depressive syndromes.

3. Length of psychotropic drug-free interval.

4. Entrainment and adaptation effects.

5. Computer-assisted analysis of phasic phenomena [e.g., rapid eye movements (REMs) and delta activity] and their temporal distribution.

Third, although considerable controversy exists whether patients on any type of psychotropic medication can be studied and, if not, how long the drug-free period needs to be, an accepted compromise position has been the use of a two-week, drug-free period. This two-week period has been the usual practice despite the fact that some critics have argued that a minimum six-week, drug-free state is necessary to deal with the metabolism and excretion of psychotropic drugs administered to patients prior to sleep studies. A psychotropic drug-free interval of less than six weeks could theoretically confound the results with residual drug-withdrawal phenomena, thereby masking the basic phenomena related to depressive psychopathology. However, studies in which a placebo was administered and all-night sleep EEG studies were performed nightly over a period of six weeks demonstrated that hospitalized patients with no significant clinical change showed stable sleep findings over the six-week period (Coble, et al., 1979) further supporting the contention that two weeks is a reasonable washout period.

Fourth, recent studies have dealt with the issue of entrainment and novelty in a more sophisticated manner. Many studies have actually been conducted in the hospital room where patients have resided for several weeks before the investigation and with strict attention to clock time. These procedures have led to a considerable degree of entrainment; thus, issues raised in the early 1970s on adaptation and the stress of the first period of studies have been resolved to some extent. Nevertheless, even though adaptation has been made easier, because current approaches often include simultaneous measurement of several variables (such as the conduct of sleep, neuroendocrine, temperature, and biochemical studies), investigators have had to remain sensitive to the burden of intensive experimental manipulation and to interactions among tests.

The fifth methodological change involves the more routine application of computers in characterizing all-night sleep. For the most part, the studies of the 1970s relied on the use of the sleepstaging schema published in the late 1960s (Rechtschaffen and Kales, 1968). Such investigations led primarily to the reporting of whole-night values. While these studies were important and the results led to considerable replication in the late 1970s and early 1980s, a trend has now emerged toward examining the distribution of sleep throughout the night, both by stages and by phasic phenomena. In particular, the examination of the number and distribution of REM waves or the number and distribution of delta waves has necessitated an increased reliance on the computer, not so much for computerized stage scoring, but for characterizing these phasic phenomena.[1]

In addition to these five methodological advances, it has also become clear that to investigate EEG sleep in affective disorders as an isolated biological rhythm is somewhat limiting; therefore, other biological rhythms should be studied simultaneously with sleep. In this monograph current studies and approaches on temperature control are reviewed elsewhere and the reader is referred to several inferences on motor activity, another biological rhythm which is altered in depressed states. Finally, it should be stressed that the relationship of sleep to neuroendocrine measures is extremely important; and this theme is discussed in detail later in this chapter.

SLEEP CHANGES IN DEPRESSION – AREAS OF CONSENSUS

At this time four major areas of consensus on the most characteristic EEG sleep changes in depression have emerged from clinical sleep research in the 1970s (Kupfer, 1982a; Table 2).

The majority of depressed patients demonstrate hyposomnia (a sleep continuity disturbance usually associated with increased wakefulness and frequent early morning awakening; Figure 1). A minority of depressed patients (15% to 20%) shows hypersomnia, a feature usually associated with other psychophysiological phenomena such as anergia. Thus, nearly all depressed patients demonstrate a change in their sleep continuity.

Considerable agreement has now emerged that a reduction in slow-wave sleep is found in depressed states, usually reported as a reduction or absence of stages 3 and 4 sleep. More recent data has demonstrated that delta sleep, as measured by computerized procedures, is lower in depressed patients than normals. First, in young adult and middle-aged depressives reduction both in the absolute number of EEG delta waves during NREM sleep and in the rate of production of such delta activity (average delta wave

TABLE 2

GLOSSARY OF EEG SLEEP VARIABLES

Sleep Latency: Time from lights out until the appearance of stage 2 sleep.

Early Morning Awakening: Time spent awake from the final awakening until the subject gets out of bed.

Awake: Time spent awake after sleep onset and before the final awakening in the morning.

Time Spent Asleep (TSA): Time spent asleep less any awake time during the night after sleep onset.

Awake/TSA: The percentage of awake time over time spent asleep.

TSA/Total Recording Period (Sleep Efficiency): The ratio of time spent asleep to total recording period.

Sleep Architecture: The various percentages of each stage of sleep: stage 1, stage 2, stage 3, and stage 4 (stages 3 and 4 are combined to yield delta sleep), stage 1-REM percentage and stage 2-REM percentage (the portion of the night when REMs are present during stage 1 and stage 2 sleep respectively).

REM Latency: Number of minutes asleep until the onset of the first REM period.

REM Activity (RA): Each minute of REM sleep is rated on a nine-point scale (0 to 8) for the relative amount of REM occurring; the sum for the whole night provides the REM activity.

RA/TA (Average REM Activity): The ratio of REM activity to time spent asleep.

RA/REM Time (REM Density): The ratio of REM activity to REM time.

Kupfer, et al.

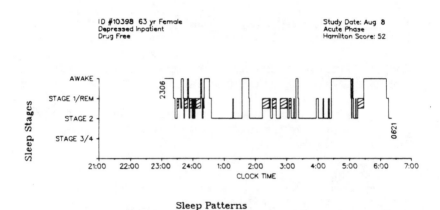

Sleep Patterns

Figure 1   EEG sleep stages of a patient with endogenous depression.

count), that is, a decrease in the number of slow waves per each
minute of NREM sleep, occurs (Kupfer, et al., 1986b). Although
such reductions may characterize all NREM periods, they are most
pronounced in the first NREM sleep period. Secondly, while
nondepressed healthy controls show a linear decrease in the rate of
production of slow-wave activity across consecutive NREM sleep
periods, with highest rates in the first NREM period, by contrast,
an altered temporal distribution of slow-wave activity is often
evident in NREM sleep of major depressives. Depressed patients
show a reduction in delta activity particularly during the first
NREM sleep period compared with the second (Kupfer, et al.,
1986b; Reynolds 3d, et al., 1985a). The finding of weakened
slow-wave activity, particularly in the first NREM period, is
extremely interesting since it is the length of the first NREM
period that also defines the shortened REM latency in the majority

of patients with depressive illnesses, especially the endogenous forms (Rush, et al., 1982; Figure 1).

This redistribution of slow-wave activity from the first to the second NREM period, as well as the increased rate of production of REMS in the first REM period, are relatively more specific to endogenous depression compared, for example, with Alzheimer's dementia (Reynolds 3d, et al., 1985b) and schizophrenia (Ganguli, Reynolds 3d and Kupfer, 1987). Since it is also true that considerably more stage 1 sleep is present in depressed patients, one might conclude that the major change is the presence of lighter stages of sleep, such as stages 1 and 2, to the exclusion of stages 3 and 4.

A key finding (one that has become most prominent because of its considerable replicability and the relative ease with which it can be scored and interpreted) has been a shortened onset to the first REM period. While this finding is somewhat contingent upon the criteria used to determine sleep onset, in the majority of patients with clinically significant depression the REM latency (or first NREM sleep period) is shortened. Specifically, the distribution of REM latency is determined by several independent but probably interactive factors including the age range of the sample studied, the severity of the depressive symptoms, and finally the subtype of depressive illness. Thus, very abbreviated REM sleep latencies (i.e., less than 20 minutes) have been found in association with delusional depression (Thase, Kupfer and Ulrich, 1986b; Coble, Kupfer and Shaw, 1981), but also in association with elderly nondelusional depression (Reynolds 3d, et al., 1985b).

A developing area that has received considerable attention has been REM sleep temporal distribution. In addition to our contributions in this area, the work of Gillin and colleagues (1979) and Vogel (1981) has also demonstrated an abnormal distribution of REM sleep compared with both normal controls and patients suffering from other psychiatric illnesses or sleep disorders. While an increased amount of REM sleep in the first third to first half of the night is present, it is even more apparent that depressed patients show a marked increase in the number of eye movements. It may be that the most significant REM sleep alteration is a change in the REM density (concentration of eye movements) in the sleep of these depressed patients. With respect to REM sleep, the major change in depressive states may be the redistribution of REM activity in all age groups. However, only in older depressives is a predictable absolute increase in REM density and number of REM movements routinely found.

These conclusions are now based on the application of automated procedures which tend to be more precise than visual estimates. The four features described above represent the area of consensus among sleep investigators in both the United States and Europe.

Our studies demonstrate that at least one (and usually more) of these abnormalities is found in 90% of all patients with major depressive disorder (Kupfer, et al., 1982b; Kupfer and Reynolds 3d, 1983a). This constellation of changes is apparently distinct from that which is found in other kinds of insomnia, sleep deprivation, free–running conditions, and different psychiatric illnesses. The pattern of sleep change is unique to depression. As other disorders show only one or two of these abnormalities (e.g., narcolepsy is associated with a reduced REM latency), the constellation of changes is probably not a nonspecific effect of mental illness, but must point in some way to pathogenetic changes in depression.

USE OF PHARMACOLOGICAL PROBES

Since a long–standing "love–affair" between proposed neurochemical abnormalities in depression and sleep regulation mechanisms has been present, the neurochemical basis for various sleep EEG changes must be further clarified. Furthermore, each sleep EEG change correlates poorly with the other in depressed patients (e.g., some show reduced REM latency, some show a lack of slow–wave sleep, and some show both). For heuristic purposes, one might try to elucidate mechanisms that underlie the following sleep EEG events: sleep onset, REM onset, subsequent REM–NREM cycle; REM sleep (amount and density); NREM sleep (amount and density); and sleep maintenance. For example, cholinergic antagonists improve sleep continuity, whereas agonists disrupt sleep continuity (depending upon dosage and timing of administration). Thus, the cholinergic system might be involved in several but not all of the sleep EEG changes in depression.

Several sleep parameters may be studied by pharmacological probes to identify altered central neurotransmission in depression. These studies should be conducted in normal, depressed, and remitted depressed populations. In view of the paucity of alternative strategies for examining central serotonin functions in man, the role of serotonin in sleep is especially important. L-tryptophan may be an inappropriate tool for this purpose as it disturbs the uptake of a number of amino acids into the brain and hence causes nonspecific effects. The recently developed selective inhibitors of 5-HT uptake are more suitable and have been reported to reduce rather than increase total sleep time.

In summary, disturbances of sleep may relate to the pathogenesis of depression. Apart from their empirical value in clinical studies, they appear to be opening a new window into brain function in man. To date, there is some evidence for cholinergic control of the onset or timing of the first and subsequent periods of REM sleep: the onset of REM sleep is delayed by atropine and hastened by arecoline (a muscarinic cholinergic agonist). Interestingly, recovered bipolar depressives may be unduly sensitive to the ability of cholinergic agonists to induce REM sleep (cholinergic REM induction test). However, the interpretation of this finding is necessarily tentative because both noradrenaline and serotonin appear to have effects upon REM which oppose those of acetylcholine. Thus, an altered balance of activity between neurotransmitter systems in depression may be hypothesized.

MODELS OF SLEEP REGULATION IN DEPRESSION

Several models have been proposed to deal with possible mechanisms of sleep regulation, psychophysiological and neurochemical aspects of sleep–wake rhythms, and depression. Most depressed patients demonstrate a change in their sleep–wake habits which are reflected both in the sleep continuity alteration and the daytime level of arousal. Whether these changes represent a 24–hour (global circadian) abnormality or are just limited to the sleep–wake process remains unresolved. Preliminary evidence suggests that one EEG sleep "marker" of depression, shortened REM latency, is present in daytime naps of depressives (Kupfer, et al., 1981b). Elsewhere in this monograph are described the models of McCarley and Hobson (1975; see also McCarley, 1982), the phase–advance hypothesis of circadian rhythm disturbance, and, to some extent, the model proposed with respect to Process S by Alex Borbély (1987).[2]

Abnormalities in a two–process model of sleep regulation (a sleep–dependent process termed Process S and a sleep–independent circadian process termed Process C) have been proposed to account for sleep abnormalities in depressive states (Borbély and Wirz–Justice, 1982b). The major tenets of the two–process model of sleep regulation as applied to depression are: the level of Process S, as reflected by the EEG slow–wave activity, corresponds to the sleep–dependent facet of sleep propensity; the pathognomonic changes of sleep in depressives are a consequence of a deficiency in the build–up of Process S. The application of automated REM and delta wave analyses in normal subjects and depressed patients supports the model to some extent: The time spent asleep is positively correlated with total delta waves (normals and depressives) and average delta waves (depressives); delta sleep is lower in depressives than in normals; the average delta wave count is significantly reduced in younger depressives over the total night and in NREM period 1. The model also postulates that measures of phasic REM activity are inversely related to Process S, suggesting that Process S can be regarded as exerting an inhibitory influence on phasic REM activity.

Borbély's hypothesis posits that the sleep–dependent process of sleep regulation (namely Process S) is deficient in depression; thus, impairment in sleep onset and sleep maintenance in depression and diminution of slow–wave sleep are attributed to reduced sleep propensity, a consequence of a low level of Process S. Hence, also, REM sleep is disinhibited or allowed to appear earlier after sleep onset. The model thus predicts that an increased level of Process S, attained by sleep deprivation, should be correlated with clinical improvement following sleep deprivation. In other words, depressed patients who improve symptomatically following sleep deprivation should also show improvement in sleep initiation and maintenance and increased slow–wave sleep during recovery sleep. Conversely, if clinical improvement after sleep deprivation is not accompanied by improved sleep continuity and enhanced slow–wave sleep, this would suggest that Process S is not relevant to the regulation of mood in depression. To test this prediction, we carried out a sleep deprivation experiment in 15 hospitalized endogenously depressed patients (Reynolds 3d, et al., 1987). As predicted by the model, responders to sleep deprivation (but not nonresponders) showed significant improvement in sleep latency, sleep efficiency, and slow-wave sleep during recovery sleep.

The advantage of such a model is that it "explains" or accounts for much of the data now available. Our recent work on phasic REM activity suggests that the security of the illness and also the likelihood of response to acute treatment can be predicted by examining phasic REM components prior to treatment (Kupfer, et al., 1982b). The immediate drug response based on examining the first two nights of sleep suggests that responsivity in the NREM system may reflect how well an antidepressant drug is going to "operate" in producing a satisfactory clinical response. Final clinical response should be (and in fact is) correlated with reduction in sleep latency onset, the prolongation of the REM latency, and also an immediate increase in delta waves.

In depressives the reduction of the intensity of the delta waves could affect the timing of the first REM period. Therefore, the weakening of the NREM system may be responsible for the shortening of REM latency. Indeed, our data points to the possible misnaming of REM latency. As shown previously (Kupfer, et al., 1984), REM latency is more strongly associated with delta-wave features of the first NREM period than any of the features in the first REM period, such as length in minutes or REM activity. However, since the sleep of patients with a number of illnesses other than depression is characterized by reduced delta-sleep time, the timing of the REM onset needs to be more specifically explained in depression (i.e., other diseases are associated with NREM "slowdown," but for the most part they do not have shortened REM latency). This finding is also reflected to some extent in the fact that depression can be associated with an increased amount of REM activity in other stages of sleep, such as stage 2 sleep. In fact, stage 2 REM sleep is significantly and positively correlated with the REM activity of the first REM period.

While SWS decreases have been discussed for many years in relationship to depressive syndromes, it is only with the advent of computerized measures that the issues of specificity with respect to delta wave decreases and their relationship to the process of aging can truly be addressed. For example, it has now become clear that there is a significant decrease in delta sleep in the first NREM period which is more profound in delusional and nondelusional depression than in either patients with schizophrenia or normal controls (Ganguli, Reynolds 3d and Kupfer, 1987).

Most recently, an examination of relationships between first NREM period delta wave counts and first REM period measures showed few significant findings in both the younger and middle–aged depressed patients (Kupfer, et al., 1986b). However, as expected, significant differences in sleep continuity between younger and middle–aged depressives were present. The increased amount of stage 1 found in the middle–aged depressives can also be interpreted as a measure of arousal and greater sleep discontinuity in this group of depressed patients as compared to younger depressed patients.

The average delta wave counts throughout the night were approximately doubled in the younger depressives as compared to the middle–aged depressives. The NREM distribution appeared to be relatively "flat" between first and second NREM period in the younger depressives, but an inverse relationship was present in the middle–age depressives, with the first NREM period having a lower average delta count than the second. When the average period lengths were examined in the younger and middle–aged depressives, as expected, there appeared to be a shorter first NREM period in the older depressives, with the REM periods themselves being approximately the same length in both groups throughout the night. REM latency/average delta count correlations for the first NREM period yielded the expected relationships between total delta counts and REM latency and a higher relationship in average delta counts with REM latency in the younger depressives.

These data, taken from two different points in the life cycle, suggest the presence of important interactions between age and disease in determining the EEG sleep characteristics of depression. These interactions will need to be examined in continuous age groups in order to understand, for example, where major shifts in slow–wave activity may occur and how increasing sleep maintenance difficulty with advancing age affects the amount and temporal distribution of slow-wave sleep.

Based on the considerable amount of data available on sleep and other biological rhythms after sleep onset, it would appear that the first 100 minutes of sleep represent an important "window" into central nervous system functioning. As more age-related changes occur in REM and NREM sleep in the first 100 minutes after sleep onset, which is a period of time associated with the usual sleep abnormalities found in depressed patients, we would hypothesize that the similarity of the two "processes" (aging and depression) can be tested in a large sample over an extended age range and that the results would help to clarify a number of issues. Specifically, at what age (if ever) in the life cycle of a normal individual does the sleep pattern of a depressed individual look similar (i.e., is there a twenty-year or a thirty-year "lag" between the sleep pattern of normals and depressives)? Second, are there periods in the life cycle in which the major differences in sleep patterns between patients and normals are less pronounced (e.g., sleep continuity differences in young depressives versus normal controls). Third, do the differences between normals and depressives at each decade demonstrate similar rates of aging (e.g., decrease in average delta count as a function of age)? Fourth, within the depressed or normal cohorts, are there gender differences at any decade using automated as well as nonautomated sleep analytic techniques?

As we have stated earlier, the basic hypothesis of a weakened NREM system implies that strengthening this system may be a necessary but not sufficient condition in which clinical response can occur. It has been suggested that sleep deprivation leads to a transient increase in slow-wave sleep (Borbély, et al., 1981) and we (Reynolds 3d, et al., 1987) have found that those depressed patients who show the best antidepressant response to sleep deprivation are individuals with the highest slow-wave increase. It is tantalizing to think that strengthening the NREM system is a prerequisite for the clinical response. If this were true, then during drug administration periods an increase in slow-wave sleep cannot be transient but must be persistent at least through the immediate clinical response period. It should be further predicted that those patients showing only a transient increase in slow-wave sleep density would be the patients showing the poorest clinical response. By extension, therefore, regardless of continued drug treatment, patients with reduced slow–wave sleep density would be more prone to relapse or vulnerable to the onset of a new episode.

The confirmation of this hypothesis and the generalizability of the phenomenology of enhancing slow–wave sleep during clinical improvement means that other modalities [such as electro-convulsive treatment (ECT) and lithium carbonate] should also foster the increase of slow–wave sleep (Kupfer, et al., 1974). Certainly, the limited data available for lithium carbonate supports such an effect on delta sleep. There are, however, no data on ECT–treated patients. Another testable notion is that clinical improvement induced by nonpharmacological treatments in depressed patients (such as cognitive therapy or interpersonal therapy) should also be associated with persistent increases in slow–wave sleep and/or delta activity. Finally, clinical remission should be associated with increased slow–wave density. Such studies would be best performed on a longitudinal basis in outpatients.

NEUROENDOCRINE RHYTHMS AND DEPRESSION

While this chapter is not intended to represent a comprehen-sive overview of sleep, biologic rhythms, and affective disorders, the emphasis on slow–wave activity and NREM sleep also points to the need for integrating data on other biologic rhythms with data on NREM sleep. Our own laboratory's recent endeavors in this area have focused on the relationship of selected neuroendocrine changes in depressed patients. Even though it is well accepted that both EEG sleep and neuroendocrine alterations are commonly found in affective disorders, most of the investigations published to date have focused on each area separately, rather than any detailed examination of their interrelationships. Systematic investigations of the interrelationships between selected neuroendocrine and EEG sleep measures should lead to the development of more precise and, at the same time, comprehensive psychobiologic profiles.

Quabbe's report of a nocturnal elevation in the plasma concentrations of human growth hormone (hGH; Quabbe, Schilling and Helge, 1966) and Sassin's polygraphic confirmation of a sleep–

linked peak for GH (Sassin, et al., 1969) marked the beginning of endocrinological sleep research and opened a field of insights into the neurochemistry of sleep (Parker, et al., 1980). Growth hormone, prolactin, luteinizing hormone, testosterone, thyrotropin, and cortisol all show a rhythmicity that is synchronized across time and between subjects. Sleep, itself being part of a circadian rhythm, may be masking the overt rhythm of these hormones. In fact, the intensity of this masking effect, i.e., the resistance of hormonal rhythms to the influence of sleep, is revealing. For example, the influence of sleep is maximal on hGH but minimal on the adrenocorticotrophic hormone (ACTH)/cortisol rhythms; the masking effect of sleep is stimulatory for hGH, prolactin, and testosterone but inhibitory for ACTH/cortisol and thyrotropin. Growth hormone release, which is temporally associated with SWS under basal conditions, produces a peak under free-running conditions which coincides both with the fall of cortisol and with SWS (Weitzman, et al., 1981b). Finally, the hormones that are stimulated by sleep have anabolic effects, whereas those that are inhibited have catabolic properties.

Growth hormone secretion has frequently been associated with the first NREM period of sleep, although there is a growing body of evidence in controls to suggest that this occurrence may be fortuitous. We and others (Jarrett, et al., 1985) have shown that even though nocturnal growth hormone secretion can occur before sleep onset, the serum concentration at sleep onset is often significantly greater than the value forty minutes previously. In an examination of the sleep of twenty-three normals whose sleep was relatively unperturbed by intravenous cannulation (Jarrett, et al., 1984) we re-examined 0.1 Hz to 2.0 Hz delta waves and their relationship to plasma growth hormone concentration. As in previous studies, we compared the average delta count to cortisol and growth hormone on the basis of twenty-minute sampling epochs throughout the night. We also conducted a precise examination of individual subject correlations throughout the night. Indeed, the female group (N = 15) failed to demonstrate any consistent relationship between growth hormone and delta activity. While delta activity was similar for both men and women, growth hormone secretion was less in women than in men. This set of findings stand in contrast to the males studied in this group (N = 8) in whom the first 160 minutes provided a significant correlation between growth hormone and either average delta count or total delta count. These sets of correlations are consistent with the apparently positive relationship between the peaking of growth hormone and of delta wave density in the first part of the night. Such findings would suggest that increased attention to sex differences, as well as to the age of the groups, is essential in future studies.

Second, it is apparent that growth hormone is secreted at a time when secretory activity in the hypothalamic pituitary adrenal (HPA) axis is relatively quiescent. Indeed, there is frequently a specific inverse relationship between the serum concentrations of growth hormone and cortisol in both depressed patients and healthy control subjects. Using twenty-minute sampling epochs, we examined the relationship between serum cortisol and growth hormone concentration. Individual subject correlations throughout the night were used to provide an average correlation. Using the test of homogeneity, it became apparent that this inverse relationship was most significant during the first NREM period ($r = -0.59$, $p < 0.01$).

Recent investigations on both healthy controls and depressed patients have drawn attention to several major tentative conclusions: (a) the complexity of the interaction between growth hormone and slow-wave sleep is considerably greater than previously thought; (b) the 24-hour distribution of growth hormone in the preliminary Belgian studies suggests a further need for studies on growth hormone release (Mendlewicz, et al., 1985); and (c) hGH peaking and SWS can be dissociated under clinical and pharmacological conditions in humans, as well as under normal conditions in the rat, cat, and dog.

In summary, since the original observation of Takahashi and colleagues (1968), the nocturnal secretion of growth hormone has been associated with the first NREM period of sleep and, in particular, the first burst of slow-wave sleep. However, using automated delta wave analysis and acknowledging individual variability, we have been unable to establish any simple linear statistical relationship between delta wave activity and growth hormone secretion even in the first 100 minutes of sleep when these two events appear to be temporally related, suggesting more complex mediating factors. This lack of simple combination has led to the hypothesis that sleep onset is permissive to both processes, and the relationship of delta wave activity to growth hormone secretion may be mediated by neuroendocrine pathways involving growth hormone releasing factor (GRF) and somatostatin (SRIF).

Since we would assert these neuroendocrine measures are tied into the sleep–wake cycle, we propose that a potential application may be their use as long–term indicators of relapse and perhaps as predictors of new episodes in depressed patients. Evidence is accumulating to support the concept that shifts occur in the normal cycle of both the sleep and neuroendocrine rhythms and that these disturbances may persist following clinical recovery from the illness. Furthermore, such abnormalities may serve as trait characteristics for the illness and thereby signify a level of vulnerability. Indeed, further research may ultimately establish the prognostic value of longitudinally following these measures in remitted recurrent depressives. The advantage of studying sleep–endocrine interactions is that they both represent circadian rhythm disturbances which may, in turn, be related to changes in neurotransmitter and receptor activity in affective disorders.

A MODIFIED MODEL OF SLEEP AND NEUROENDOCRINE PROCESSES

Recently, Ehlers and Kupfer (1987) have proposed a refinement of the two–process model of sleep to include the neuropeptide and neuroendocrine pathways that may be involved in affective disorders (Table 3).

This model is based upon the following empirical findings. A considerable body of data on the first part of the night suggests that both slow–wave sleep (delta wave density) and growth hormone are decreased in depressed patients, that the nadir of nocturnal cortisol levels is blunted, and that REM sleep and REM activity distribution are shifted to the earlier hours of sleep. Probes are now needed to assess how these variables can be altered independently in both normals and in depressed patients. Any probe that specifically affects any one of these four sets of variables merits consideration. For example, Ehlers and colleagues (1986) have demonstrated EEG effects following intracerebro ventricular growth hormone releasing factor (GRF) administration to animals, suggesting that slow-wave sleep changes may be stimulated by the GRF-GH axis. It is on the basis of this current

TABLE 3

CRF/GRF AND THE TWO-PROCESS MODEL
OF SLEEP IN DEPRESSION

	PROCESS S	PROCESS C
Definition	A sleep-dependent process that builds up during the day and is released at night	A sleep-independent circadian process
Sleep Stage Relationship	Slow-wave sleep-related	REM sleep-related
Neuroendocrine Relationship	GRF and/or GRF/CRF Ratio	CRF-HPA axis
Alteration in Depression	Deficient	Increased
Physiological Consequences in Depression	GH hyposecretion after sleep onset, decreased delta density, delayed sleep onset, lighter overall sleep pattern	Cortisol hyper-secretion over 24-hour period, increased REM activity and density provides the REM activity

data base that further investigative activity of possible alterations in growth hormone secretion would be valuable, especially since the mechanisms for the nocturnal release of growth hormone are probably different from growth hormone release during the day in response to a variety of metabolic probes. Thus, our strategies are predicated on the assumption that growth hormone releasing factors may alter sleep EEG patterns and nocturnal growth hormone releasing secretory activity.

Although this model is capable of simulating several aspects of the sleep disturbance in depression, it does not offer any insights into the physiological mechanisms that may "drive" the described dynamic processes. As a first approximation, we would suggest that the neurohormones CRF and GRF may actively participate in the two processes with GRF representing the Process S and CRF the Process C. Thus, lowered levels of GRF would be seen as inducing a weakened or impaired slow-wave (delta) sleep generator. When the S system is somewhat weakened, less of stages 3 and 4 is seen and also a lighter overall sleep pattern. Growth hormone increases during the day may reflect the increased level of Process S during the day in terms of "leakage" and, therefore, may lead to a decrease in Process S during sleep time. The increased levels of CRF over the 24-hour period would produce not only an elevated and a flattened appearance of the C process, but might also result in increased REM activity and density during the night. The CRF/GRF ratio may, in fact, reflect the strength of Process S.

Although further studies are needed to confirm or refute this hypothesis, the advantage of the "extended" model are severalfold: (a) it provides additional experimental tools to test the hypothesis, so that neuropeptide challenge strategies on sleep EEG may be employed; (b) it facilitates the examination of interactions among various biological rhythms; and (c) the application of the model provides an opportunity to make specific predictions concerning the level of dissociation among selected biological rhythms in the depressive state and in the state of clinical recovery.

ACKNOWLEDGMENTS

This work was supported in part by National Institute of Mental Health Grants MH–30915 and MH–24652, as well as a grant from the John D. and Catherine T. MacArthur Foundation Research Network on the Psychobiology of Depression.

FOOTNOTES

1   As indicated previously, it is important to realize that advances in understanding sleep physiology, especially in psychopathological states, will probably necessitate the application of more automated techniques. We have previously described the increasing application of automated REM and delta sleep analyses. Our automated measures are derived by the application of software programs which are implemented on a PDP–11/44 minicomputer using the LPS–11 laboratory peripheral system. Compressed analog tapes of each subject's sleep record are played directly into an analog–to–digital converter; the program yields both a minute–by–minute printout and a disk file. The disk file is later matched by a DEC–10 system computer to the visually–scored minute–by–minute record so that non–sleep minutes as well as measurement artifact can be accounted for and removed.

The REM analyzer has a software routine to detect REM wave forms and measure their characteristics, and has been described in an earlier publication. A REM is detected when there are simultaneous (within 115 msec) threshold crossings of opposite polarity by two EOG potentials. Each EOG biopotential has two thresholds set at $\pm$ 25 µV. After recognizing a REM wave form, its voltage integral over time, time of occurrence, and interocular latency are measured. The interocular latency is the time interval separating the movement of each eye for the same REM and is by definition less than 15 msec. For automated analyses each REM period contained a minimum of five minutes, although the REM onset time was derived in the usual fashion where the first REM period needed to be only 3 minutes in length. Other automated REM sleep measures are described in our previous publications (Kupfer, et al., 1982b; McPartland, et al., 1978a; McPartland and Kupfer, 1978b; McPartland, et al., 1979).

The delta analyzer program currently used in our sleep laboratory is implemented on a PDP-11/44 minicomputer using the LPS-11 Laboratory Peripheral System (Kupfer, et al., 1981a). There are two main sections in the program's structure. The first is written in FORTRAN and provides the operator interaction for program start-up as well as all disk I/O functions; the second section is written in PDP-11 assembly language and provides the real-time data collection functions.

The compressed analog tape recordings of the patients' EEG waveforms are played directly into the analog-to-digital converter of the LPS-11 at a speed of 16 times that of the recording speed, allowing an eight-hour period to be processed in only 30 minutes. The EEG channel is monitored and data collected at a real-time rate of 200 samples per second. Each sample is first stored in a buffer until 200 samples have been collected. The average of these stored samples is computed and then subtracted from the oldest sample in the buffer. (The effect is to filter the signal digitally with a high-pass characteristic and a roll-off frequency of 0.1 Hz, thereby eliminating any problems associated with baseline drifts.) The standard delineation of delta waves indicative of stages 3 and 4 sleep are 0.5 Hz to 2.0 Hz at 75 μv to 200 μv. The adjusted samples (from the buffer) go directly to a baseline-crossing detector and then to an amplitude (peak) detector. With each baseline crossing, the period of the preceding half-wave is computed from the prior crossing and the peak noted and checked. The program normally runs between two calibration marks (which the program detects at the start and end of a record) and provides both a minute-by-minute printout and a disk file. Whole night counts can then be examined or the average delta counts per minute analyzed, correlations with visually-scored sleep can be made for each minute of the night during NREM or REM periods or on any other subset of the EEG sleep recording.

2   In addition, to further interpret the sleep-wake disturbances in affective states, the reciprocal interaction model of sleep-cycle control proposed by McCarley and Hobson (1975) can be applied. This model has been extended to suggest the presence of an abnormal sleep initiation point different in depressed patients from nondepressed patients.

REFERENCES

American Psychiatric Association. 1980. Diagnostic and Statistical Manual of Mental Disorders, Third Edition. Washington, D.C.: American Psychiatric Association Press, Inc.

American Psychiatric Association. 1987. Diagnostic and Statistical Manual of Mental Disorders, Third Edition (Revised). Washington, D.C.: American Psychiatric Association Press, Inc.

Borbély, A.A. 1987. The S-deficiency hypothesis of depression and the two-process model of sleep regulation. Pharmacopsychiatry 20:23-29.

Borbély, A.A., F. Baumann, D. Brandeis, I. Strauch and D. Lehmann. 1981. Sleep deprivation: effect of sleep stages and EEG power density in man. Electroencephalogr Clin Neurophysiol 51:483-495.

Borbély, A.A. and A. Wirz-Justice. 1982b. Sleep, sleep deprivation, and depression. A hypothesis derived from a model of sleep regulation. Hum Neurobiol 1:205-210.

Coble, P.A., D.J. Kupfer, D.G. Spiker, J.F. Neil and R.J. McPartland. 1979. EEG sleep in primary depression: longitudinal placebo study. J Affect Disord 1:131-138.

Coble, P.A., D.J. Kupfer and D.H. Shaw. 1981. Distribution of REM latency in depression. Biol Psychiatr 16:453-466.

Ehlers, C.L., T.K. Reed and S.J. Hendriksen. 1986. Effects of corticotropin-releasing factor and growth hormone-releasing factor on sleep and activity in rats. Neuroendocrinology 42:467-474.

Ehlers, C.L. and D.J. Kupfer. 1987. Hypothalamic peptide modulation of EEG sleep in depression: a further application of the S-process hypothesis. Biol Psychiatr 22:513-517.

Foster, F.G., D.J. Kupfer, P. Coble and R.J. McPartland. 1976. Rapid eye movement sleep density. An objective indicator in severe medical-depressive syndromes. Arch Gen Psychiatr 33:1119-1123.

Ganguli, R., C.F. Reynolds 3d and D.J. Kupfer. 1987. Electro-encephalographic sleep in young, never–medicated schizophrenics: a comparison with delusional and nondelusional depressive and with healthy controls. Arch Gen Psychiatr 44:36–44.

Gillin, J.C., W. Duncan, K.D. Pettigrew, B.L. Frankel and F. Snyder. 1979a. Successful separation of depressed, normal, and insomniac subjects by EEG sleep data. Arch Gen Psychiatr 36:85–90.

Jarrett, D.B., J.B. Greenhouse, S.B. Thompson, A. McEachran, P. Coble and D.J. Kupfer. 1984. Effect of nocturnal intrave-nous cannulation upon sleep–EEG measures. Biol Psychiatr 19:1537–1550.

Jarrett, D.B., P. Coble, D.J. Kupfer and J.B. Greenhouse. 1985. Sleep–related hormone secretion in depressed patients. Acta Psychiatr Belg 85:603–614.

King, D., H.S. Akiskal, H. Lemmi, J. Belluomini and B.I. Yerevanian. 1981. REM density in the differential diagnosis of psychiatric from medical–neurologic disorders: a replication. Psychiatr Res 5:267–276.

Kupfer, D.J. 1982. EEG sleep as biological markers in depression. In Biological Markers in Psychiatry and Neurology (A Symposium on Biological Markers in Psychiatry and Neurology, New Orleans, May 1981), Usdin, E. and Hanin, I. (eds.). New York: Pergamon Press, pp. 387–396.

Kupfer, D.J., C.F. Reynolds 3d, B.L. Weiss and F.G. Foster. 1974. Lithium carbonate and sleep in affective disorders: further considerations. Arch Gen Psychiatr 30:79–84.

Kupfer, D.J., D.G. Spiker, P.A. Coble, J.F. Neil, R. Ulrich and D.H. Shaw. 1981a. Sleep and treatment prediction in endogenous depression. Am J Psychiatr 138:429–434.

Kupfer, D.J., J.C. Gillin, P.A. Coble, D.G. Spiker, D. Shaw and B. Holzer. 1981b. REM sleep, naps, and depression. Psychiatr Res 5:195–203.

Kupfer, D.J., D.H. Shaw, R.F. Ulrich, P.A. Coble and D.J. Spiker. 1982a. Application of automated REM analysis in depression. Arch Gen Psychiatr 39:569-573.

Kupfer, D.J. and C.F. Reynolds 3d. 1983a. Neurophysiologic studies of depression: state of the art. In The Origins of Depression: Current Concepts and Approaches (Report of the Dahlem Workshop on the Origins of Depression: Current Concepts and Approaches; Berlin, 1982), Angst, J. (ed.). Berlin: Springer-Verlag, pp. 235-253.

Kupfer, D.J., R.F. Ulrich, P.A. Coble, D.B. Jarrett, V. Grochocinski, J. Doman, G. Matthews and A.A. Borbély. 1984. Application of automated REM and slow wave sleep analysis: II. Testing the assumptions of the two-process model of sleep regulation in normal and depressed subjects. Psychiatr Res 13:335-343.

Kupfer, D.J., C.F. Reynolds 3d, R.F. Ulrich and V.J. Grochocinski. 1986b. Comparison of automated REM and slow-wave sleep analysis in young and middle-aged depressed subjects. Biol Psychiatr 21:189-200.

McCarley, R.W. 1982. REM sleep and depression: common neurobiological control mechanisms. Am J Psychiatr 139:565-570.

McCarley, R.W. and J.A. Hobson. 1975. Neuronal excitability modulation over the sleep cycle: a structural and mathematical model. Science 189:58-60.

McPartland, R.J., D.J. Kupfer, P. Coble, D. Spiker and G. Matthews. 1978a. REM sleep in primary depression: a computerized analysis. Electroencephalogr Clin Neurophysiol 44:513-517.

McPartland, R.J. and D.J. Kupfer. 1978b. Computerised measures of electro-oculographic activity during sleep. Int J Biomed Comput 9:409-419.

McPartland, R.J., D.J. Kupfer, P. Coble, D.H. Shaw and D.G. Spiker. 1979. An automated analysis of REM sleep in primary depression. Biol Psychiatr 14:767-776.

Mendlewicz, J., P. Linkowski, M. Kerhofs, D. Desmedt, J. Golstein, G. Copinschi and E. van Cauter. 1985. Diurnal hypersecretion of growth hormone in depression. J Clin Endocrinol Metab 60:505–512.

Parker, D.C., L.G. Rossman, D.F. Kripke, J.M. Hershman, W. Gibson, C. Davis, K. Wilson and E. Pekary. 1980. Endocrine rhythms across sleep–wake cycles in normal young men under basal state conditions. In Physiology in Sleep (Research Topics in Physiology, Volume 2), Orem, J. and C.D. Barnes (eds.). New York: Academic Press, pp. 145–179.

Quabbe, H.J., E. Schilling and H. Helge. 1966. Pattern of growth hormone secretion during a 24–hour fast in normal adults. J Clin Endocrinol Metab 26:1173–1177.

Rechtschaffen, A. and A. Kales. 1968. A Manual of Standardized Terminology, Techniques and Scoring System for Sleep Stages of Human Subjects (Publication No. 204). Washington, D.C.: National Institutes of Health.

Reynolds 3d, C.F., D.J. Kupfer, L.S. Taska, C.C. Hoch, D.E. Sewitch and V.J. Grochocinski. 1985a. Laboratory note: Slow wave sleep in elderly depressed, demented, and healthy subjects. Sleep 8:155–159.

Reynolds 3d, C.F., D.J. Kupfer, L.S. Taska, C.C. Hoch, D.J. Spiker, D.E. Sewitch, B. Zimmer, R.S. Marin, J.P. Nelson, D. Martin and R. Morycz. 1985b. EEG sleep in elderly depressed, demented, and healthy subjects. Biol Psychiatr 20:431–442.

Reynolds 3d, C.F., D.J. Kupfer, C.C. Hoch, J.A. Stack, P.A. Houck and S.R. Berman. 1987. Sleep deprivation effects in older endogenous depressed patients. Psychiatr Res 21:95–109.

Rush, A.J., D.E. Giles, H.P. Roffwarg and C.R. Parker. 1982. Sleep EEG and dexamethasone suppression test findings in outpatients with unipolar major depressive disorders. Biol Psychiatr 17:327–341.

Sassin, J.F., D.C. Parker, J.W. Mace, R.W. Gotlin, L.C. Johnson and L.G. Rossman. 1969. Human growth hormone release: relation to slow-wave sleep and sleep-waking cycles. Science 165:513-515.

Spitzer, R.L., J. Endicott and E. Robins. 1978. Research diagnostic criteria: rationale and reliability. Arch Gen Psychiatr 35:773-782.

Takahashi, Y., D.M. Kipnis and W.H. Daughaday. 1968. Growth hormone secretion during sleep. J Clin Invest 47:2079-2090.

Thase, M.E., D.J. Kupfer and R.F. Ulrich. 1986b. Electroencephalographic sleep in psychotic depression: a valid subtype. Arch Gen Psychiatr 43:886-893.

Vogel, G.W. 1981. The relationship between endogenous depression and REM sleep. Psychiatr Ann 11:423-428.

Weitzman, E.D., C.A. Czeisler, J.C. Zimmerman and M.C. Moore-Ede. 1981b. Biological rhythms in man: relationship of sleep-wake, cortisol, growth hormone, and temperature during temporal isolation. In Neurosecretion and Brain Peptides (Advances in Biochemical Psychopharmacology, Volume 28), Martin, J.B., S. Reichlin and K.L. Bick (eds.). New York: Raven Press, pp. 475-499.

2

THE SLEEP DISTURBANCES OF DEPRESSION: CLUES TO PATHOPHYSIOLOGY WITH SPECIAL REFERENCE TO THE CIRCADIAN RAPID EYE MOVEMENT RHYTHM

J. Christian Gillin
Wallace B. Mendelson
David J. Kupfer

INTRODUCTION

Loss of sleep has been known to be a symptom of depression for thousands of years. Modern electroencephalographic (EEG) sleep studies confirm the strong association of insomnia with most types of depression, but, in addition, have strongly suggested that even more specific disturbances of rapid eye movement (REM) sleep, and perhaps, delta sleep (stages 3 and 4), may be involved.

The major reported disturbances of sleep in primary or endogenous depression are summarized in Table 1 (taken from references: Akiskal, et al., 1980, 1982; Bell, et al., 1983; Coble, Foster and Kupfer, 1976; Coble, et al., 1979; Duncan, Pettigrew and Gillin, 1979; Feinberg, et al., 1982; Foster, et al., 1976; Gillin, et al., 1979a, 1981; Gillin, 1983a; Gresham, Agnew, Jr. and Williams, 1965; Hartmann, Verdone and Snyder, 1966; Hauri and Hawkins, 1971; Hauri, et al., 1974; Kupfer, 1976; Kupfer, et al., 1980, 1981a; Kupfer and Thase, 1983c; Lange, Burr and von Aswege, 1976; McNamara, et al., 1984; Mendels and Hawkins, 1967b, 1971; Reynolds 3d, et al., 1983c; Rush, et al., 1982; Schulz, et al., 1979; Schulz and Tetzlaff, 1982; Snyder, 1969a; Spiker, et al., 1978; and Vogel, et al., 1980). The relatively nonspecific disturbances include reduced total sleep time and sleep efficiency, and increased wakefulness. The disturbances reported to be more closely associated with depression include short REM latency and perhaps less well-established, increased duration and increased eye

TABLE 1

MAJOR SLEEP ABNORMALITIES OF DEPRESSION

Subjective: Insomnia (occasionally hypersomnia); early morning awakening

Objective: Total sleep: Usually reduced and inefficient; decreased sleep maintenance

Non–rapid eye movement sleep (NREM) | Decreased stage 3 and 4; decreased power density; increased stage 1; increased sleep spindles; short first NREM period (REM latency)

REM sleep: Increased REM density; increased duration of first REM period

---

movement activity in the first REM period, and a redistribution of REM across the night so that more is found in the first third, and less in the last third of the night. Although loss of stage 3 and 4 sleep has been reported in various psychiatric, neurological, and medical conditions (schizophrenia, insomnia, dementia, normal aging, mental retardation, Cushing's syndrome, hypothyroidism, alcoholism, Gilles de la Tourette's Syndrome and others), its importance in depression has recently been emphasized by Borbély and Wirz–Justice (1982b).

Electroencephalographic sleep patterns in depression and normals change with age (Gillin, et al., 1981; Ulrich, Shaw and Kupfer, 1980). REM latency, delta sleep, sleep time, and sleep efficiency tend to fall in two groups with advancing age, whereas early morning awake times tend to increase in depressives.

Various hypotheses have been proposed to account for these objective sleep disturbances in major depressive disorders (Snyder, 1969a; Hartmann, 1968; Vogel, et al., 1980; Gillin, et al., 1979a; Kripke and Atkinson, 1974; Papousek, 1975; see Snyder in Weitzman, et al., 1968; McCarley, 1982; and Borbély and Wirz-Justice, 1982b). The major theoretical emphasis has focused on REM disturbances (especially short REM latency) in major depression, but loss of delta sleep and fragmented sleep have also been emphasized.

CHOLINERGIC ACTIVITY IN SLEEP AND DEPRESSION

One particular set of theories has been based on neuropharmacological and neurophysiological considerations regarding normal sleep physiology (Gillin, et al., 1973, 1979a,b; Karczmar, Longo and de Caroh, 1970; McCarley, 1982; McGinty and Drucker-Colin, 1982; Oswald, et al., 1975; and Sitaram and Gillin, 1980a). These views suggest that shortened REM latency and other features of the sleep of depressed patients may result from an enhanced ratio of cholinergic to aminergic (particularly, noradrenergic) functional activity (Gillin, et al., 1979a). This model is consistent with earlier speculation that depressed mood is directly related to cholinergic activity and indirectly related to aminergic activity (Janowsky, et al., 1972). A model of muscarinic supersensitivity in normal volunteers, achieved by administration of scopolamine for three consecutive mornings, mimics the sleep disturbances of depressed patients (Gillin, Sitaram and Duncan, 1979b). Furthermore, in the Cholinergic REM Induction Test (CRIT), which measures the latency to REM induction by arecoline (a direct muscarinic agonist), patients with primary affective disorder enter REM sleep significantly faster than normal controls (Sitaram, et al., 1980b, 1982).

This is consistent with other data indicating cholinergic supersensitivity in patients with affective illness. For example, when challenged with cholinomimetic agents, such as physostigmine or arecoline, depressed patients show a greater increase in plasma levels of ACTH, beta-endorphin, and prolactin than patients with other psychiatric illnesses (Janowsky, et al., 1980; Risch, et al., 1981). Depression during withdrawal from antidepressants have been attributed to "cholinergic overdrive" (Dilsaver, et al., 1983).

Despite these observations, cholinergic mechanisms do not appear to be solely responsible for either the depressed mood or for the depressive sleep patterns in patients with major affective disorder (Gillin, Sitaram and Mendelson, 1982). Although physostigmine may induce depressive–like symptoms in depressed patients (Modestin, Hunger and Schwartz, 1973) and normal subjects (Risch, et al., 1981), the changes are not robust. Furthermore, mood changes were not observed in normal volunteers who showed the sleep abnormalities of depression following morning administration of scopolamine (Gillin, et al., 1979b), nor is there strong evidence that anticholinergic therapy relieves depression. Yet other neurotransmitters may also be involved. For example, inhibition of tyrosine hydroxylase with alpha methyl paratyrosine induces sleep and mood changes in normals similar to bipolar illness, i.e., short REM latency (Sitaram, Gillin and Bunney, Jr., 1984).

The muscarinic supersensitivity hypothesis of affective disorders was supported by a report by Nadi, Nurnberger, Jr. and Gershon (1984) on muscarinic receptors on adult skin fibroblasts. They claimed that receptor density, measured by 3H–QNB, was increased within pedigrees in members who had major affective disorder in contrast to nonaffected family members or normal controls. Unfortunately, this finding has not been supported by subsequent research. We have not been able to measure significant numbers of skin fibroblasts in many cell lines (Kelsoe, et al., 1985). Even in those who do show measurable numbers (Bmax), preliminary data indicates no difference between patients with either unipolar or bipolar affective illness compared with normal controls. Moreover, we also found no difference in muscarinic receptor number in brain autopsy material from suicides as compared with controls (Kaufman, et al., 1984).

CHRONOBIOLOGICAL APPROACHES AND MODELS

Chronobiological considerations have had an increasingly important role in theories of normal sleep physiology and in speculations about the pathophysiology of depression. For example, Borbély and Wirz–Justice (1982b) have interpreted the sleep disturbance of depression on the basis of Borbély's two–process model of sleep regulation (Borbély, 1982a). In this model, it is hypothesized that normal sleep is regulated by two processes: (1) Process S, a homeostatic factor reflecting increased propensity to sleep as duration of prior wakefulness increases; and (2) Process C, reflecting the circadian propensity to sleep at various times around the clock. The intensity of Process S is roughly reflected in the power density of the EEG (i.e., stage 4 distribution over the sleep period). In depression, it is postulated that Process S is deficient or accumulates slowly, thus accounting for loss of stage 4 sleep and the clinical benefits of sleep deprivation. Furthermore, since Process S is thought to be inhibitory to REM sleep, it accounts for the short REM latency. Daan and colleagues (1984) have developed a mathematical model based on the Borbély hypothesis which permits computer simulations of sleep disturbance in depression.

Another major chronobiological hypothesis has been the phase–advance hypothesis, which suggests that the circadian rhythm of REM sleep and perhaps other variables, such as temperature and cortisol, are advanced relative to clock time and sleep onset. This hypothesis goes back to the similarities noted by Frederick Snyder (see Weitzman, et al., 1968) between the sleep of depressives and normals whose sleep time had been inverted by 180°. Kripke and Atkinson (1974) also proposed the phase–advance hypothesis and Papousek (1975) reviewed the literature and presented the hypothesis in greater detail a year later. Wehr and his associates (1979b, 1980) have elaborated upon it and reviewed published data favoring this hypothesis. MacLean, Cairns and Knowles (1983) used this hypothesis to simulate the shortening of REM latency in normals by delaying sleep onset by varying degrees. Another chronobiological perspective was initiated by Halberg (1968), who suggested that internal desynchronization between different rhythms would give rise to "beat phenomena" occurring as various rhythms go in and out of phase with one another. These "beats" might be responsible for the periodic nature of affective illness. Consistent with this hypothesis are reports that some circadian rhythms in depression have period lengths differing from 24 hours, such as, for example, Kripke's finding of a faster temperature rhythm in some bipolar patients (Atkinson, Kripke and Wolf, 1975; and Kripke, Mullaney and Atkinson, 1978).

While Dirlich and colleagues (1981) did not find evidence of a faster than normal cycle length for the temperature rhythm in a 48-hour cycling unipolar patient during both entrained and free-running conditions, they did observe that the sleep-activity cycle was unusually fast, about 18.6 hours, under free-running conditions. In general, sleep appeared to have a deleterious effect on the patient's mood.

In a study of two schizophrenics and an investigator living in a time-free environment, Mills and colleagues (1977) found that the schizophrenics developed a sleep-wake cycle of about 23.5 hours. As in the case study of Dirlich and associates (1981), it is highly unusual for subjects to show sleep-activity rhythms with cycle lengths less than 24 hours in free-running conditions.

In contrast to the free-running laboratory type of exper-iment, Jenner and partners (1968) lived with a patient having a 48-hour bipolar mood disorder in a special chamber where the light-dark cycle was surreptitiously shortened from 24 hours to 22 hours. The patient's mood cycle was reported to shorten from 48 hours to 44 hours. Again, it is unusual for normal subjects to easily adjust to light-dark cycles with such a short cycle length, i.e., a 22-hour light-dark cycle usually exceeds the limits of entrainment. These three studies (Mills, et al., 1977; Dirlich, et al., 1981; and Jenner, et al., 1968) suggest that the limits of entrainment may be biased in the direction of a shorter endogenous tau in some psychiatric patients. If this were true, it could lead to the development of beats between various rhythms (Halberg, 1968).

On the basis of studies of normal volunteers living under free-running conditions for extended periods of time, Kronauer and co-workers (1982) hypothesized the existence of two major, mutually-coupled, self-sustaining oscillators, a so-called "strong" oscillator, controlling the circadian rhythms of temperature, REM sleep, and cortisol, and the so-called "weak" oscillator, controlling the sleep-wake cycle. This model is somewhat similar to one proposed by Wever (1979a). Under free-running conditions, the phase relationship between the two oscillators was hypothesized to change, i.e., the onset of REM sleep, the onset of cortisol secretion, and the nadir of the body temperature rhythm occurred sooner relative to sleep onset than under entrained 24–hour conditions. Zulley (1979) also has similar data. It was also postulated that the endogenous cycle length of the "weak" oscillator gradually increased under free–running conditions. As a consequence, at certain points, the phase relationships between the oscillators changed rapidly and dramatically, with the result that the subject exhibited long sleep–wake cycles (i.e., 48–hour, or "bicircadian days").

The two–oscillator model has theoretical implications for the phase–advance hypothesis. It implies, for example, that short REM latency could reflect a phase advance of the strong oscillator relative to clock time. Moreover, as Wehr and Goodwin (1981b) have speculated, the development of a "bicircadian day" in free–running conditions is analogous to the loss of sleep for a night which typically occurs with the "switch" process from depression to mania in bipolar manic–depressive patients. As previously noted, however, in several single EEG sleep case studies associated with a pattern of sleeping every other night or every third night (Gillin, 1977b; Gillin, et al., 1977a; Gillin and Wyatt, 1975; Mendelson, Gillin and Wyatt, 1977; Post, et al., 1977). One difference, however, should be noted: individuals exhibiting the bicircadian day in "free–running" conditions and the switch process in bipolar illness often display little or no REM sleep on the nights when they do sleep, whereas normal volunteers do have REM sleep when they sleep during the free–running bicircadian days (Wever, 1979a; Zulley, 1979). This observation strongly suggests that the mechanisms responsible for the sleep–wake cycle during the switch process in manic–depressive patients is not entirely similar to that responsible for the bicircadian day in free–running patients. In addition, of course, the switch process has been studied only under entrained conditions, in hospitals where it is likely that many environmental factors — light–dark cycles, scheduled meals, nursing staff rules and interactions, patient activities — modify the endogenous sleep–wake cycle.

Finally, in light of chronobiological considerations, it is of interest that both manic–depressive patients with fast transitions between mood states and patients with 48-hour mood cycles tend to "switch" preferentially at certain times of the 24-hour day (Sitaram, Gillin and Bunney, Jr., 1978a,b). In a study of hospitalized bipolar patients, Sitaram and colleagues (1978a) found that rapid switchers were most likely to switch into and out of mania during the nursing shift between 7 a.m. and 3 p.m. Patients who switched at night, however, showed higher ratings of mania and less sleep (based on nurses' bed checks at night) than patients switching at other times of the day. In contrast to the usual bipolar patient, however, patients with 48-hour mood cycles — about 20 case studies have been reported in the world's literature — typically switch at night (Sitaram, Gillin and Bunney, Jr., 1978b).

The age-related changes in sleep in depressives and normals might be understood from several of these theoretical positions. For example, circadian temperature rhythms may become advanced with increasing age (Weitzman, 1982a) and this process could be amplified in association with depression. Additionally, Process S (Borbély, 1982a) might be inversely related to age which would be consistent with an accelerated reduction of stage 4, total sleep time, and REM latency in aging patients with depression, as well as the progressive increase in early morning awakening noted in depressives with increasing age.

A STUDY OF SLEEP IN DEPRESSION

Little evidence is currently available on the circadian rhythm of REM sleep in patients with affective disorders. As an initial approach to investigating this issue in depressives, we studied both naps and nocturnal sleep in a group of 15 unmedicated depressed patients meeting the Research Diagnostic Criteria (RDC) for major depressive disorder (Spitzer, Endicott and Robbins, 1978; Kupfer, et al., 1981b). Each patient was studied for four consecutive nights. After the second baseline night, patients were asked to take a nap at 10 a.m., and after the third night, patients were requested to take a nap at 4 p.m. If no sleep occurred within 60 minutes, the nap study was stopped, but if the patient fell asleep, he was permitted to sleep until he had been recorded for two hours.

The results showed that all patients had some stage 1 in both naps; sleep latency to stage 1 averaged 13 minutes in the morning nap and 14 minutes in the afternoon nap. Twelve of the fifteen patients had some stage 2 in the morning and 14 had some in the afternoon. Morning and afternoon naps did not differ significantly in total sleep time, stages 1, 2, 3, or 4 sleep in those patients who entered stage 2 sleep.

Nine patients had REM sleep in the morning and six in the afternoon. Mean REM latency (from stage 2 to REM sleep, minus intermittent awake time) was the same in nocturnal, morning, and afternoon sleep, averaging 37 minutes, 36 minutes, and 44 minutes, respectively. REM latency at night tended to correlate with that in the morning ($r = 0.55$, $p = NS$, $n = 9$) and was significantly correlated with that in the afternoon ($r = 0.81$, $p < 0.05$, $n = 6$).

Although REM latency was similar at each of the three time periods, the propensity for REM sleep appeared to be greater during the morning nap than in the afternoon nap or during a comparable period of sleep early at night. In the five patients who had REM sleep in both morning and afternoon naps, REM time was greater in the morning (15 minutes vs. 14 minutes, $p < 0.01$; 23.9% vs. 9.2%; $p < 0.02$); mean total sleep time was nearly identical in the morning and afternoon naps, 78 minutes and 72 minutes, respectively. REM density showed a nonsignificant trend to be greater in the morning than the afternoon (1.7 vs. 1.4). Despite the greater amount of REM in the morning compared with the afternoon nap, REM latency was the same at the two times (39 minutes vs. 42 minutes). REM latency in these five subjects was positively, but not significantly, correlated at the two naps ($r = 0.61$, $p < 0.1$).

To examine the differences between morning and afternoon naps in a slightly different way, we looked at seven patients who exhibited at least 26 minutes total sleep time from onset of stage 2 in both the morning and afternoon naps. Total sleep time averaged 56 minutes in both morning and afternoon naps, but measures of REM sleep were significantly greater in the morning than in the afternoon (REM time, 19 minutes vs. 7 minutes; REM%, 25.1% vs. 13.7%, $p < 0.05$).

In order to compare REM propensity during the naps with that during nocturnal sleep, we calculated the number of minutes of REM accumulating between the onset of stage 2 and the end of a sleep period identical in duration to the sleep period in the patient's morning or afternoon naps. Again, the results suggest that REM propensity is greatest in the morning nap, compared with the early evening or the afternoon nap. Average REM time was 15 minutes in the morning nap compared with six minutes at night ($p < 0.05$) and four minutes in the afternoon ($p < 0.05$).

The design of this study was modified from a previous investigation of naps in normal volunteers (Karacan, et al., 1970). In contrast to the present results in depressed patients, Karacan and colleagues found that REM latency in normals varied with the time of day; it was lowest in the morning nap, greatest at night, and in between in the afternoon. Indeed, REM latency in the morning nap was about the same in their normals and our depressives, approximately 40 minutes. Consistent with the findings of Karacan and associates, we observed a circadian propensity for REM sleep, with a peak in the morning nap.

These observations imply that REM latency in depressives is short whenever depressives sleep independent of clock time, in contrast to what has been reported in normals. Moreover, it tends to be correlated during naps with that at night. Since Kupfer (1976) and Spiker and partners (1978) have previously shown that nocturnal REM latency varies inversely with severity of depression, this may also be true during naps. Moreover, the results indicate that there is a circadian propensity for REM sleep in depressed patients, as measured by the amount of REM sleep per unit of sleep time rather than by REM latency, and that the peak occurs in the morning period at approximately the same time as has been previously reported in normals. The results suggest, therefore, that the mechanisms controlling the timing of REM sleep with reference to sleep onset differ from those controlling the amount of REM sleep. We previously reached a similar conclusion in a study comparing the effects of REM deprivation in schizophrenic and control patients (Gillin and Wyatt, 1975).

The latency to stage 1 in the morning nap, 13 minutes, is virtually the same as that reported at the same time of day in

normal volunteers. In the afternoon nap, ↑   38
stage 1, 14 minutes, was approximately t↑
value. The latter finding would be consisten.
of over-arousal and deficient Process S.

Three findings in the nap study raise the possibility that the
sleep of depressed patients is "normal" during the 10 a.m. nap: the
latency to stage 1, and in the patients who slept enough, the
latency to REM, and the greater propensity for REM sleep.
Further studies comparing depressives with normal controls are
required to evaluate this hypothesis and the possibility of subtle
differences in the phase angle of the circadian rhythm of REM
sleep or in the mean level of REM propensity.

Studies by Avery, Wildschiodtz and Rafaelsen (1982) and
Schulz and Lund (1983) suggest that body temperature is normal
during daytime hours in depressed patients compared with normals,
although patients are significantly "hotter" at night. If it is shown
by further studies that REM sleep and temperature are normal at
10 a.m., this would be quite interesting in view of other studies
indicating hypersecretion of cortisol at this time in many
depressives.

The importance of circadian changes in sleep within the
depressed group was also indicated in another area. Patients who
slept poorly during the naps were more likely to respond well to
tricyclic antidepressant therapy than were patients who slept
better during naps. Responders showed a significantly lower sleep
efficiency in both morning (29.3% vs. 58.2%, p < 0.05) and
afternoon naps (21.4% vs. 58.4%, p < 0.05) than nonresponders.
Furthermore, responders had less total sleep time (23 minutes vs.
48 minutes, p < 0.05) and longer sleep latency (30 minutes vs. 18
minutes, p < 0.05) in the afternoon nap than nonresponders.
Responders and nonresponders did not differ in any sleep parameter
at night. These results suggest that responders to tricyclic therapy
differ from nonresponders in being over-aroused (less sleepy)
during the daytime, but not at night. The concept that responders
have objective evidence of over-arousal is also consistent with
clinical judgments that responders are more likely than
nonresponders to exhibit motor agitation and absence of motor
retardation (Kupfer, et al., 1981a).

Since responders and nonresponders to tricyclic antidepressant therapy differ in the amount of daytime sleep, it is premature
to conclude from this study that naps conclusively reveal a
significant peak of REM propensity in the 10 a.m. period in all
depressed patients. It may be that responders and nonresponders
have different distributions of REM sleep propensity around the
clock. In this study, two of seven responders showed REM sleep in
their naps (in these two cases, in both the morning and afternoon),
whereas all-night nonresponders had REM in either a morning or an
afternoon nap (three in both). Further studies are needed to
establish the circadian distribution of REM sleep in depression.

DISCUSSION OF SLEEP DISTURBANCES IN DEPRESSION

Although EEG sleep studies currently provide important
biological markers of affective illness, it should be emphasized
that the databases are meager when comparisons are made
between unmedicated, well-diagnosed depressives and age-sex
matched normal controls. Furthermore, relatively few published
studies exist of sleep in other psychiatric or medical illnesses,
especially since new diagnostic criteria have been proposed. Thus,
it is difficult to specify the exact qualitative and quantitative
sleep abnormalities in depression or the specificity and sensitivity
of these abnormalities in comparison with other diagnostic
conditions. Although short REM latency in primary and endogenous
depression has been replicated by numerous investigators, its
specificity is not entirely clear since it has been reported by some,
but not all, investigators in acute and chronic schizophrenia (Stern,
et al., 1969; Jus, et al., 1973), in some adult patients with anorexia
nervosa (Neil, et al., 1980), in some obsessive-compulsive disorders
in children (Rapoport, et al., 1981), and adults (Insel, et al., 1982),
in characterological depression (Akiskal, et al., 1980), in chronic
pain syndrome (Blumer, et al., 1982), in Korsakoff's syndrome
(Martin, et al., 1986) and narcolepsy. In all of these clinical
conditions, however, depressive symptoms may be prominent and
severe, and antidepressant medications have often been useful.

In contrast, very little data is available on the duration of the
first REM period, REM density of the first REM period, of the
distribution of REM over the first and last third of the night in

depressive normals. Duncan and colleagues (1979) found duration of the first REM period to be increased in unipolar, but not bipolar, depressed patients, compared with normals. The distribution of REM by thirds of the night has not, apparently, been systematically reported in both depressives and normals in any study other than by Gresham, Agnew, Jr. and Williams (1965), when the patients had only recently been withdrawn from medication. Kupfer, Foster and Detre (1973), also documented the increase of REM in the first third of the night in patients with low sleep efficiency.

Theories about depression, based upon sleep studies, must also recognize that clinical status and sleep change are not always linked together. Some normals spontaneously have an occasional short REM latency, for example, without being depressed, while some depressed patients may not have short REM latency. Moreover, patients may continue to have short REM latency, perhaps even shorter than usual, and increased "REM pressure" after they recover from depression; for example, after electro-convulsive therapy (Green and Stajduhar, 1966). Snyder (1969a) and Mendels and Hawkins (1971) also remarked that REM sleep pressure increased as depressed patients recovered. Although Vogel and colleagues (1980) found that responders to experimental REM deprivation showed increased "late REM %" (a measure of REM sleep distribution towards the end of the night) several days before nonresponders, both responders and nonresponders eventually increased "late REM %". These observations suggest that clinical improvement in depression may be partially independent of achieving the proper alignment between REM sleep and sleep onset.

Various manipulations can produce depressive–like sleep patterns in normals without major mood changes. These include, for example, experimental REM deprivation (Dement, et al., 1960), the scopolamine–induced muscarinic supersensitivity model of sleep in depression (Gillin, Sitaram and Duncan, 1979b), free–running experiments (Czeisler, 1978; and Zulley, 1979), or shifts of the sleep period (Weitzman, et al., 1968). It is true that the psychological effects of some of these manipulations have not been fully evaluated, and that dysphoric reactions are common with jet lag, shift work, or occasionally, in free–running conditions.

Nevertheless, it does not appear that any of the above-mentioned procedures predictably induce major mood disturbances in normal subjects. It is possible, however, that there are people who are vulnerable to these manipulations. The depressed patients studied by Dirlich and associates (1981), however, did not apparently show an intensification of depressive symptoms under free–running conditions. Lund (1974), on the other hand, found that internal desynchronization under free–running conditions in normal volunteers was associated with pathological personality test scores before the study.

The sleep changes in depression appear, therefore, to be somewhat nonspecific, at least as they have been measured up until now. To take an example, REM latency can be shortened in a variety of conditions, some pathological, others not. The pathophysiological interpretation of a short REM latency must be, therefore, cautiously approached. This is no different than most tests associated with disease. Diagnosis and clinical severity may have associated laboratory abnormalities, but the entire clinical picture must be considered. Neither short REM latency nor "escape" on the dexamethasone test are sufficient to establish the diagnosis of a particular type of depression in the absence of appropriate clinical features. It is naïve to assume that these biological measures define depression. Moreover, a variety of physiological mechanisms could, for example, shorten REM latency. These might include enhanced cholinergic activity, decreased noradrenergic (and possibly serotonergic) activity, phase advance of a circadian oscillator, a history of prior REM deprivation, advancing age, or a combination of these and other factors.

Despite considerable research up to this time, there is still no convincing data establishing a specific abnormality of circadian rhythms in affective illness. Obviously, however, more carefully controlled and comprehensive studies are still required. In the case of REM, short REM sleep latency has repeatedly been reported in major depressive disorder, as well as perhaps increased duration and intensity of REM density in the first REM period, but it is far from clear that these findings represent a shifted phase of circadian REM sleep or a change in the amplitude, waveform, or mean of the circadian REM rhythm. As Borbély (1982a) suggests, it may even be a mistake to postulate a specific circadian REM sleep system, and may be more parsimonious to consider the circadian distribution of REM sleep from alternate viewpoints, such as the interaction of Processes S and C. Thus, the shortening of nocturnal REM latency in depression may be independent of any circadian alteration. The normal increase in REM latency in normal volunteers from morning to afternoon to evening (Karacan, et al., 1970) may be consistent with the progressive accumulation of Process S (Borbély, 1982). The apparent "normal REM latency" we found at 10 a.m. in depressed patients and failure to increase REM latency from morning to afternoon to evening would be entirely consistent with Borbély's and Wirz–Justice's model (1982b) that the elaboration of Process S is deficient over the day in depression.

In the case of the circadian temperature curve, it is also far from clear that there is a phase advance. In one of the clearest studies, Avery, Wildschiodtz and Rafaelsen (1982) found no difference in the waking temperature curve between depressives and normal controls; at night, however, the depressives failed to show the normal sleep–related fall in body temperature to the same extent as normals and, consequently, exhibited a higher mean temperature throughout the night. The interpretation of this study could be in doubt, however, since the normals may have had an unusually early temperature minimum compared to previous studies. Upon recovery, depressives had a significantly lower mean temperature curve during sleep than they had while ill. Schulz and Lund (1983) and Beersma, van den Hoofdakker and van Berkestijn (1983b) recently presented preliminary data supporting Avery and colleagues (1982).

All investigators agree that nocturnal temperature is elevated in depression. The temperature at night appears to be negatively correlated with REM latency (the "hotter" the patient, the shorter the REM latency). The temperature minimum did not occur early to a statistically significant degree in any study, although there appeared to be greater likelihood of this in depression. Subjects with early temperature minimum tended to have short REM latency, but not necessarily vice versa. In summary, the studies on temperature in the depressed have not yet provided evidence of a robust phase advance in depression. The data tends to favor a change toward flattening of the 24–hour temperature waveform with an elevation of mean body temperature as a result of higher nocturnal temperature than normal.

In the case of cortisol, Jarrett, Coble and Kupfer (1983) found that the onset of cortisol secretion followed sleep onset more rapidly in depressives than in normals. Since sleep onset was significantly later in the depressives than in the normals, it does not appear that either the onset of the first REM period or of cortisol secretion was advanced relative to clock time in depression. Reynolds also showed delayed sleep onset time in depression, but normal REM onset time by the clock in depressives compared with normals (Reynolds 3d, et al., 1983c). The nadir of cortisol secretion, however, was significantly higher in depressives than normals (Jarrett, Coble and Kupfer, 1983). In a separate study, Asnis and colleagues (1983) reported that depressed patients with hypersecretion of cortisol had significantly shorter REM latency than those without hypersecretion. These results would appear to be more consistent with the loss of a homeostatic process rather than a shift of circadian phase, i.e., processes regulating wakefulness, cortisol secretion, core body temperature, and REM are disinhibited in depression.

In some sense which remains ill-defined at this time, depressed patients may be described as being "over-aroused" (Gillin, et al., 1984). If these concepts are expressed in chronobiological terms, it would suggest that depression is associated with a weakened Process S (Borbély and Wirz-Justice, 1982b). The evidence does not yet strongly support a phase advance of nocturnal REM onset or the circadian REM rhythm in depression relative to clock time. It is possible, however, that the waveforms or mean levels ("mesor") for REM sleep, temperature, or cortisol are altered in depression. At this time, however, there have apparently been no published studies of depressives in either entrained or free-running conditions in which data is simultaneously collected for sleep, REM sleep, temperature, cortisol, or thyroid indices (i.e., TSH), to name five biological measures relevant to depression which have circadian patterns. Thus, little is known about the phase relationships between circadian systems in depression.

The study of sleep disturbances in depression is the beneficiary of current exciting developments in the theoretical understanding of sleep–wake control, chronobiology, neuroendo-crinology, neuropharmacology, and the clinical studies. We can hope for new insights into the specific and nonspecific pathophys-iological mechanisms involved in the best documented biological marker of affective illness.

REFERENCES

Akiskal, H.S., T.L. Rosenthal, R.F. Haykal, H. Lemmi, R.H.
Rosenthal and A. Scott–Strauss. 1980. Characterological
depressions. Clinical and sleep EEG findings separating
"subaffective dysthymias" from "character spectrum disorders".
Arch Gen Psychiatr 37:777–783.

Akiskal, H.S., H. Lemmi, B.I. Yerevanian, D. King, J. Belluomini.
1982. The utility of the REM latency test in psychiatric diagnosis:
a study of 81 depressed outpatients. Psychiatr Res 7:101–110.

Asnis, G.M., U. Halbreich, E.J. Sackar, R.S. Nathan, L.C. Ostrow,
H. Novacenko, M. Davis, J. Endicott and J. Puig–Antich. 1983.
Plasma cortisol secretion and REM period latency in adult
endogenous depression. Am J Psychiatr 140:750–753.

Atkinson, M., D.F. Kripke and S.R. Wolf. 1975. Autorhythm–
ometry in manic–depressives. Chronobiologia 2:325–335.

Avery, D.H., G. Wildschiodtz and O. Rafaelsen. 1982. REM
latency and temperature in affective disorder before and after
treatment. Biol Psychiatr 17:463–470.

Beersma, D.G.M., R.H. van den Hoofdakker and J.W.B.M. van
Berkestijn. 1983b. Circadian rhythms in affective disorders: body
temperature and sleep physiology in endogenous depressives. In
Advances in Biological Psychiatry (Volume 11), Mendlewicz, J. and
H.M. van Praeg (eds.). Basel: S. Karger, A.G., pp. 114–127.

Bell, J., H. Lycaki, D. Jones, S. Kelwala and N. Sitaram. 1983.
Effect of pre–existing borderline personality disorder on clinical
and EEG sleep correlates of depression. Psychiatr Res 9:115–123.

Blumer, D., F. Zorick, M. Heilbronn and T. Roth. 1982. Biological
markers for depression in chronic pain. J Nerv Ment Dis
170:425–428.

Borbély, A.A. 1982a. A two–process model of sleep regulation.
Hum Neurobiol 1:195–204.

Borbély, A.A. and A. Wirz-Justice. 1982b. Sleep, sleep deprivation, and depression. A hypothesis derived from a model of sleep regulation. Hum Neurobiol 1:205-210.

Coble, P., F.G. Foster and D.J. Kupfer. 1976. Electroencephalographic sleep diagnosis of primary depression. Arch Gen Psychiatr 33:1124-1127.

Coble, P.A., D.J. Kupfer, D.G. Spiker, J.F. Neil and R.J. McPartland. 1979. EEG sleep in primary depression: longitudinal placebo study. J Affect Disord 1:131-138.

Czeisler, C.A. 1978. Human circadian physiology: internal organization of temperature, sleep-wake and neuroendocrine rhythms monitored in an environment free of time cues. (Doctoral dissertation, Stanford University.) Palo Alto: University Microfilms (No. 79-05, 838).

Czeisler, C.A., J.C. Zimmerman, J.M. Ronda, M.C. Moore-Ede and E.D. Weitzman. 1980. Timing of REM sleep is coupled to the circadian rhythm of body temperature in man. Sleep 2:329-346.

Daan, S., D.G.M. Beersma and A.A. Borbély. 1984. Timing of human sleep: recovery process gated by a circadian pacemaker. Am J Physiol 246:R161-R178.

Dement, W.C. 1960. The effect of dream deprivation. Science 131:1705-1707.

Dilsaver, S.C., Z. Kronfol, J.C. Sackellares and J.F. Greden. 1983. Antidepressant withdrawal syndromes: evidence supporting the cholinergic overdrive hypothesis. J Clin Psychopharmacol 3:157-164.

Dirlich, G., A. Kammerloher, H. Schulz, R. Lund, P. Doerr and D. von Zerssen. 1981. Temporal coordination of rest-activity cycle, body temperature, urinary free cortisol, and mood in a patient with 48-hour unipolar-depressive cycles in clinical and time-cue-free environments. Biol Psychiatr 16:163-179.

Duncan, W.C., K.D. Pettigrew and J.C. Gillin. 1979. REM architecture changes in bipolar and unipolar depression. Am J Psychiatr 136:1424–1427.

Feinberg, M., J.C. Gillin, B.J. Carroll, J.F. Greden and A.P. Zis. 1982. EEG studies of sleep in the diagnosis of depression. Biol Psychiatr 17:305–316.

Foster, F.G., D.J. Kupfer, P. Coble and R.J. McPartland. 1976. Rapid eye movement sleep density. An objective indicator in severe medical–depressive syndromes. Arch Gen Psychiatr 33:1119–1123.

Gillin, J.C. 1977b. Electroencephalographic sleep alterations during the switch process, pp. 324–325, In **The switch process in manic–depressive psychosis,** Bunney, Jr., W.E., Moderator (Transcription of a Combined Clinical Staff Conference, National Institute of Mental Health, Bethesda, Maryland, February 1976). Ann Intern Med 87:319–335.

Gillin, J.C. 1983a. Sleep studies in affective illness diagnostic, therapeutic and pathophysiological implication. Psychiatr Ann 13:367–384.

Gillin, J.C., R.M. Post, R.J. Wyatt, F.K. Goodwin, F. Snyder and W.E. Bunney, Jr. 1973. REM inhibitory effect of L–DOPA infusion during human sleep. Electroencephalogr Clin Neurophysiol 35:181–186.

Gillin, J.C. and R.J. Wyatt. 1975. Schizophrenia: perchance a dream? Int Rev Neurobiol 17:297–342.

Gillin, J.C., C. Mazure, R.M. Post, D. Jimerson and W.E. Bunney, Jr. 1977a. An EEG sleep study of a bipolar (manic–depressive) patient with a nocturnal switch process. Biol Psychiatr 12:711–718.

Gillin, J.C., W. Duncan, K.D. Pettigrew, B.L. Frankel and F. Snyder. 1979a. Successful separation of depressed, normal, and insomniac subjects by EEG sleep data. Arch Gen Psychiatr 36:85–90.

Gillin, J.C., N. Sitaram and W.C. Duncan. 1979b. Muscarinic supersensitivity: a possible model for the sleep disturbance of primary depression? Psychiatr Res 1:17–22.

Gillin, J.C., W.C. Duncan, D.L. Murphy, R.M. Post, T.A. Wehr, F.K. Goodwin, R.J. Wyatt and W.E. Bunney, Jr. 1981. Age–related changes in sleep in depressed and normal subjects. Psychiatr Res 4:73–78.

Gillin, J.C., N. Sitaram and W.B. Mendelson. 1982. Acetylcholine, sleep, and depression. Hum Neurobiol 1:211–219.

Gillin, J.C., N. Sitaram, T.A. Wehr, W. Duncan, R.M. Post, D.L. Murphy, W.B. Mendelson, R.J. Wyatt and W.E. Bunney, Jr. 1984. Sleep and affective illness. In Neurobiology of Mood Disorders (Frontiers of Clinical Neuroscience, Volume 1), Post, R.M. and J.C. Ballenger (eds.). Baltimore: Williams & Wilkins, pp. 157–189.

Green, W.J. and P.P. Stajduhar. 1966. The effect of ECT on the sleep–dream cycle in a psychotic depression. J Nerv Ment Dis 143:123–134.

Gresham, S.C., H.W. Agnew, Jr. and R.L. Williams. 1965. The sleep of depressed patients. An EEG and eye movement study. Arch Gen Psychiatr 13:503–507.

Halberg, F. 1968. Physiological considerations underlying rhythmometry with special reference to emotional illness. In Cycles Biologiques et Psychiatrie (Symposium Bel–Air 3d, Geneva, 1967), de Ajuriaguerra, J. (ed.). Paris: Masson et Cie, pp. 73–126.

Hartmann, E. 1968. Longitudinal studies of sleep and dream patterns in manic–depressive patients. Arch Gen Psychiatr 19:312–329.

Hartmann, E., P. Verdone and F. Snyder. 1966. Longitudinal studies of sleep and dreaming patterns in psychiatric patients. J Nerv Ment Dis 142:117–126.

Hauri, P. and D.R. Hawkins. 1971. Phasic REM, depression, and the relationship between sleeping and waking. Arch Gen Psychiatr 25:56–63.

Hauri, P., D. Chernik, D. Hawkins and J. Mendels. 1974. Sleep of depressed patients in remission. Arch Gen Psychiatr 31:386-391.

Insel, T.R., J.C. Gillin, A. Moore, W.B. Mendelson, R.J. Loewenstein and D.L. Murphy. 1982. The sleep of patients with obsessive-compulsive disorder. Arch Gen Psychiatr 39:1372-1377.

Janowsky, D.S., M. Khaled El-Yousef, J.M. Davis and H.J. Sekerke. 1972. A cholinergic-adrenergic hypothesis of mania and depression. Lancet 2:632-635.

Janowsky, D.S., C. Risch, D. Parker, L. Huey and L. Judd. 1980. Increased vulnerability to cholinergic stimulation in affective disorder patients. Psychopharmacol Bull 16:29-31.

Jarrett, D.B., P.A. Coble and D.J. Kupfer. 1983. Reduced cortisol latency in depressive illness. Arch Gen Psychiatr 40:506-511.

Jenner, F.A., J.C. Goodwin, M. Sheridan, I.J. Tauber and M.L. Lobban. 1968. The effect of an altered time regime on biological rhythms in a 48-hour periodic psychosis. Br J Psychiatr 114:215-224.

Jus, K., M. Bouchard, A.K. Jus, A. Villeneuve and R. Lachance. 1973. Sleep EEG studies in untreated, long-term schizophrenic patients. Arch Gen Psychiatr 29:386-390.

Karacan, I., R.L. Williams, W.W. Finley and C.J. Hursch. 1970. The effects of naps on nocturnal sleep: influence on the need for stage-1 REM and stage 4 sleep. Biol Psychiatr 2:391-399.

Karczmar, A.G., V.G. Longo and S. de Caroh. 1970. A pharmacological model of paradoxical sleep: the role of cholinergic and monoamine systems. Physiol Behav 5:175-182.

Kaufman, C.A., J.C. Gillin, B. Hill, T. O'Laughlin, I. Phillips, J.E. Kleinman and R.J. Wyatt. 1984. Muscarinic binding in suicides. Psychiatr Res 12:47-55.

Kelsoe, J.R., J.C. Gillin, D.S. Janowsky, J.H. Brown, S.C. Risch and B. Lumkin. 1985. Letter to the Editor: Failure to confirm muscarinic receptors on skin fibroblasts. N Engl J Med 312:861–862.

Kripke, D.F. and M. Atkinson. 1974. Circadian phase disorders in manic depressives. In Proceedings of the 127th Annual Meeting of the American Psychiatric Association. Washington, D.C.: American Psychiatric Association Press, Inc.

Kripke, D.F., D.J. Mullaney, M. Atkinson and S. Wolf. 1978. Circadian rhythm disorders in manic–depressives. Biol Psychiatr 13:335–351.

Kronauer, R.E., C.A. Czeisler, S.F. Pilato, M.C. Moore–Ede and E.D. Weitzman. 1982. Mathematical model of the human circadian system with two interacting oscillators. Am J Physiol 242:R3–R17.

Kupfer, D.J. 1976. REM latency: a psychobiologic marker for primary depressive disease. Biol Psychiatr 11:159–174.

Kupfer, D.J., F.G. Foster and T.P. Detre. 1973. Sleep continuity changes in depression. Dis Nerv Syst 34:192–195.

Kupfer, D.J., D. Broudy, P.A. Coble and D.G. Spiker. 1980. EEG sleep and affective psychosis. J Affect Disord 2:17–25.

Kupfer, D.J., D.G. Spiker, P.A. Coble, J.F. Neil, R. Ulrich and D.H. Shaw. 1981a. Sleep and treatment prediction in endogenous depression. Am J Psychiatr 138:429–434.

Kupfer, D.J., J.C. Gillin, P.A. Coble, D.G. Spiker, D. Shaw and B. Holtzer. 1981b. REM sleep, naps, and depression. Psychiatr Res 5:195–203.

Kupfer, D.J. and M.E. Thase. 1983c. The use of the sleep laboratory in the diagnosis of affective disorders. Psychiatr Clin North Am 6:3–25.

Lange, H., W. Burr and J. von Aswege. 1976. Sleep–stage shifts in depressive illness. Biol Psychiatr 11:239–243.

Lund, R. 1974. Personality factors and desynchronization of circadian rhythms. Psychosom Med 36:224–228.

MacLean, A.W., J. Cairns, J.B. Knowles. 1983. REM latency and depression: computer simulations based on the results of phase delay of sleep in normal subjects. Psychiatr Res 9:69–79.

Martin, P.R., R.J. Loewenstein, W.H. Kaye, M.H. Ebert, H. Weingartner and J.C. Gillin. 1986. Sleep EEG in Korsakoff's psychosis and Alzheimer's disease. Neurology 36:411–414.

McCarley, R.W. 1982. REM sleep and depression: common neurobiological control mechanisms. Am J Psychiatr 139:565–570.

McGinty, D.J. and R.R. Drucker–Colin. 1982. Sleep mechanisms: biology and control of REM sleep. Int Rev Neurobiol 23:391–436.

McNamara, E., C.F. Reynolds 3d, P.H. Soloff, R. Mathias, A. Rossi, D. Spiker, P.A. Coble and D.J. Kupfer. 1984. EEG sleep evaluation of depression in borderline patients. Am J Psychiatr 141:182–186.

Mendels, J. and D.R. Hawkins. 1967b. Sleep and depression. A follow–up study. Arch Gen Psychiatr 16:536–542.

Mendels, J. and D.R. Hawkins. 1971. Sleep and depression. IV. Longitudinal studies. J Nerv Ment Dis 153:251–272.

Mendelson, W.B., J.C. Gillin and R.J. Wyatt. 1977. Human Sleep and its Disorders. New York: Plenum Press.

Mills, J.N., R. Morgan, D.S. Minors, J.M. Waterhouse. 1977. The free–running rhythms of two schizophrenics. Chronobiologia 4:353–360.

Modestin, J.J., R.B. Hunger and R.B. Schwartz. 1973. Uber die depressogene Wirkung von Physostigmin. Arch Psychiatr Nervenkr 218:67–77.

Nadi, N.S., J.I. Nurnberger, Jr. and E.S. Gershon. 1984. Muscarinic cholinergic receptors on skin fibroblasts in familial affective disorders. N Engl J Med 311:225–230.

Neil, J.F., J.R. Merikanges, F.G. Foster, K.R. Merikanges, D.G. Spiker and D.J. Kupfer. 1980. Waking and all–night sleep EEGs in anorexia nervosa. Clin Electroencephalogr 11:9–15.

Oswald, I., V.R. Thacore, K. Adam, V. Brezinova and R. Burack. 1975. Alpha–adrenergic receptor blockade increases human REM sleep. Br J Clin Pharmacol 3:107–110.

Papousek, M. 1975. Chronobiologische aspekte der Zyklothymie. Fortschr Neurol Psychiatr 43:381–440.

Post, R.M., F.J. Stoddard, J.C. Gillin, M. Buchsbaum, D.C. Runkle, K. Black and W.E. Bunney, Jr. 1977. Alterations in motor activity, sleep, and biochemistry in a cycling manic–depressive patient. Arch Gen Psychiatr 34:470–477.

Rapoport, J., R. Elkins, D.H. Langer, W. Sceery, M.S. Buchsbaum, J.C. Gillin, D.L. Murphy, T.P. Zahn, R. Lake, C. Ludlow and W. Mendelson. 1981. Childhood obsessive–compulsive disorder. Am J Psychiatr 138:1545–1554.

Reynolds 3d, C.F., L.S. Taska, D.B. Jarrett, P.A. Coble and D.J. Kupfer. 1983c. REM latency in depression: is there one best definition? Biol Psychiatr 18:849–864.

Risch, S.C., R.M. Cohen, D.S. Janowsky, N.H. Kalin, N. Sitaram, J.C. Gillin and D.L. Murphy. 1981. Physostigmine induction of depressive symptomatology in normal human subjects. Psychiatr Res 4:89–94.

Rush, A.J., D.E. Giles, H.P. Roffwarg and C.R. Parker. 1982. Sleep EEG and dexamethasone suppression test findings in outpatients with unipolar major depressive disorders. Biol Psychiatr 17:327–341.

Schulz, H., R. Lund, C. Cording and G. Dirlich. 1979. Bimodal
distribution of REM sleep latencies in depression. Biol Psychiatr
14:595–600.

Schulz, H. and W. Tetzlaff. 1982. Distribution of REM latencies
after sleep interruption in depressive patients and control
subjects. Biol Psychiatr 17:1367–1376.

Schulz, H. and R. Lund. 1983. Sleep onset REM episodes are
associated with circadian parameters of body temperature. A
study in depressed patients and normal controls. Biol Psychiatr
18:1411–1426.

Sitaram, N., J.C. Gillin and W.E. Bunney, Jr. 1978a. The switch
process in manic–depressive illness. Circadian variation in time of
switch and sleep and manic ratings before and after switch. Acta
Psychiatrica Scand 58:267–278.

Sitaram, N., J.C. Gillin, W.E. Bunney, Jr. 1978b. Circadian
variation in the time of "switch" of a patient with 48–hour
manic–depressive cycles. Biol Psychiatr 13:567–574.

Sitaram, N. and J.C. Gillin. 1980a. Development and use of
pharmacological probes of the CNS in man: evidence of
cholinergic abnormality in primary affective illness. Biol Psychiatr
15:925–955.

Sitaram, N., J.I. Nurnberger, Jr., E.S. Gershon and J.C. Gillin.
1980b. Faster cholinergic REM sleep induction in euthymic
patients with primary affective illness. Science 208:200–202.

Sitaram, N., J.I. Nurnberger, Jr., E.S. Gershon and J.C. Gillin.
1982. Cholinergic regulation of mood and REM sleep: potential
model and marker of vulnerability to affective disorder. Am J
Psychiatr 139:571–576.

Sitaram, N., J.C. Gillin, W.E. Bunney, Jr. 1984. Cholinergic and
catecholaminergic receptor sensitivity in affective illness:
strategy and theory. In Neurobiology of Mood Disorders (Frontiers
of Clinical Neuroscience, Volume 1), Post, R.M. and J.C. Ballenger
(eds.). Baltimore: Williams & Wilkins, pp. 629–651.

Snyder, F. 1969a. Dynamic aspects of sleep disturbance in relation to mental illness. Biol Psychiatr 1:119–130.

Spiker, D.G., P.A. Coble, J. Cofsky, F.G. Foster and D.J. Kupfer. 1978. EEG sleep and severity of depression. Biol Psychiatr 13:485–488.

Spitzer, R.L., J. Endicott and E. Robins. 1978. Research diagnostic criteria: rationale and reliability. Arch Gen Psychiatr 35:773–782.

Stern, M., D. Fram, R.J. Wyatt, L. Grinspoon and B. Tursky. 1969. All-night sleep studies of acute schizophrenics. Arch Gen Psychiatr 20:470–477.

Ulrich, R.F., D.H. Shaw and D.J. Kupfer. 1980. Effects of aging on EEG sleep in depression. Sleep 3:31–40.

Vogel, G.W., F. Vogel, R.S. McAbee and A.J. Thurmond. 1980. Improvement of depression by REM sleep deprivation. New findings and a theory. Arch Gen Psychiatr 37:247–253.

Wehr, T.A., A. Wirz–Justice, F.K. Goodwin, W. Duncan and J.C. Gillin. 1979b. Phase advance of the circadian sleep–wake cycle as an antidepressant. Science 206:710–713.

Wehr, T.A., G. Muscettola and F.K. Goodwin. 1980. Urinary 3–methoxy–4–hydroxyphenol–glycol circadian rhythm. Early timing (phase–advance) in manic–depressives compared with normal subjects. Arch Gen Psychiatr 37:257–263.

Wehr, T.A. and F.K. Goodwin. 1981b. Biological rhythms and psychiatry. In American Handbook of Psychiatry, Second Edition (Volume VII), Arieti, S. and H.K.H. Brodie (eds.). New York: Basic Books, Inc., pp. 46–74.

Weitzman, E.D. 1982a. Chronobiology of man. Sleep, temperature and neuroendocrine rhythms. Hum Neurobiol 1:173–183.

Weitzman, E.D., D. Goldmacher, D. Kripke, P. MacGregor, J. Kream and L. Hellman. 1968. Reversal of sleep–waking cycle: effect on sleep stage pattern and certain neuroendocrine rhythms. Trans Am Neurol Assoc 93:153–157.

Weitzman, E.D., M.L. Moline, C.A. Czeisler and J.C. Zimmerman. 1982c. Chronobiology of aging: temperature, sleep–wake rhythms and entrainment. Neurobiol Aging 3:299–309.

Wever, R.A. 1979a. The Circadian System of Man: Results of Experiments Under Temporal Isolation. New York: Springer–Verlag.

Zulley, J. 1979. Der Einfluß von Zeitgebern auf den Schlaf des Menschen. (Doctoral dissertation, Universitat Tübingen.) Frankfurt am Main: Rita Fischer–Verlag.

3

THE TWO–PROCESS MODEL OF SLEEP REGULATION: IMPLICATIONS FOR SLEEP IN DEPRESSION

Alexander A. Borbély

INTRODUCTION

The relationship between sleep and depression has an intriguing aspect: on one hand, sleep disturbances are among the most common symptoms in depression, and on the other hand, sleep deprivation induces often a distinct, though short–lived, remission (for recent reviews, see Gillin, 1983b; and van den Hoofdakker and Beersma, 1984). It is difficult to understand why the denial of an apparently impaired sleep process should have an antidepressant effect.

The "phase–advance hypothesis" has recently been proposed to account for the relationship between sleep and depression (Wehr and Wirz–Justice, 1981a; Wehr and Goodwin, 1983b; and Wehr, Gillin and Goodwin, 1983c). Its main tenet is the existence of an abnormal phase relationship between a circadian oscillator controlling rapid eye movement sleep (REMS), body temperature and cortisol, and a second circadian oscillator controlling the sleep–wake cycle. The hypothesis is able to account for the REMS abnormalities (i.e., early REMS latency, prolonged first REMS period) in depression, yet offers no explanation for the reduction of slow–wave sleep (SWS), another major and consistent abnormality in depressive sleep (Kupfer and Foster, 1978). Wehr and co–workers (1983c) have summarized the evidence supporting the advance of the body temperature rhythm relative to sleep in depressives. However, as the authors themselves point out, the evidence is not entirely consistent. Thus recent studies did not reveal a phase–advance of body temperature with respect to the sleep–wake cycle (Avery, et al., 1986a,b; Beersma, van den Hoofdakker and van Berkestijn, 1983b; and Lund, Kammersloher and Dirlich, 1983). Methodological problems contribute to the difficulty of obtaining a clearer picture. Thus, sleep onset and SWS lower body temperature and thereby mask the "true minimum" of the temperature rhythm (Weitzman, et al., 1983). Sleep disturbances in depression may alter the timecourse of nighttime body temperature. A further methodological difficulty arises from the flat temperature rhythm in some depressives (Beersma, van den Hoofdakker and van Berkestijn, 1983b; and Wehr, Gillin and Goodwin, 1983c), which renders the reliable identification of the temperature minimum almost impossible. Finally, while a main tenet of the phase–advance hypothesis is the altered phase relationship of the REMS rhythm with respect to the sleep–wake rhythm, a nap study in depressive patients did not reveal an altered REMS propensity (Kupfer, et al., 1981b). Therefore stronger and more direct evidence is needed to support the phase–advance hypothesis.

According to Wehr and co–workers (1983c), the abnormal phase relationship between the circadian oscillators is not only responsible for the abnormalities of depressive sleep, but may be causally related to the depressive symptoms. The authors have attempted to correct this deficiency by phase–advancing the sleep period relative to the body temperature rhythm. While the first experiment in a depressive patient was spectacularly successful (Wehr, et al., 1979b), phase–shifts in subsequent experiments were only partly effective (Wehr and Goodwin, 1983b).

In the following sections, an alternative hypothesis is presented to account for the relationship between sleep and depression. Main features of the two hypotheses are summarized in Table 1.

SOME BASIC ASPECTS OF SLEEP REGULATION

Sleep is regulated as a function of prior waking time. In a first approximation, one could state that the longer a subject stays

TABLE 1

A COMPARISON OF TWO HYPOTHESES ON
SLEEP AND DEPRESSION

	Circadian phase–shift hypothesis	S–deficiency hypothesis
Main tenet	Abnormal phase position (phase advance of circadian body temperature/REMS rhythm relative to sleep-wake oscillator)	Deficient Process S
Main evidence	Abnormal phase relations in depressives	Reduction of SWS in depressives
Features of sleep in depression	REMS abnormalities	– Shortened sleep – SWS reduction – REMS abnormalities in conjunction with the reciprocal interaction model
Additional assumptions to account for sleep–deprivation therapy	Existence of a depressogenic sleep phase	Causal relationship between clinical symptoms and level of S
Main limitation	Abnormal phase position can occur without depression	SWS reduction can occur without depression

awake, the longer he will sleep. However, as experiments have shown, the "sleep debt" incurred during a prolonged vigil is only to a small part compensated by a prolongation of recovery sleep. This was dramatically demonstrated in an experiment in which a young man stayed awake for 264 hours, and then slept only 14.4 hours (Gulevich, Dement and Johnson, 1966). This and other observations led to the question of whether sleep loss can be compensated for by an increase in sleep intensity. Electroencephalographic (EEG) slow-wave activity appeared to be a good candidate for a sleep-intensity parameter, since it occurs predominantly in the first part of a sleep period, when the arousal threshold is high (see Borbély, 1982a, for references). Moreover, SWS is markedly enhanced by sleep deprivation (SD; Borbély, et al., 1981). The situation is quite different for REMS: unlike SWS, the proportion of REMS typically increases in the course of a nighttime sleep period, and is little affected by a moderate SD (Nakagawa, et al., 1978; and Borbély, et al., 1981). Although prolonged selective REMS deprivation leads to a REMS rebound (e.g., Dement, 1960), REMS does not respond as sensitively to a deficit as does SWS.

Sleep and sleep propensity are not exclusively determined by prior waking time. A 24-hour rhythm of sleep propensity has been early recognized (Patrick and Gilbert, 1896) and repeatedly documented. Recently, Akerstedt and Gilberg (1981) have impressively demonstrated the prominent role of circadian factors in sleep regulation: when the time of sleep onset was successively delayed by four-hour intervals, the duration of sleep first decreased below its regular level and then increased well beyond baseline.

REMS is the sleep stage that is most prominently influenced by circadian factors. Thus, naps taken early in the day contain more REMS than naps during later daytime hours (Maron, Rechtschaffen and Wolpert, 1964; and Webb, Agnew, Jr. and Sternthal, 1966), a trend that prevailed even after a night without sleep (Endo, et al., 1981). In several studies, a coincidence was noted between the maximum of the circadian rhythm of REMS and the minimum of the body temperature rhythm (see Borbély, 1982a, for references).

THE TWO–PROCESS MODEL OF SLEEP REGULATION

The Timing of Sleep

The model is based on the assumption that two separate processes underlie sleep regulation. One process is determined by sleep and waking, while the other is controlled independently of the sleep–wake cycle by a circadian oscillator. According to the model, sleep propensity is determined by the combined action of the two processes.

The timecourse of the sleep–dependent process was estimated from power density values which had been derived from all–night spectral analysis of the sleep EEG. The mean integrated values (corresponding largely to slow–wave activity) were calculated for each nonREMS–REMS cycle, standardized with respect to the first cycle (equivalent to 100%), and plotted at the cycle midpoint times. The points shown in the upper part of Figure 1 represent the average values from eight subjects. The decline over the first three nonREMS–REMS cycles was closely approximated by an exponential function (Borbély, et al., 1981). After a continuous waking period of 40.5 hours, the initial power density value was increased by approximately 40%, but still showed the exponential decline over the subsequent cycles (Figure 1, upper right). The thin interrupted lines interpolate the values between two consecutive sleep periods on the basis of an exponential process and thus represent the rising level of SWS propensity in the course of waking. Note that the time constant for the rising part of the process is longer than for the declining part. The lower part of Figure 1 shows the timecourse of Process S, which is based on the measured values of slow–wave activity during sleep and on the interpolated values during waking. In the model, Process S is regarded as the major sleep–dependent component of total sleep propensity, which is assumed to correspond to the sum of Process S and Process C. The latter represents the circadian component of sleep propensity, which is controlled by a circadian oscillator and is unaffected by the occurrence of sleep and waking.

The phase position of Process C can be derived from the

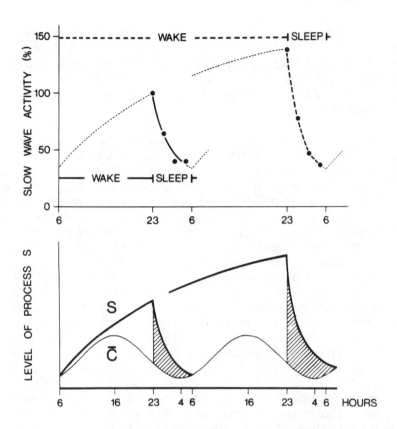

Figure 1   Timecourse of sleep processes after regular
and extended waking periods. Upper part: Exponential
decline of slow-wave activity over four consecutive
sleep cycles (value of first cycle = 100%) for a baseline
night (continuous line) and after sleep deprivation
(interrupted line). The exponential increase of
slow-wave sleep propensity during wake time is
indicated by the dotted line. Lower part: Timecourse
of Process S and the negative function of Process C
(curve $\overline{C}$; from Borbély, 1982a.)

circadian rhythm of vigilance during prolonged SD (Akerstedt and Fröberg, 1977). As a first approximation, Process C was represented by a sine function with the minimum at 1600 hours and the maximum at 0400 hours. To facilitate the visualization of the combined action of the two processes, the negative function (mirror image) of Process C (designated by C̄) has been plotted in Figure 1. Total sleep propensity is therefore represented by the difference between S and C̄. Curve C̄ may be regarded as reflecting the level of "wake–up propensity", which is lowest when the circadian sleep propensity is highest (i.e., in the early morning hours). It should be also noted that curve C̄ corresponds closely to the circadian rhythm of body temperature which is inversely related to the circadian rhythm of sleep propensity (see Borbély, 1982a, for references). The widening gap between the two curves in the evening hours of a regular waking period (see Figure 1) represents the increase in total sleep propensity. After sleep onset, at 2300 hours, the difference between the curves (hatched area) diminishes progressively until it reaches zero at the time of awakening. When the wake period is extended beyond its regular duration, the gap between the curves narrows during the morning and early afternoon hours, and then widens during the evening hours. Thus, in accordance with experimental data, sleep propensity is a nonmonotonic function of elapsed wake time. At the end of the SD period, sleep propensity is markedly higher than after a regular wake period. However, due to the exponential decline of S, recovery sleep is not much longer than a regular sleep period (Figure 1).

Recently, the model has been further elaborated to simulate the timing of human sleep under a variety of different paradigms (Daan, Beersma and Borbély, 1984). Quantitative estimates for the time constants of Process S were obtained from rates of change of EEG power density during regular sleep and during recovery from SD, while the characteristics of C̄ were derived from the spontaneous wake–up times after partial SD. In addition to curve C̄, which represents the fluctuating level of wake–up propensity, a second, analogous curve was defined (by shifting curve C̄ upward), whose intersection with S corresponds to the time of sleep onset. Computer simulations based on this extended model have allowed accounting for observations such as internal desynchronization in the absence of time cues, sleep fragmentation during continuous bedrest, circadian phase dependence of sleep duration during isolation from time cues, recovery from SD, and shift work. The model also showed that a single circadian pacemaker is sufficient to account for experimental data obtained under temporal isolation.

Presently, we are performing simulations based on a Rayleigh oscillator where Process S is regarded as being part of a limit cycle (Abraham, Borbély and Wirz-Justice, in preparation). An interesting aspect of this novel approach arises from the stiffness term whose reduction transforms the relaxation oscillation into a sinusoidal oscillation. Thus, it seems possible that this mathematical approach might integrate parts of a previous model based on two circadian oscillators of the Van der Pol type (Kronauer, et al., 1982) with those of the two-process model.

The NonREMS-REMS Cycle

So far, Process S has been described as a continuously declining exponential function which does not reflect the cyclic alternation of nonREMS and REMS. The model was therefore extended to include this salient feature of sleep. In Figure 2, REMS propensity (R) is represented by a horizontal interrupted line during waking and by the upper boundary of the black areas during sleep.

The constant level of R during the sleep-wake cycle indicates that, in contrast to Process S, REMS propensity is little influenced by moderate variations in the duration of prior sleep or waking. Consequently, REMS propensity largely corresponds to the circadian component of total sleep propensity (Process C) which, in Figure 2, is represented by the difference between R and $\overline{C}$.

The nonREMS-REMS cycles are represented by the succession of white and black areas. The upper boundary of the white areas is defined by the exponentially declining Process S, the upper boundary of the black areas by the constant level of R, while the lower boundaries of both are delimited by curve $\overline{C}$. The white and black rectangles below the curve indicate the duration of nonREMS and REMS periods in successive cycles. It is assumed that the duration of nonREMS and REMS periods is determined by

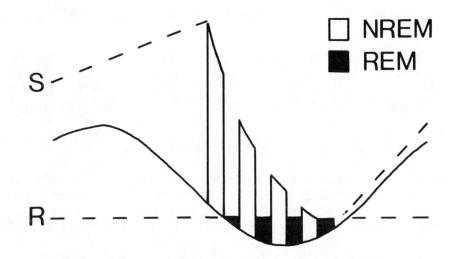

Figure 2 Extended model incorporating the nonREMS–REMS cycle. S and R are plotted relative to C̄. The rectangles below the curve indicate the decreasing duration of nonREMS periods (white) and the increasing duration of REMS periods (black) during sleep. (Modified from Borbély, 1982a.)

the ratio of nonREMS and REMS propensity. Thus, while at sleep onset nonREMS propensity (S − C̄) is clearly larger than REMS propensity (R − C̄), the two are practically equal at the end of the sleep period. Consequently, the first REMS period represents only a small fraction of the entire sleep cycle, while the fourth period occupies 50%.

To account for the cyclic alternation between nonREMS and REMS, I have invoked the reciprocal interaction model (Borbély, 1982a) which McCarley and Hobson (1975) had originally used to simulate the dynamic relationship of brainstem neurons during sleep. The nonREMS-controlling process is assumed to exert a self-inhibitory action and to inhibit also the REMS-controlling process, while the latter exerts a self-excitatory action and agitates the nonREMS-controlling process. This interaction can be described by two sets of differential equations of the Lotka-Volterra type.

Computer simulations of human sleep have been performed by Beersma and co-workers (1984a,b) based on values that had been originally used by Hobson, McCarley and Wyzinski (1975), for simulating the interaction between neuronal populations in the cat. In their simulation, Beersma and colleagues assumed that REMS is present whenever the rate of one process (corresponding in the neuronal model to the discharge rate of the x-cells) exceeds one-third of the maximum. It turned out that the REMS latency distribution is strongly influenced by the initial value of the other process (corresponding in the neuronal model to y_0, the initial discharge rate of the y-cells). Reducing y_0 had two effects: first, it markedly shortened REMS latency, resulting in a bimodal latency distribution; second, it enhanced the duration of the short-latency REMS episodes. Both changes represent typical features of depressive sleep. Since, in the model, parameters x and y correspond to REMS- and nonREMS-controlling processes, respectively, a reduced initial value y_0 could be regarded as corresponding to a reduced SWS propensity. Therefore, the typical REMS alterations in depressive sleep can be viewed as a direct consequence of a SWS deficiency. Further implications of this hypothesis will be discussed below.

There is recent evidence supporting an association between the level of SWS and the distribution of REMS. Thus the reduced percentage of SWS in healthy elderly persons in their 80s was paralleled by a fairly uniform distribution of REMS throughout the night, whereas in young subjects with a prominent SWS, REMS showed a progressive increase (Hayashi and Endo, 1982). The authors suggested that the forward shift of REMS in aged subjects might be due to the diminished SWS level in the earlier part of the night. Gillin and co-workers (1981) have previously documented the age-related decrease of SWS and the shortening of REMS latency in healthy subjects as well as in depressives. In two other studies conducted in healthy subjects, REMS latency also showed a significant positive correlation with the amount of SWS (Gillin, et al., 1979a) and with the amount of the average delta wave count, an EEG measure for slow–wave activity (Kupfer, et al., 1984). Short–latency REMS periods or even sleep onset REM periods (SOREMP) were observed in healthy subjects during morning naps when, due to the preceding nighttime sleep period, their SWS propensity was low (Globus, 1966; Nakagawa, 1980; and Endo, et al., 1981). Also the amount of REMS was increased and SWS decreased when nighttime sleep followed closely upon a prolonged daytime sleep period (Weitzman, et al., 1983), even though REMS latency was unchanged (Weitzman, et al., 1982c). This data also supports the suggestion by Vogel and colleagues (1980) that, in depression, a short REMS latency and a long intense first REMS period reflects a low sleep onset REMS inhibition. On the other hand, it must be kept in mind that correlations between SWS and REMS are insufficient evidence for a direct interaction of the two variables, since both could be controlled by a third factor.

In conclusion, the data is consistent with the proposition that REMS latency and the length of the first REMS episode are determined by two factors: SWS propensity and REMS propensity. The latter is primarily controlled by a circadian oscillator, and only under exceptional circumstances (e.g., following prolonged SD or selective REMS deprivation) by homeostatic mechanisms (i.e., an increase in "REMS pressure"). The circadian influence on REMS was clearly evident in experiments where subjects lived in temporal isolation. Under these circumstances, a short REMS latency and a prolonged first REMS episode was seen when sleep onset coincided with the minimum of the circadian body temperature rhythm (Webb and Agnew, Jr., 1974; Zulley, 1979; and Czeisler, et al., 1980).

THE TWO–PROCESS MODEL AND DEPRESSION

Depressive Sleep: The S–Deficiency Hypothesis

By assuming that the sleep–dependent component of sleep regulation (Process S) is deficient and therefore does not rise to its usual level in the course of waking, various pathognomonic features of depressive sleep can be accounted for within the framework of the two–process model (Borbély and Wirz–Justice, 1982b). Figure 3 shows the reduced interval between curves S and C̄ for the depressive patient.

Since in the model this change corresponds to a decreased sleep propensity, it follows that sleep latency is prolonged and sleep itself shallow and easily disrupted by external or internal stimuli. Moreover, since the intersection of the two curves defines the time of awakening, the length of the sleep period is reduced. Thus the extension of the two–process model can account for the disturbances in sleep onset and sleep continuity in depressives. According to the model, a deficiency in S should affect also sleep organization. First, since by definition, the level of S is a measure of SWS propensity, a reduction of S corresponds to a reduced amount of SWS. Second, as a result of the reciprocal interaction of the REMS– and nonREMS–controlling processes (see page 62), a reduction of S alters the REMS distribution across the night. In particular, due to the reduced inhibitory action of S after sleep onset, the latency to the first REMS episode is shortened and the duration of the first episode prolonged. Therefore, the assumption of an S deficiency is sufficient to account for the main features of depressive sleep.

While in the two–process model the characteristics of Process S were derived from experimental EEG data, the reduced rise rate of S in depression had to be inferred on the basis of circumstantial evidence. We have therefore recently attempted to directly test some of the assumptions of the model by performing all–night spectral analysis of the sleep EEG of drug–free depressive patients and comparing the data with those obtained from age and sex–matched normals (Borbély, et al., 1984). Both groups contained nine subjects (mean age 32) for each of whom the sleep stages were scored and the spectra computed for one night. To study the evolution of sleep throughout the night, the power density values were integrated over the entire frequency rate (0.25 Hz – 25 Hz) for each nonREMS–REMS cycle and plotted at the cycle midpoint times. Due to the high power density values in the low frequency range, the integration yielded essentially a measure of EEG slow–wave activity. A consistent decreasing trend over the first three sleep cycles was present in both depressives and normals. However, for each cycle the power density of depressives

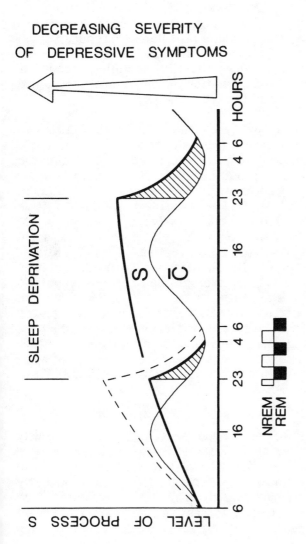

Figure 3   Sleep processes in a healthy subject (interrupted curve) and in a depressive patient (continuous curve) plotted for a regular sleep–wake cycle and for sleep deprivation (cp. Figure 1). The sleep periods of the depressive patient are indicated by shading. Due to the deficiency of Process S, the sleep propensity and the amount of SWS are reduced in depression, and the sleep period is shortened. Due to the disinhibition of the REMS–controlling process in the first part of the night, REMS latency is shortened and the duration of the first episode increased (white and black rectangles below the curve; cp. Figure 2). Sleep deprivation normalizes not only the depressive sleep pattern, but induces a remission of depressive symptomatology. (From Borbély and Wirz–Justice, 1982b.)

67

was significantly below the value of the normals. The differences could not be attributed to a more disrupted sleep in the depressives, since the number and duration of wake periods did not differ between the groups. The results are therefore consistent with the S–deficiency hypothesis which postulates a reduced level of slow–wave activity and a consistent decreasing trend over the sleep cycles. It should be mentioned that the declining trend was not readily apparent from the distribution of the sleep stages, since SWS was virtually absent beyond the first sleep cycle.

As described on page 62 (and following), the depressive changes of the first REMS period (i.e., shortened REMS latency, prolonged first REMS episode) can be simulated in a reciprocal interaction model by reducing the initial value of parameter y which may be regarded as representing SWS propensity (Beersma, Daan and van den Hoofdakker, 1984a,b). This implies a positive correlation between REMS latency and slow–wave activity. In our study (Borbély, et al., 1984), no such relationship was seen. However, studying a larger sample of depressives (N = 41), Kupfer and co–workers (1986b) obtained a significant positive correlation between REMS latency and the average delta wave count (a measure of EEG slow–wave activity) in the first nonREMS period. Interestingly, a negative correlation was found for nonREMS period 3. This suggests that REMS latency is primarily determined by the slow–wave activity in the first sleep cycle, an assumption that could explain the absence of a significant correlation between REMS latency and total SWS in another study (Gillin, et al., 1979a).

Alternative Hypotheses

Although the S–deficiency hypothesis can parsimoniously account for typical features of depressive sleep, it is interesting to consider alternative explanations within the framework of the two–process model. Beersma and co–workers (1985) have recently performed computer simulations to determine the parameters of the model whose variation yields a depressive sleep pattern. Here I shall mainly discuss some implications of reducing the circadian amplitude of C.

Figure 4 illustrates the timecourse of S with (top) and without (bottom) circadian modulation of $\overline{C}$. Abolishing circadian

ORIGINAL MODEL

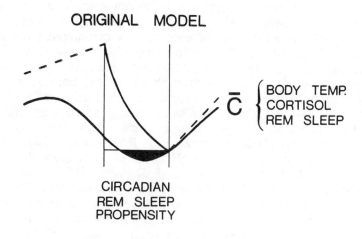

$\overline{C}$ { BODY TEMP.
CORTISOL
REM SLEEP

CIRCADIAN
REM SLEEP
PROPENSITY

NO CIRCADIAN MODULATION

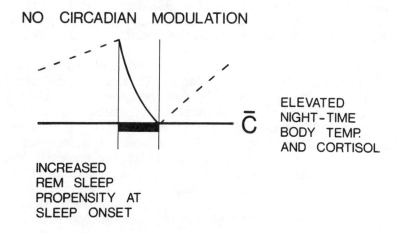

$\overline{C}$ ELEVATED
NIGHT-TIME
BODY TEMP.
AND CORTISOL

INCREASED
REM SLEEP
PROPENSITY AT
SLEEP ONSET

Figure 4 Abolition of circadian modulation. Sleep is shortened, REMS propensity becomes uniform throughout the night, and the level of nighttime body temperature and cortisol is elevated.

rhythmicity has two obvious sequelae: sleep duration is shortened and the REMS propensity (black area) becomes uniform throughout the night. The raised level of REMS propensity at sleep onset results in a shortened REMS latency and a prolonged first REMS episode in comparison to the original model. However, according to the model, the abolition of circadian modulation does not affect only sleep structure, but also other physiological parameters such as body temperature and cortisol. In accordance with this prediction the 24-hour rhythm of body temperature was markedly attenuated and nighttime temperature elevated in some depressives (Avery, Wildschiodtz and Rafaelsen, 1982; Avery, et al., 1986b; Beersma, van den Hoofdakker and van Berkestijn, 1983b; and Lund, Kammersloher and Dirlich, 1983). Moreover, Avery and colleagues (1986b) reported that depressed patients showed a significantly higher nocturnal body temperature and lower amplitude of the 24-hour temperature rhythm when compared either to themselves after recovery or to healthy controls. Also the significant negative correlation between REMS latency and nocturnal temperature (Avery, Wildschiodtz and Rafaelsen, 1982; and Avery, et al., 1986b) and the occurrence of SOREMP in patients exhibiting a flat temperature rhythm (Schulz and Lund, 1983) are consistent with the model.

Similar considerations apply to cortisol which is also markedly influenced by circadian factors (Moore-Ede, Sulzman and Fuller, 1982). Thus, curve C may represent not only body temperature, but also the level of plasma cortisol. Jarrett, Coble and Kupfer (1983) reported for depressive patients an elevated nighttime level of cortisol as well as a precocious increase after sleep onset (see also Sachar, et al., 1970, for an early paper). Jarrett and co-workers concluded from their findings that the cortisol-suppressing effect of sleep onset is less effective in depressives and that therefore an early "breakthrough" occurs. If SWS would be mainly responsible for the cortisol suppressing action at sleep onset, a parallelism between the SWS-cortisol and the SWS-REMS relationship could be seen. However, the data on this problem do not provide a clear picture. Thus while long sleep periods in non-entrained subjects showed an increased amount of SWS and a reduced level of cortisol (Weitzman, 1982a), SWS and cortisol were not negatively correlated in another study (Weitzman, et al., 1983). In depressive patients cortisol hypersecretion was associated with a shortened REMS latency (Asnis, et al., 1983), a finding that is consistent with the model. Kupfer and Jarrett (1983b) proposed that the depressive state may be associated with a "flattening" or diminished amplitude in hormone rhythms which may account for abnormalities in cortisol, prolactin and growth hormone secretion.

In conclusion, the attenuated circadian modulation of Process C in depressives could account not only for the changes in sleep, but also for the typical alterations of body temperature and cortisol. Nevertheless, there is one aspect in this version of the model which is difficult to reconcile with the data: since the reduction of the circadian amplitude of C does not affect the timecourse of Process S, this parameter alone cannot account for the reduction of SWS in depressives. Hence a combination of both hypotheses — the reduction of S and the flattening of C — could be considered as a further possibility to explain physiological and endocrine changes in depression.

There are additional ways of simulating depressive sleep within the framework of the model. For example, a shortening of sleep duration could be obtained by raising the level of curve $\overline{C}$. In fact, the resulting situation would largely correspond to the S–deficiency hypothesis. Moreover, if the level of $\overline{C}$ is assumed to correspond to the level of body temperature and cortisol, the elevated nighttime values of these parameters in depression would find an explanation. On the other hand, since the level of S at sleep onset remains unchanged, it would again be difficult to explain the reduction of SWS. Beersma and co–workers (1985) have recently proposed a further interesting possibility. By superimposing random fluctuations upon curve $\overline{C}$ they were able to simulate the shortening of sleep as well as the frequent sleep interruption which are both seen in depressives. The enhanced fluctuation of $\overline{C}$ could reflect an increased susceptibility to external or internal stimuli during sleep. Beersma and colleagues suggested that the reduction of SWS may not be due to an intrinsic deficiency in Process S, but to the frequent interruptions of the sleep process by arousals. Although, as previously mentioned (Borbély, et al., 1984; see page 65 [and following]), the reduction of slow–wave activity cannot always be attributed to arousal, this hypothesis deserves further examination. As a final point, it should be emphasized that the various hypotheses are not mutually exclusive. Nevertheless, assuming a combination of altered parameters in depression is certainly less appealing than a hypothesis where a single change can account for a multitude of clinical symptoms.

Sleep Deprivation Therapy

To explain the antidepressant effect of sleep deprivation we have proposed that the S-deficiency may be causally related to the disease process (Borbély and Wirz-Justice, 1982b). Consequently, if depressive symptoms are linked to the low level of S, its elevation should lead to clinical improvement. By prolonging the waking period, S can rise in spite of its reduced rise rate to near normal levels (Figure 3). However, since the basic deficiency is not corrected by this procedure, a regular sleep period or even a nap (Knowles, et al., 1979) restores the low level of S, thereby causing a relapse into depression. It should be noted that the frequently observed 24-hour rhythm of depressive symptoms, with a maximum in the morning hours and a minimum in the evening hours, is fully consistent with the model. Thus the same basic deficiency, which has been proposed to account for the major aspects of depressive sleep, is able to explain the rapid yet short-lasting antidepressive action of sleep deprivation.

According to the present hypothesis the improvement of depression is dependent on the passage of a critical duration of waking, a conclusion that has also been reached in a detailed single-case study (Knowles, et al., 1979). On the other hand, as has been pointed out previously (Daan, Beersma and Borbély, 1984), the interaction of S with C introduces a circadian factor. For this reason, it is not irrelevant whether a partial sleep deprivation period is placed in the first or in the second four-hour period of the night (Figure 5) since, in the latter case, S reaches a higher level. Clinical data is consistent with the prediction of the model that partial sleep deprivation in the first part of the night is the least effective type of treatment (Schilgen, et al., 1976; Schilgen and Tölle, 1980; and Goetze and Tölle, 1981).

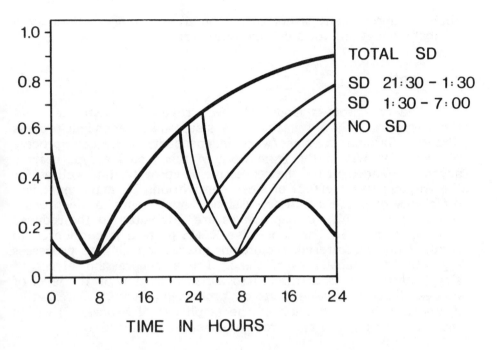

Figure 5   Effect of various sleep deprivation (SD) schedules on the subsequent level of S during waking. Deprivation time (hours:min) correspond to schedule in clinical studies. Total SD (Pflug and Tölle, 1971); partial SD in the second part (Schilgen, et al., 1976); and in the first part of the night (Goetze and Tölle, 1981). (Modified from Daan, Beersma and Borbély, 1984.)

So far we have assumed that the level of S alone constitutes the critical variable determining the clinical state. However, apart from parsimony there is no reason to exclude Process C as a contributing variable. One may speculate that the close proximity of S and C (Figure 3) may induce a depressogenic action, and that clinical improvement is contingent on S exceeding $\bar{C}$ both by a critical amount and for a critical time period.

SUMMARY

The two–process model of sleep regulation postulates that sleep propensity is a function of a sleep/wake–dependent process (Process S) and a sleep/wake–independent, circadian process (Process C). Within the framework of this model a hypothesis is advanced to account for the depressive sleep pattern as well as for the antidepressant effect of sleep deprivation. Its main tenet is a deficiency of process S in depression. Impairments in sleep onset and sleep continuity in depressives are attributed to the reduced level of Process S. The depressive REMS pattern is considered to result from an altered reciprocal interaction of the processes regulating the substrates of sleep. The antidepressant effect of sleep deprivation is attributed to a normalization of the level of Process S as a consequence of prolonged waking. Alternative hypotheses (e.g., reduction of the amplitude of Process $\bar{C}$) within the framework of the two–process model are discussed.

ACKNOWLEDGMENT

The study was supported by the Swiss National Science Foundation, grants 3.171–0.81 and 3.518–0.83.

REFERENCES

Akerstedt, T. and J.E. Fröberg. 1977. Psychophysiological circadian rhythms in females during 75 hours of sleep deprivation with continuous activity. Waking Sleeping 4:1-8.

Akerstedt, T. and M. Gillberg. 1981. The circadian variation of experimentally displaced sleep. Sleep 4:159-169.

Asnis, G.M., U. Halbreich, E.J. Sachar, R.S. Nathan, L.C. Ostrow, H. Novacenko, M. Davis, J. Endicott and J. Puig-Antich. 1983. Plasma cortisol secretion and REM period latency in adult endogenous depression. Am J Psychiatr 140:750-753.

Avery, D.H., G. Wildschiodtz and O. Rafaelsen. 1982. REM latency and temperature in affective disorder before and after treatment. Biol Psychiatr 17:463-470.

Avery, D.H., G. Wildschiodtz, R.G. Smallwood, D. Martin, O.J. Rafaelsen. 1986a. REM latency and core temperature relationships in primary depression. Acta Psychiatr Scand 74:269-280.

Avery, D.H., R.G. Smallwood, P.N. Prinz, M. Vitiello, D. Martin and D.L. Dunner. 1986b. Circadian temperature rhythm in primary depression. Submitted.

Beersma, D.G.M., R.H. van den Hoofdakker and J.W.B.M. van Berkestijn. 1983b. Circadian rhythms in affective disorders: body temperature and sleep physiology in endogenous depressives. In Advances in Biological Psychiatry (Volume 11), Mendlewicz, J. and H.M. van Praeg (eds.). Basel: S. Karger, A.G., pp. 114-127.

Beersma, D.G.M., S. Daan and R.H. van den Hoofdakker. 1984a. Sleep structure in depression. In Sleep Mechanisms (Experimental Brain Research, Supplement 8), Borbély, A. and J.-L. Valatx (eds.). Berlin: Springer-Verlag, pp. 285-296.

Beersma, D.G.M., S. Daan and R.H. van den Hoofdakker. 1984b.
Distribution of REM latencies and other sleep phenomena in
depression as explained by a single ultradian rhythm disturbance.
Sleep 7:126–136.

Beersma, D.G.M., S. Daan and R.H. van den Hoofdakker. 1985.
The timing of sleep in depression: theoretical considerations.
Psychiatr Res 16:253–262.

Borbély, A.A. 1982a. A two–process model of sleep regulation.
Hum Neurobiol 1:195–204.

Borbély, A.A., F. Baumann, D. Brandeis, I. Strauch and
D. Lehmann. 1981. Sleep deprivation: effect on sleep
stages and EEG power density in man. Electroencephalogr
Clin Neurophysiol 51:483–495.

Borbély, A.A. and A. Wirz–Justice. 1982b. Sleep, sleep
deprivation, and depression. A hypothesis derived from a model of
sleep regulation. Hum Neurobiol 1:205–210.

Borbély, A.A., I. Tobler, M. Loepfe, D.J. Kupfer, R.F. Ulrich,
V. Grochocinski, J. Doman and G. Matthews. 1984. All–night
spectral analysis of the sleep EEG in untreated depressives and
normal controls. Psychiatr Res 12:27–33.

Czeisler, C.A., J.C. Zimmerman, J.M. Ronda, M.C. Moore–Ede and
E.D. Weitzman. 1980. Timing of REM sleep is coupled to the
circadian rhythm of body temperature in man. Sleep 2:329–346.

Daan, S., D.G.M. Beersma and A.A. Borbély. 1984. Timing of
human sleep: recovery process gated by a circadian pacemaker.
Am J Physiol 246:R161–R178.

Dement, W.C. 1960. The effect of dream deprivation. Science
131:1705–1707.

Endo, S., T. Kobayashi, T. Yamamoto, H. Fukuda, M. Sasaki and
T. Ohta. 1981. Persistence of the circadian rhythm of REM sleep:
a variety of experimental manipulations of the sleep–wake cycle.
Sleep 4:319–328.

Gillin, J.C. 1983b. The sleep therapies of depression. Prog Neuropsychopharmacol Biol Psychiatr 7:351–364.

Gillin, J.C., W. Duncan, K.D. Pettigrew, B.L. Frankel and F. Snyder. 1979a. Successful separation of depressed, normal, and insomniac subjects by EEG sleep data. Arch Gen Psychiatr 36:85–90.

Gillin, J.C., W.C. Duncan, D.L. Murphy, R.M. Post, T.A. Wehr, F.K. Goodwin, R.J. Wyatt and W.E. Bunney, Jr. 1981. Age–related changes in sleep in depressed and normal subjects. Psychiatr Res 4:73–78.

Globus, G.G. 1966. Rapid eye movement cycle in real time. Implications for a theory of the D–state. Arch Gen Psychiatr 15:654–659.

Goetze, U. and R. Tölle. 1981. Antidepressive Wirkung des partiellen Schlafentzuges während der 1. Hälfte der Nacht. Psychiatr Clin (Basel) 14:129–149.

Gulevich, G., W. Dement and L. Johnson. 1966. Psychiatric and EEG observations on a case of prolonged (264 hours) wakefulness. Arch Gen Psychiatr 15:29–35.

Hayashi, Y. and S. Endo. 1982. Comparison of sleep characteristics of subjects in their 70s with those in their 80s. Folia Psychiatr Neurol Jpn 36:23–32.

Hobson, J.A., R.W. McCarley and P.W. Wyzinski. 1975. Sleep cycle oscillation reciprocal discharge by two brainstem neuronal groups. Science 189:55–58.

Jarrett, D.B., P.A. Coble and D.J. Kupfer. 1983. Reduced cortisol latency in depressive illness. Arch Gen Psychiatr 40:506–511.

Knowles, J.B., S.E. Southmayd, N. Delva, A.W. MacLean, J. Cairns and F.J. Letemendia. 1979. Five variations of sleep deprivation in a depressed woman. Br J Psychiatr 135:403–410.

78   Borbély

Kronauer, R.E., C.A. Czeisler, S.F. Pilato, M.C. Moore–Ede and
E.D. Weitzman. 1982. Mathematical model of the human
circadian system with two interacting oscillators. Am J Physiol
242:R3–R17.

Kupfer, D.J. and F.G. Foster. 1978. EEG sleep and depression. In
Sleep Disorders: Diagnosis and Treatment, Williams, R.L. and
I. Karacan (eds.). New York: J. Wiley & Sons, pp. 163–204.

Kupfer, D.J., J.C. Gillin, P.A. Coble, D.G. Spiker, D. Shaw, and
B. Holzer. 1981b. REM sleep, naps, and depression. Psychiatr Res
5:195–203.

Kupfer, D.J. and D.B. Jarrett. 1983b. Sleep–neuroendocrine
interrelationships in affective disorders. Psychopharmacol Bull
19:479–481.

Kupfer, D.J., R.F. Ulrich, P.A. Coble, D.B. Jarrett,
V. Grochocinski, J. Doman, G. Matthews and A.A. Borbély.
1984. Application of automated REM and slow wave sleep
analysis: II. Testing the assumptions of the two–process model
of sleep regulation in normal and depressed subjects. Psychiatr
Res 13:335–343.

Kupfer, D.J., C.F. Reynolds 3d, R.F. Ulrich and V.J. Grochocinski.
1986b. Comparison of automated REM and slow–wave sleep
analysis in young and middle–aged depressed subjects. Biol
Psychiatr 21:189–200.

Lund, R., A. Kammersloher and G. Dirlich. 1983. Body
temperature in endogenously depressed patients during depression
and remission. In Circadian Rhythms in Psychiatry, Wehr, T.A. and
F.K. Goodwin (eds.). Pacific Grove: Boxwood Press, pp. 77–88.

Maron, L., A. Rechtschaffen and E.A. Wolpert. 1964. Sleep cycle
during napping. Arch Gen Psychiatr 11:503–508.

McCarley, R.W. and J.A. Hobson. 1975. Neuronal excitability
modulation over the sleep cycle: a structural and mathematical
model. Science 189:58–60.

Moore–Ede, M.C., F. Sulzman and C.A. Fuller. 1982. The Clocks That Time Us. New York: Raven Press.

Nakagawa, Y. 1980. Continuous observation of EEG patterns at night and in daytime of normal subjects under restrained conditions. I. Quiescent state when lying down. Electroencephalogr Clin Neurophysiol 49:524–537.

Nakagawa, Y., M. Otorii, M. Ohishima, T. Otorii and H. Hasuzawa. 1978. Changes in sleep pattern after sleep deprivation. Folia Psychiatr Neurol Jpn 32:85–93.

Patrick, G.T.W. and J.A. Gilbert. 1896. On the effects of loss of sleep. Psychol Rev 3:469–483.

Pflug, B. and R. Tölle. 1971. Disturbance of the 24–hour rhythm in endogenous depression and the treatment of endogenous depression by sleep deprivation. Int Pharmacopsychiatr 6:187–196.

Sachar, E.J., L. Hellman, D.K. Fukushima and T.F. Gallagher. 1970. Cortisol production in depressive illness. A clinical and biochemical clarification. Arch Gen Psychiatr 23:289–298.

Schilgen, B. and R. Tölle. 1980. Partial sleep deprivation as therapy for depression. Arch Gen Psychiatr 37:267–271.

Schilgen, B.W., W. Bischofs, F. Blaskiewicz, W. Bremer, G.A.E. Rudolf and R. Tölle. 1976. Totaler und partieller schlafentzug in der behandlung von depressionen: vorläufige mitteilung. Arzneim Forsch 26:1172–1173.

Schulz, H. and R. Lund. 1983. Sleep onset REM episodes are associated with circadian parameters of body temperature. A study in depressed patients and normal controls. Biol Psychiatr 18:1411–1426.

van den Hoofdakker, R.H. and D.G.M. Beersma. 1984. Sleep deprivation, mood, and sleep physiology. In Sleep Mechanisms (Experimental Brain Research, Supplement 8), Borbély, A. and J.–L. Valatx (eds.). Berlin: Springer–Verlag, pp. 297–309.

Vogel, G.W., F. Vogel, R.S. McAbee and A.J. Thurmond. 1980. Improvement of depression by REM sleep deprivation. New findings and a theory. Arch Gen Psychiatr 37:247–253.

Webb, W.B., H.W. Agnew, Jr. and H. Sternthal. 1966. Sleep during the early morning. Psychon Sci 6:277–278.

Webb, W.B. and H.W. Agnew, Jr. 1974. Sleep and waking in a time–free environment. Aerospace Med 45:617–622.

Wehr, T.A., A. Wirz–Justice, F.K. Goodwin, W. Duncan and J.C. Gillin. 1979b. Phase advance of the circadian sleep–wake cycle as an antidepressant. Science 206:710–713.

Wehr, T.A. and A. Wirz–Justice. 1981a. Internal coincidence model for sleep deprivation and depression. In Sleep 1980: Circadian Rhythms, Dreams, Noise and Sleep, Neurophysiology and Therapy (Proceedings of the Fifth European Congress on Sleep Research, Amsterdam, 1980), Koella, W.P. (ed.). Basel: S. Karger, A.G., pp. 26–33.

Wehr, T.A. and F.K. Goodwin. 1983b. Biological rhythms in manic–depressive illness. In Circadian Rhythms in Psychiatry, Wehr, T.A. and F.K. Goodwin (eds.). Pacific Grove: Boxwood Press, pp. 129–184.

Wehr, T.A., J.C. Gillin and F.K. Goodwin. 1983c. Sleep and circadian rhythms in depression. In Sleep Disorders: Basic and Clinical Research (Advances in Sleep Research, Volume 8), Chase, M. and Weitzman, E.D. (eds.). New York: S.P. Medical and Scientific Books, pp. 195–225.

Weitzman, E.D. 1982a. Chronobiology of man. Sleep, temperature and neuroendocrine rhythms. Hum Neurobiol 1:173–183.

Weitzman, E.D., M.L. Moline, C.A. Czeisler and J.C. Zimmerman. 1982c. Chronobiology of aging: temperature, sleep–wake rhythms and entrainment. Neurobiol Aging 3:299–309.

Weitzman, E.D., J.C. Zimmerman, C.A. Czeisler and J. Ronda. 1983. Cortisol secretion is inhibited during sleep in normal man. J Clin Endocrinol 56:352–358.

Zulley, J. 1979. Der Einfluß von Zeitgebern auf den Schlaf des Menschen. (Doctoral dissertation, Universitat Tübingen.) Frankfurt am Main: Rita Fischer–Verlag.

4

MODELING THE ALTERNATIONS OF RAPID EYE MOVEMENT SLEEP TIMING AND PHARMACOLOGY IN DEPRESSION

Robert W. McCarley
Steven C. Massaquoi

INTRODUCTION

Other contributions to this volume have described the rapid eye movement (REM) sleep changes characteristic of depressed sleep, their reversal with antidepressant treatment, and the altered pharmacological responsiveness to cholinergic compounds in depressives. Taken together, these findings both suggest the importance of REM sleep signs as indicators of biological status in depression and also the rather high degree of commonality of biological control systems important for REM sleep control and for depression. This chapter proposes a unifying hypothesis for the REM sleep alterations in depression that is derived from a formal mathematical and physiological model for REM sleep. We first describe the model and its operation in normals.

Background of the Model

In 1975, McCarley and Hobson proposed a model of REM sleep that was physiologically based on the observed time course of discharge activity in two neuronal populations: (1) "REM-on" neurons in the pontine reticular formation (PRF) which became active in REM sleep and appeared to act to promote this sleep phase; and (2) "REM-off" neurons in the locus ceruleus (LC) and dorsal raphe (DR) nuclei whose discharge activity had a reciprocal time course to the REM-on cells. LC/DR cells slowed and nearly ceased discharge activity with the approach and advent of REM sleep and appeared to act in a permissive, disinhibitory fashion in REM control. It was proposed that the periodic occurrence of REM sleep might be a function of reciprocal interaction between these two groups of neurons, and the Lotka–Volterra (LV) equations were used to describe this interaction.

Advances in physiology since 1975 have indicated reticular neurons in addition to those of the pontine giant cell field (FTG) are important for REM functions but the concept of a REM–promoting, cholinergic cholinoceptive brainstem reticular group remains useful. Similarly, the concept of the functional role of LC/DR cells has now been expanded to include many general behavioral regulatory functions as well as a role in REM sleep, and other REM–off neurons, also probably biogenic amine–containing, have been recorded in the brain stem. The original model aroused interest as the only systematic mathematical model of REM sleep oscillation, and has formed the basis of attempts to model the characteristic REM sleep changes associated with depression (Vogel, et al., 1980; Beersma, Daan and van den Hoofdakker, 1984b).

We thus thought it useful to refine and extend the model mathematically so that it would be both physiologically more realistic and also applicable to human sleep. A central formal problem was the neutral stability of the simple LV system; this meant that there was no inherent limit on the amplitude of neuronal discharge and even oscillations of infinite amplitude were possible. A reasonable first step in modeling was thus to add terms to the equation which reflected realistic physiological limits on neuronal firing rates. In addition, terms were added that better described neuronal firing characteristics at low discharge rates. These changes led to a model which displayed limit cycle stability, and the new model will be hereafter described as the limit cycle model. The limit cycle of this physiological system can be thought of as the time course of the neuronal discharge activity of system components which is approached regardless of the starting point (initial conditions) or presence of perturbations. Our initial description of the limit cycle model as a "Karma" model expressed the limit cycle concept as the "fate" of the system components to follow a particular time course. The presence of limit cycle stability opened the possibility of modeling and thus studying mechanisms by which exogenous influences, such as pharmaco-logical agents and circadian variation, affect the REM oscillator.

Specifically, this new limit cycle model shows that the marked differences in latency, amplitude and duration of the first REM sleep period seen with circadian variation and depressive pathology can be modeled by beginning the REM oscillation at different initial points relative to the final position in the limit cycle, as illustrated in Figures 3 and 4 in the Results section, and here summarized: 1) beginning from a point that is graphically interior to the limit cycle produces a long–latency, short–duration, and less intense first REM period (Figure 3); and 2) beginning from a point graphically exterior to the limit cycle produces a short-latency, long–duration and more intense first REM period (Figure 4). In the model the determinant of whether the oscillation begins exterior or interior to the limit cycle is the rate of change in the REM–off population discharge activity at sleep onset. When this time course is made to depend on circadian phase, the model produces a very close match to the observed large shifts between the first and second REM period in duration (often a 50% change) and intensity also matches the observed shifts in first REM period latency as human sleep begins at different circadian phases. This variation accounts for the major changes in REM sleep over the night. In addition, the model postulates a continuous but small circadian variation (of the order of $\pm 5\%$ change in REM parameters) acting throughout the course of a night's sleep.

Because the model is derived from actual physiological data, rather than being a purely ad hoc or phenomenological construct, it offers the possibility of direct tests of its postulates through neurobiological studies in animals, by circadian phase–related manipulations of the sleep cycle, and through perturbations of the system in humans by the use of drugs. Indeed, an explicit phase response curve of the system to cholinergic agonists has been developed and is presented here; this will permit experimental tests of the model in both animals and humans. Preliminary version of this model have been presented (Massaquoi and McCarley, 1982; Massaquoi, 1983; and McCarley and Massaquoi, 1985a) and a full exposition is in McCarley and Massaquoi, 1986.

MODEL CONSTRUCTION

Reciprocal Interaction of REM–on and REM–off Cells

A simple structural diagram of the model is presented in Figure 1. In viewing the figure, our emphasis on the REM–on and REM–off neurons being used as exemplars of what are likely larger populations of neurons involved in REM cycle generation must be kept in mind. Evidence for the connections indicated have been summarized elsewhere (McCarley, 1978, 1980) and thus will be only briefly reviewed here. Data on mPRF–mPRF positive feedback (connection "a" in Figure 1) is now quite extensive and includes intracellular evidence from both direct microstimulation of mPRF neurons (McCarley, 1981) and of axon collaterals. There is in addition very strong evidence of pontine linkage to bulbar and mesencephalic reticular formations. Within the LC and DR the presence of recurrent inhibitory synapses is also well–established, both anatomically and physiologically (connection "c" in the structural model). There is auto–radiographic anatomical evidence for DR to mPRF projections and also evidence for norepinephrine–containing varicosities in the pontine reticular formation (connection "b" in the model). With respect to connection "d" in the model, there is Golgi evidence for reticular projections to LC, and recently (Lydic, McCarley and Hobson, 1983b) there has been obtained physiological evidence in the unanesthetized cat for mPRF–DR excitatory projections. The pathway observed in this study was not monosynaptic but we note that in terms of the model dynamics whether the connections postulated are monosynaptic or oligo–synaptic is not critical, since these terms in the model represent "lumped" effects for the influence of one population upon another or feedback upon itself.

The Simple LV Equations and the Time Course of Neuronal Activity

Figure 2 is derived from McCarley and Hobson (1975) and Lydic, McCarley and Hobson (1983a), and shows that the simple LV equations (equations 1 and 2) yield time courses of activity that mimic the time course of mPRF neuronal discharge and also of DR discharge. Each of the constants in the simple LV model and the new limit cycle model is, as noted before, associated with a

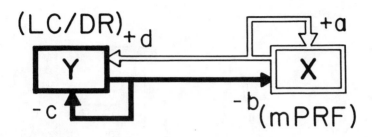

Figure 1   Structural model of the X and Y population interconnections postulated by the model, with the connectivity constants corresponding to those in text equations 1 through 4. The X population is REM–promoting, excitatory and cholinoceptive/cholinergic; mPRF neurons are used as exemplars. The Y population is REM–suppressive, inhibitory and uses biogenic amines as neurotransmitters; LC and DR neurons are used as exemplars of this population. Solid lines and "–" signs indicate inhibitory connections and open lines and "+" signs indicate excitatory connections.

particular connection in the structural model. The data fitting for the cat neuronal data to the simple LV model was done by setting the strengths of the equations constants to match the observed time course of rise of mPRF neuronal activity at the approach of REM sleep (see description in McCarley and Hobson, 1975; see also Hobson, et al., 1974b). The new limit cycle model as applied to human polygraphic sleep data continues to use the same relative values of model constants and thus does not introduce any different assumptions about the dynamics of underlying neuronal activity through changes in the values of these constants.

In both the simple LV and in the new limit cycle model the sleep cycle dynamics can be described in words in the following manner: after the end of one REM period LC/DR neuronal discharge activity is high; this diminishes over time because of the negative feed back (auto–inhibition). As this proceeds further, mPRF cells are released from inhibition and because of the

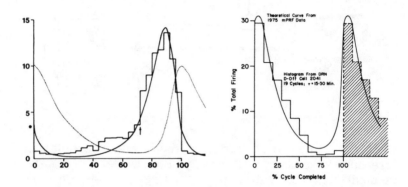

Figure 2A Match of the time course of averaged mPRF
neuronal activity (data in bins) to time course of
activity from model simulation using the simple LV
equations (equations 1 and 2). For model: solid line = X
population; broken line = Y population. Ordinate =
discharge activity in spikes per second. Point 0 on the
graph represents the end of one REM episode (the start
of the cycle) and 100 represents the end of the next
REM episode (cycle end, 100% complete). The arrow
points to the start of the bin with the most probable
time of REM sleep onset. Initial conditions and the
values of model constants were set to match the
observed modulation during the sleep cycle. (From
McCarley and Hobson, 1975.)

Figure 2B Theoretical curve (smooth line) for the Y
population derived from data for the X population
described in part A compared with averaged neuronal
activity data from 10 cycles of a DR neuron (from
Lydic, McCarley and Hobson, 1983a; τ = sleep cycle
duration). Abscissa as in A. Averages from LC neurons
showed approximately the same goodness of fit.
(McCarley and Hobson, 1975.) We emphasize that the
values of constants used in the new limit cycle model
presented in this paper are approximately the same as
those derived from cat neuronal data.

positive feedback increase their discharge rate. When their activity reaches a certain critical threshold REM sleep occurs. The activity of mPRF cells gradually turns on the LC/DR neurons and they in turn inhibit mPRF neurons causing termination of the REM episode. We suggest that the time durations of both the feline (24 min) and human (90 min) sleep cycles indicate that the neurotransmitters involved are those that act with a long time duration. This long time duration is most likely related to the production of "second messengers", such as cyclic–adenosine monophosphate (AMP) in the case of LC/DR synaptic input and of cyclic–guanosine monophosphate (GMP) in the case of mPRF. These second messengers, as emphasized by Bloom (1975), act to extend the time range of neuronal interaction by several orders of magnitude.

The simple LV equations are, with X representing REM–on (mPRF) and Y REM–off (LC/DR) activity:

$$(1) \quad X'(t) = aX - bXY$$
$$(2) \quad Y'(t) = -cy + dXY$$

The LV system was named after two mathematical ecologists who explored the interaction between prey and predator populations in isolated ecosystems. It was thus a logical starting point for descriptions of interaction between inhibitory ("predator") and excitatory ("prey") neuronal populations.

The New Limit Cycle Model: Summary of Major Features and Changes from the Simple LV Model

The limit cycle feature of the new model results from the addition of the following postulates to the simple LV equations: 1) limitation on maximal neuronal firing rate in both REM–on (X) and REM–off (Y) populations; further, the strength of inhibition of the REM–off population on the REM–on population is limited when the REM–on population activity is at low levels; and 2) the term for growth rate of the mPRF population resulting from excitatory feedback is now a function of X level, and is less for lower values of X whereas it was constant in the simple LV model.

The other major category of change in the model is the addition of circadian variation, not treated at all in the original model. All circadian sleep fluctuation is modeled by: a) circadian variation in the way the system begins oscillation, modeled by variation in the rate of decline of the REM–off (Y) population at sleep onset; this "start–up" variation accounts for most of the observed circadian changes in REM sleep percentage; and b) a small continuous circadian modulation (accounting for about ± 5% variation in REM parameters) that results from changing the constant "d" in the simple LV equations to a sinusoidally modulated circadian variable, d(circadian time phase) = d(circ). The equations for the limit cycle model are:

(3) $X'(t) = a(X) * X * S_1(X) - b(X) * X * Y$
(4) $Y'(t) = -c * Y + d(circ) * X * Y * S_2(Y)$

Where:

$*$ = multiplication.
X = mPRF activity; Y = LC/DR activity.
S_1 and S_2 are saturation functions limiting X and Y.
$a(X) \rightarrow$ X growth rate higher with larger X.
$b(X) \rightarrow$ limitation on inhibitability of X by Y for low X values.
d(circ) = d(circadian time) $\rightarrow$ circadian variation in amplitude of d.

The graphs and details of construction for S_1, S_2, a(X), b(X) and d(circ) are given in McCarley and Massaquoi, 1986.

Phase Plane Graphs

The study of the dynamic behavior of such a two–component system is greatly facilitated by plotting the level of activity of one component (X) versus that of the other (Y) at successive points in time. The resulting graph of system activity levels ("system points") over time becomes a trajectory through the X–Y plane; this X–Y plane is referred to as the phase plane and the trajectory through the phase plane captures the evolution of the X–Y interaction. Any stable oscillation of X and Y populations is represented graphically as a single closed orbit which is traversed repeatedly over time. In particular, the simple LV solutions appear as families of simple oval orbits in the phase plane. The limit cycle model solutions are quite similar except that they are families of spirals which all converge to the same kind of oval seen in the simple LV equations; the oval trajectory to which they converge is termed the limit cycle, and the presence of such a limiting oval graphically demonstrates the stability of the oscillatory system (Figure 3, top portion). Because of the power of such graphs, we frequently use phase plane as well as time domain representations.

Circadian Variation and Events at the Onset of Sleep

Neuronal recordings in cats indicate that during waking the activity of the REM–off population is generally elevated ($1 \leq Y \leq 2$) and intracellular recordings indicate population activity and excitability of the X population is low, with X typically < 0.2, although, as discussed above, subsets of mPRF neurons may be phasically active during waking. Thus, in the phase plane graph (Figure 3, top portion), the system points (X–Y values) cluster in the upper left–hand corner during waking (high Y values, low X values). At sleep onset there is falling Y activity and rising X activity and thus the graph shows a downward and rightward drift and eventually begins to orbit. In a limit cycle system all orbits, by definition, eventually converge to the limit cycle, and the graph of later cycles is insensitive to the details of the trajectory of the initial transition into sleep. However, the shape of the first cycle is critically dependent on the precise trajectory taken from the waking state region into sleep.

Although no specific physiological mechanism has yet been clearly identified as maintaining the system in the upper left portion of the phase plane in waking, our model proposes a simple and plausible explanation. We suggest that tonic excitatory input to LC/DRN maintains the system at high Y values during waking, and that physiologically the ultimate control of the strength of this input may be circadian influences arising from the hypothalamus. Computer simulations show that such an input suppresses oscillations by keeping Y high and thus X activity low. In our limit cycle model the circadian waxing and waning of this input turns the REM sleep oscillator on and off. We hasten to add that we do not wish to suggest that other physiological mechanisms having the equivalent mathematical effect are ruled out, but only that this currently appears the most plausible postulate.

With this model the trajectory into sleep cycling is controlled by the time course of the decline in excitatory input to Y. Slow withdrawal allows the system very slowly to begin a gentle oscillation which increases in amplitude as the limit cycle is approached. In the phase plane graph this corresponds to an initial trajectory that is interior to the limit cycle with a subsequent outward spiraling to reach the limit cycle (cf., Figure 3, results). In contrast, rapid withdrawal of excitation from Y allows the system to accelerate into a rapid, large amplitude oscillation which then decays slightly to the limit cycle amplitude; this is represented in the phase plane graph as an external approach to the limit cycle (cf., Figure 4, results).

The experimentally observed circadian phase sensitivity of the initial sleep cycle parameters (cycle period duration, REM intensity, REM latency, and REM duration) are simply modeled by varying the time course of withdrawal of excitatory influences on the Y population with circadian phase: withdrawal is more rapid near a temperature minimum and slower at a temperature maximum.

Specifically, this is modeled by having a constant rate of decay of excitation of Y but having the starting amplitude of Y excitation at sleep onset vary sinusoidally and in phase with the circadian temperature oscillator (Czeisler, et al., 1980; Zulley, Wever and Aschoff, 1981; Akerstedt and Gillberg, 1981; Endo, et al., 1981; and Kronauer, et al., 1982). For sleep onset at all circadian phases the rate of decline of Y excitation is 0.05 Y units/time unit (10.7 min) but the higher starting amplitude with sleep onset at Tmax leads to a slower time course of decay of Y and an internal approach to the limit cycle, resulting in a longer latency, shorter duration, and lesser intensity first REM period. In contrast, with sleep onset near Tmin there is a lower starting level of Y excitation that leads to a more rapid decay of Y and an external entry into the limit cycle. An earlier version of this limit cycle model was termed the "Karma" model to emphasize that the "fate" of the system depended on the way in which it was set into motion (Massaquoi and McCarley, 1982).

A further refinement of this initial Karma model was the introduction of continuous circadian variation of the parameter "d", which describes the sensitivity of the Y population to activity in the X population. This allows: 1) modeling of small amounts of sleep cycle parameter variation that occur in concert with the temperature rhythm after the first sleep cycle and are especially visible in humans in extended sleep (for example, circabidean days); and 2) a more accurate modeling of the shorter latency of REM near sleep onset near temperature minima. Specifically the amplitude of "d" sinusoidally covaries with temperature; d = 1.1 at temperature maximum and is 0.85 at temperature minimum.

We note that it is the difference in the time course of decline of Y at sleep onset which determines whether the limit cycle is entered from the interior (slow time course of decline) or from exterior (rapid time course of decline), and thus this parameter is by far the most critical one for determining changes in REM sleep values, since it is the first REM cycle that varies the most from all others.

Fixed and Variable Parameters

In computer simulation of sleep of normals, only circadian phase was varied, and this affected only the time course of decline of the Y population and d(circ). All other parameters were fixed save for "a" in simulations of injections of cholinergic agonists. (In depressives Yi was also varied.) In all simulations the time scaling remained the same; the initial time scale was fixed by a match to normal human data. Similarly, REM threshold remained the same for all simulations, 1.4 X units, a value compatible with cat neuronal data showing the zone of X values of most probable REM onset; within this zone the exact threshold was set at the value producing the most realistic rapid eye movement/non–rapid–eye–movement (REM/NREM) ratios for normal human sleep cycles. In the simulation of pre–stage 2 sleep conditions X was always initially set to 0.2 units; at normal Y values ($\geq$ 0.35 Y units) the system dynamics (i.e., inhibition of X by Y) led to a decrease to about 0.1 X units in the time before stage 2 onset for all circadian phases. As discussed in detail in the Results, only with the lower Y values in the simulations of depressives' pre–stage 2 condition did the X population increase; all of these simulations for depressives were begun with X = 0.2 while the level of Y was systematically varied. Terminology: Sleep Cycle = REM cycle = end of one REM episode to the end of the next REM episode.

RESULTS – NORMAL SUBJECTS

This section describes the results of model simulations for normal human subjects, for REM sleep alterations in depression, and REM sleep cycle phase response curve predictions for cholinergic agonist administration.

Entrained Normal Subjects

Figure 3 describes the phase plane and time domain results derived from the model and based on a setting of circadian phase at 2.3 radians as the starting point; this is soon after the occurrence of a temperature maximum at 90° or 1.57 radians. For the reader unfamiliar with phase plane charts we note that the phase plane represents X–Y values as 1 point for any single time value. The passage of time is represented by a sequence of X–Y values. In this graph the first sleep cycle begins at the X–Y value indicated by the dot and then the X–Y sequence moves in the trajectory indicated by the arrow; the successive X–Y values over the first sleep cycle are indicated by the "1" label in the figure, and in those the second sleep cycle are indicated by the "2" label and so on. The phase plane representation is best for providing a good overview of the relative amplitude of successive REM episodes and the trend toward larger or smaller values while the time domain representation is useful for study of REM duration: it is to be noted that the phase plane representation does not provide an explicit indication of the time duration of the X–Y values, merely the order in which they occur. In the time domain representation X values are indicated by solid lines and Y values by dotted lines.

The phase plane chart provides a useful illustration for description of the system dynamics. During waking the X–Y values remain in the upper left portion of the phase plane, at a high activity level (> 1.75 units, and thus higher than that seen during the sleep oscillation) of the Y population (the REM–inhibitory,

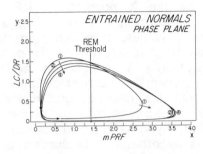

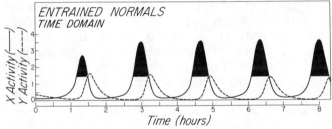

Figure 3   Model simulation of night's course of REM sleep in entrained normal humans. The top part is the phase plane and the bottom part the time domain representation of this data. At the bottom the dark portions of the X (mPRF) graph show those portions of the night with REM sleep and the height of these peaks indicates the intensity of the REM sleep episode. Note the short-duration, lesser intensity first REM episode with subsequent variations being slight. The activity of the Y (REM inhibitory) population is indicated by the dotted line. In the phase plane representation at the top, each point on the graph represents the X-Y values at a particular time. The dot represents the starting point and the interior curve with the arrow shows the first REM episode values, with this curve being interior to the limit cycle values obtained in subsequent REM cycles, labeled 2,4, in the order of their occurrence (for simplicity, sleep cycle 5 has not been graphed in the phase plane). The smaller variations in sleep cycles 2 through 4 are due to circadian modulation.

LC/DRN population). This high activity level of the Y population holds the value of the X population (REM promoting) at low values. Thus, our conception is that during waking the system is "clamped" at high Y values, at which point no oscillations occur. The model postulates that as the result of circadian influences before sleep onset the Y population activity level declines. Although there is currently no direct cellular evidence bearing on the mechanism for this decline, our model uses the simplest assumption of a withdrawal of excitation. Our physiological hypothesis is that hypothalamic influences mediate circadian effects; while this hypothalamic brainstem connectivity is known to be present the sign of influence has not yet been defined. In addition to this circadian input, the model provides for the possibility of prevention of sleep onset by exogenous input activating the Y population and also for a "wake-up" through exogenous activation of the Y population; in this paper we will not model these events in any further detail.

System Unlocking

Our computer simulations show that when Y population activity declines below a certain critical level the X-Y population oscillations begin. This decline may be viewed as an "unlocking" of an oscillatory system. The critical feature for circadian alterations in the first REM cycle have to do with the time course of Y decline at the time the sleep cycle oscillation begins. For all computer runs simulating normal human subjects the level of Y was always set at a fixed value (0.35 units) at the beginning of the simulation. All of our figures begin at a time point corresponding to stage 2 of human sleep, which is the usual starting point for REM latency measurements in humans. We note that in cat studies the 0.35 level of Y neuronal activity is reliably associated with the presence of sleep.

When the night of sleep is begun at a circadian phase of 2.3 radians (just after a temperature maximum) this means that the level of circadian-determined excitation of Y at sleep onset is near maximum. While our model posits that the rate of decrease of this excitation is constant across circadian phase, the high initial level of the excitation at this phase means that the decay of excitation takes longer and that consequently Y remains at higher levels longer than near a circadian minimum. The rate of Y decay determined by the X–Y interaction alone without this circadian excitatory input is much faster. This prolonged time course of decay in Y results in the first sleep cycle beginning on a trajectory interior to that of the limit cycle, as illustrated by the phase plane graph in Figure 3. Note that the X–Y trajectory of the first cycle has a much smaller X amplitude but that the second cycle goes very close to the final limit cycle. The small changes observed in cycles 2 through 4 are the result of the small continuous circadian variation which alters slightly the shape of the limit cycle by variation of "d" amplitude. The time domain chart shows the first REM episode is of low amplitude (low intensity) and short duration and has a long latency value. These value follow from the slow rate of Y decline and consequent approach to the limit cycle from the interior (cf., the phase plane graph). The relatively similar time domain values in subsequent cycles reflect the fact that by the second cycle the limit cycle trajectory has been attained. The smaller differences that are present between the second and subsequent REM cycles in the time domain graph reflect the continuous circadian modulation of "d" and hence of cycle values: over the night REM episodes become slightly longer and the sleep cycle period duration (measured from end of REM to end of REM) becomes slightly shorter.

Comparisons with Experimental Data

Table 1 summarizes experimental data from several polygraphic sleep studies on REM latency (= first NREM episode duration) and REM and NREM episode duration for the first three cycles in normal male subjects under conditions of two–hour entrainment both in sleep labs and when living in underground bunkers (Zulley, 1979); also tabulated is data from free–running subjects who went to sleep near temperature maxima. This is paralleled by the data derived from model simulations for these two conditions. In general the fit between model and data is good. Note specifically that in the entrained condition model simulation and the human sleep data both show: 1) a large increase in REM duration between the first and second episode; and 2) an increase in REM episode duration as sleep progresses. The model slightly over–estimates the duration of the first REM episode (model = 19 min vs. experimental median = 15 min) but the duration of

TABLE 1

MATCH BETWEEN MODEL AND EXPERIMENTAL VALUES
FOR NORMAL MALES UNDER SEVERAL CONDITIONS

			DURATION IN MINUTES				
STUDY	CONDITION		NREM 1 = "REM LATENCY"	REM 1	NREM 2	REM 2	NREM 3	REM 3
Zulley (1980)	24 hr Entrained	Median Mean		12 15		30 30		34 35
Zulley (1980)	Free Run Near Tmax	Median Mean		16 16		23 22		24 27
Schulz, Zulley and Dirlich (1984)	Laboratory	Median	69	12	75	29	73	33
Williams, Karacan and Hursch (1974)	Laboratory Age 20–29 Age 30–39	Mean Mean		15 17	76 76	31 21	69 72	24 30
Feinberg, Koresko and Heller (1967)	Laboratory	Mean	69	11	72	21	68	26
Caille and Bassano (1975)	Laboratory	Mean	67	18		27		27
MODEL:	Entrained Match, Circadian Phase = 2.3 Radians		69	19	75	28	73	29
	Free Run, Tmax at Sleep Onset Match, Circadian Phase = 1.57 Radians		80	17	79	25	74	26

* Blanks indicate no data available.

subsequent REM episodes matches quite well. The model predicts a small but consistent lengthening of REM episode duration throughout the night which has been hard to demonstrate with statistical reliability in the quite variable human data. However, the trend in the studies reviewed here is to show an increase: 5/7 studies show an increased duration of REM 3 compared with REM 2 vs. no difference in one study and only a single study with a decrease. Furthermore, in a statistical re-analysis of the data of Schulz, Zulley and Dirlich (1984), we have demonstrated a statistically significant trend for a successive increase in REM duration for the first three REM periods by computing the probability of having REM durations ordered REM 1 < REM 2 < REM 3 for 7/11 subjects, as occurred in this dataset: p was < 0.002 for this ordering vs. the hypothesis of equiprobable random ordering.

Free-Running Normal Subjects with
Sleep Onset Near a Temperature Minimum

In contrast to the fuzziness of the data about systematic circadian alteration in the REM episodes following the second, data about circadian variation in the first REM episode parameters is much more robust and offer an excellent opportunity to test the model's performance against empirical data. Zulley (1979, 1980) has provided quantitative data on the median duration of successive REM episodes in free-running normal subjects who went to sleep at two different times, one group near a temperature minimum and the other near a temperature maximum. To model the situation of a temperature minimum we set the circadian phase parameter of the model at the temperature phase of 4.72 radians (270°, exactly at the minimum) and held all other parameters of the model the same as those for normal entrained subjects, as described in the first part of this section. Figure 4 shows the phase plane and the time domain plot of the X-Y values resulting from this condition and the subsequent changes in REM sleep parameters over the night. The main result of this condition is seen clearly in the time domain plot as a shorter latency, larger amplitude and longer duration first REM episode when compared with that of normal subjects who began their sleep nearer a temperature maximum (Figure 3).

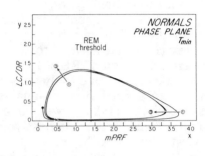

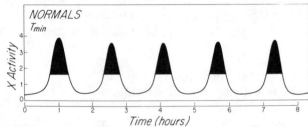

Figure 4   Phase plane (top) and time domain (bottom) representation of model: results for sleep begun near a temperature minimum (circadian phase + 4.72 radians, 270°). Note that, in contrast to Figure 3, the phase plane graph shows an entry into the limit cycle from a point _exterior_ to the cycle; arrows indicate the direction of change successive phase plane trajectories for cycles 1, 2 and 3. As can be seen this is associated with a shorter latency, longer duration, and higher intensity first REM episode than does the _interior_ entry that occurs near a temperature maximum (Figure 3, phase plane).

What is of special interest from the modeling and theoretical point of view is that this set of values is associated with an entry into the limit cycle from a point _exterior_ to the limit cycle, as seen in the phase plane of Figure 4 where the first cycle trajectory is labeled "1". Subsequent REM cycles in this graph (direction of change indicated by arrows) are of lesser amplitude. This data provides an extremely close fit to the data of Zulley (1980) on free-run normals who begin sleep at an early temperature minimum. The sequence of model predictions (data underlined) and Zulley data on REM duration in minutes was: REM1, 33 vs. 34; REM 2, 29 vs. 30; REM 3, 28 vs. 30; REM 4, 28 vs. 28; REM 5, 28 vs. 28; REM 6, 27 vs. 27. In both the model and in the empirical data the principal changes occur from the first to the second REM episode; there is a small trend toward a declining REM duration in subsequent REM episodes suggesting continuous circadian modulation in the data.

Free-Running Normals with Sleep Onset Near a Temperature Maximum (= with a Late Temperature Minimum)

This condition in free-running subjects resembles that of sleep onset in normal subjects in that a temperature minimum with both groups occurs late in the evening. For both groups the clear prediction of the model is for a longer latency, lesser intensity, shorter duration first REM episode, when compared with subsequent REM episodes and with the first REM episode of subjects with sleep onset near a temperature minimum. For simulation of sleep onset with an early temperature maximum, circadian phase was set to 1.57 radians (temperature maximum) and all other parameters were as on previous simulations. Table 1 shows the match of the model simulation to Zulley's data on duration of successive REM episodes in free-running normals. Note that the fit is good, with REM durations falling quite close to Zulley's data: both model and experimental data show the REM 1 to REM 2 duration increase is the largest, and there is a smaller increase from REM 2 to REM 3. (For this simulation we have not graphed the phase plane and time domain results since they so closely resemble those of Figure 3).

It is worth noting that Zulley's data for this free-run condition are slightly different from his data on 24-hour entrained subjects: the free-run subjects show a longer duration first REM episode and a less abrupt change from first to second REM episode duration (Table 1). While this could be random statistical variation, it also could represent subjects going to sleep at slightly different temperature phases in the two conditions and/or other factors in the 24-hour entrained condition leading to a shortened first REM episode, such as a higher body activity level and resultant higher temperature level. Our simulation matches this feature of the empirical data by assuming a slightly different circadian phase in the free-run condition (Free-Run Circadian Phase = 1.57 radians vs. 24-Hour Entrained Circadian Phase = 2.3 radians; see Table 1).

REM ALTERATIONS IN DEPRESSION

The covariance of REM sleep abnormalities and depression have strongly suggested links between the neurobiological control mechanisms for these phenomena (see other chapters in this volume and review in McCarley, 1982). Compared with age-matched normal controls, depressives show a first REM period that occurs with a shorter latency and an increased intensity (Coble, Foster and Kupfer, 1976; and Foster, et al., 1976). (REM intensity is measured as the number of rapid eye movements per unit time and is often called "REM density": combined eye movement and unit recordings show the number of EMs to be roughly correlated with the intensity of neuronal activity within the REM period - see Pivik, McCarley and Hobson, 1977; McCarley, 1978; Nelson, McCarley and Hobson, 1983). There is also data indicating the first REM period is of longer duration in depressives than normals. Whether there are alterations in later REM periods in depressives is not known with certainty; this point will later be discussed in more detail. Although endogenous depressives have other sleep abnormalities, control studies comparing depressives with nonspecific insomniacs show that only the REM sleep abnormalities appear as distinctive separators of these two groups (Vogel, et al., 1980).

The monoamine theory of depression proposes that a deficiency in monoamine activity (norepinephrine and/or serotonin systems) is responsible for the occurrence of some or all of the major depressions. While we recognize that causation of depression is undoubtedly more complex than this simple theory can accommodate, we will focus on it because of the links to the cholinergic-monoaminergic model of sleep cycle control we have presented. Studies reviewed by McCarley (1982) indicate that virtually all varieties of clinically effective tricyclic antidepressants, including those atypical ones not associated with acute blocking of monoamine re-uptake such as iprindole, act to change norepinephrine and serotonin receptor binding. Long-term administration of these agents decreases beta adrenergic and serotonin-2 (high affinity to ^{3}H-spiroperiodol) receptors. Neuronal recordings indicate that long-term administration of tricyclic antidepressants, including the atypical ones, act on monoamine systems by increasing responsiveness to iontophoretically applied monoamines. A recent study has provided some insight into the mechanism of antidepressant action at the neuronal level; after two weeks of antidepressant administration serotonergic transmission in the rat DR-hippocampal pathway was potentiated (Blier and DeMontigny, 1983).

The implication of monoamine systems in both the regulation of depression (the monoamine theory) and in REM sleep (the reciprocal interaction theory) suggest the possibility of a link between these two systems through the monoamines. Kupfer and partners (1981a,b) have shown that one of the first indications of effectiveness of the tricyclic action on depression is the abolition of the abnormally short latency of the first REM period. A study by Vogel and colleagues (1980) has indicated that REM sleep deprivation, known to increase monoamine neuronal discharge activity in animals, acts to improve depression. REM sleep deprivation has also been shown to decrease rat cortical high affinity bonding sites for the antidepressant imipramine (Mogilnicka, et al., 1980), with the likely mediating event being the deprivation-induced increased firings of monoamine neurons.

Modeling the REM Sleep Abnormalities of Depression

The above review has sketched the data supporting altered levels of monoamine activity in depression; in our modeling we shall concentrate on alterations in the Y population, composed of monoamine-containing neurons (simply labeled LC/DR in our graphs, but also including other REM-off brainstem cells, including those in the peribrachial area). We shall first address the distinctive alterations in the first REM episode, and then suggest, on the basis of our simulations, the appropriate empirical measurements to determine whether or not there are alterations in later REM periods.

Our examination of the first REM latency, intensity, and duration as sleep is begun near a temperature minimum in normal subjects (previous section) is instructive for the kind of changes that might occur in depression. As shown by Figure 4, in our model at Tmin there is a more rapid decline of the Y (monoamine) population that leads to entry into the limit cycle from the outside and hence produces a shorter latency (45 min), larger amplitude, and longer duration REM episode than in normals beginning sleep near a temperature maximum. The simulation data matches empirical findings in normals quite well with respect to the circadian changes in REM. However, the REM latency, while lower than that of sleep begun near temperature maximum, did not appear to be close enough to the very short latencies shown by depressives. We thus postulate that in depressives the changes in Y are more pronounced than those in normals at temperature minima. Thus in addition to viewing the conditions at sleep onset in depressives like those of normals at Tmin, we postulate that the value of Y (Y initial, Yi) at the beginning of the sleep cycle in depressives is lower than the normal value.

To provide an illustration for our discussion and elaboration we show the phase plane and time domain (Figure 5) result of a simulation with the model parameters set exactly the same as for the simulation for normals near Tmin but with the additional assumption that Yi is 0.24 units, compared with a normal value of 0.35 units at the onset of stage 2 sleep, the sleep stage whose onset is used to calculate REM latency and the starting point of the graphs. This produces a first REM latency of 35 min; this is almost exactly in accord with the mean values for depressives in the literature and is less than most extreme values for the first REM latency in normals as tabulated by Schulz, Zulley and Dirlich (1984). Figure 5 further indicates that alteration of Yi is not only able to mimic the shortened REM latency characteristic of depressives but also produces a first REM episode with a heightened amplitude (= heightened REM intensity) and duration, also characteristics of the first REM episode of depressives. Subsequent REM cycles tend to converge to the limit cycle, an important feature. As will be discussed later in more detail, only the limit cycle model (and not the simple LV model) preserves a realistic replica of sleep patterning after the initial short latency REM episode.

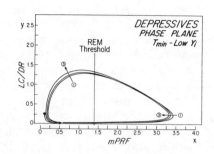

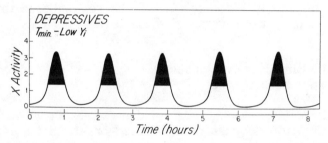

Figure 5 Phase plane (top) and time domain (bottom) representation of REM activity of depressives. Note the first REM episode has a shortened latency, increased intensity, and longer duration compared with normal REM in Figure 3; note also the tendency for less REM in subsequent REM episodes. Circadian phase as in Figure 4 for a temperature minimum (4.72 radians) and Yi is 0.25 vs. the 0.35 for all simulation of normal REM. See also description in text.

With respect to the later REM episodes, Figure 5 shows the result of modeling depression as involving both a lower Yi and a "phase advance" of the circadian rhythm in depressives with Tmin occurring near sleep onset (Kripke, et al., 1978; Wehr, et al., 1979b). As the circadian rhythm progresses from onset at Tmin, there are attendant alterations of subsequent REM cycles: a progressive increase in the time between REM episode onset and a decrease in the duration of each REM episode. The critical feature of the limit cycle model that produces a short latency REM episode is the rapid decline of the Y population. Our model is compatible with this resulting at least in part from a phase shift in circadian rhythms or, and we underline this "or", the entire rapid descent and lower value of the Y population at sleep onset could be due to intrinsic Y population pathology without a phase shift. Indeed, in our simulations we can produce short latency, higher amplitude and longer duration REM episode without assuming a phase shift. The critical test for the phase advance theory is to measure the time course of REM activity over the night: as illustrated in Figure 5, the phase advance theory predicts that REM episodes should show progressively less duration and that the time intervals between REM episodes should increase. It will be remembered that these trends are exactly the reverse of those seen in normals with sleep onset near Tmax and illustrated in Figure 3.

Modeling the Bimodal Distribution of REM Latencies in Depression

The REM latency histogram of depressives shows a "bimodal distribution" with one peak of near sleep–onset REM episodes and another peak at much longer latencies, with relatively few REM episodes in the intermediate zone of latencies (Schulz, et al., 1979). Our simulations provide some insight into a possible mechanism for this phenomenon. Under the conditions established by our model, Y values less than approximately 0.3 are progressively less able to "hold" the X population at initially low values, i.e., 0.1 and less. If the Y values drop to below this critical zone of about 0.3 in the pre–sleep period (and which also includes stage 1 since the usual REM latency is measured from stage 2 to REM), there is a progressively increasing tendency for an "escape" (i.e., a gradual increase) of the X population toward a higher value prior to onset of stage 2 (the beginning point of our graphs).

This hastens the onset of the first REM episode. Simulations show that the degree of shortening of REM latency as Y values become less depends on the pre–stage 2 duration of particular values of Y. The shape of the function relating REM latency and the level of Y before stage 2 onset (pre–sleep Y), which we shall refer to as Y^*, is highly nonlinear with a much more rapid rate of decrease of REM latencies with lower values of Y^*. To illustrate this phenomenon we have done a series of simulations in which Y^*

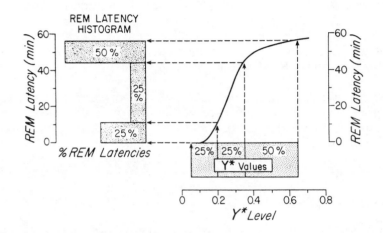

Figure 6   Model simulation of bimodal REM latency distribution for depressives. See text for description.

is held constant for 30 min prior to stage 2 onset (stage 2 onset = sleep onset is the starting point of the figures); we have used this constant level for computational simplicity but hasten to add that the true time course of Y* is probably a decreasing function. The results of these simulations are presented in Figure 6; in all cases other parameters, including circadian phase (phase = 4.72 radians at stage 2 onset) were as for Figure 5.

The non–linear, approximately sigmoid form of the relationship between different levels of Y* and the subsequent REM latency produces a bimodal histogram of REM latencies, as is illustrated in Figure 6. We assume for simplicity of illustration that the probability of a given Y* is uniformly distributed in the range 0.05 to 0.65. The resulting map of this probability distribution onto the probability distribution of REM latencies (labeled REM latency histogram in Figure 6) is highly nonlinear. Note that 50% of the Y* range from 0.35 to 0.65 but that this range maps into a much smaller latency range, 43 to 56 min or 23% of latency range, producing a peak at longer REM latencies. There is a second strongly nonlinear region at the lower end where 25% of Y* values map into a latency range of zero to 11 min (20%), producing a peak at the lower range of REM latencies. In contrast, 25% of the Y* values map into a large middle value REM latency range, 11 to 43 min (57% of entire range). Thus assuming a pre-stage 2 increase in X values secondary to low Y* values produces a bimodal REM latency distribution.

It is evident that the exact form of the distribution is contingent on the level and rate of change of Y pre-sleep, as well as the probability distribution assumed for Y*. Another publication (Massaquoi and McCarley, in preparation) will discuss these factors in more detail than can be provided here, but we note that the production of a bimodal REM latency distribution occurs under a wide variety of assumptions about the form of Y* density and the rapidity of Y* decline.

Relationship to Previous Work on Modeling REM Latency in Depression

All of the previous work has been based on the simple LV model of McCarley and Hobson (1975; equations 1 and 2 of this paper). Vogel and co-workers (1980), used cycle-to-cycle alterations of the connectivity constants "a" and "c" without explicit use of the Y population values at sleep onset. McCarley (1980) suggested that alterations in the Yi value might replicate the findings in depression, and Massaquoi and McCarley (1982) provided quantitative evidence for this in the context of the presenting the initial version of this limit cycle model. Beersma and colleagues (1983a, 1984b) also used alteration of Yi, although in the simple LV model, and were the first to point out that a stochastic model of Yi values would generate a bimodal REM latency histogram. We agree with Beersma and associates that alteration of the one parameter (Y) is to be preferred to the elaborate suppositions needed in the work of Vogel and partners. We note that the limit cycle model developed here is an improvement over the simple LV model in the modeling of REM abnormalities in depression for the following reasons: 1) in the simple LV equations with parameters used by Beersma and co-authors, lowering Yi, while shortening the REM latency, produces an initial REM episode with a less than normal intensity;

this is not at all in agreement with the higher intensity found in empirical studies of depression; 2) because of the neutral stability feature of the simple LV equations, creating a short-latency first REM episode means that distortions of the REM/NREM cycle persist throughout the night, and the REM/NREM values predicted by the LV simulation do not match those observed in empirical studies. As we noted in the introduction, this neutral stability problem with the simple LV model was one of the motivating factors in developing the limit cycle model.

Depression: Monoamines, Acetylcholine and Phase Response Abnormalities

In addition to the monoamine abnormalities in depression, Gillin, Sitaram and co-workers have found that increased sensitivity to acetylcholine agonist induction of REM sleep appears to be a hallmark of patients subject to endogenous depression (cf., next section). There are several biochemical possibilities for this effect. One is simply that there might be an abnormal sensitivity to acetylcholine agonist administered exogenously. If this were true, then the people with predisposition to affective disorder not only should have a single time point abnormality in their response to acetylcholine agonist but should also have an abnormal phase response curve, whose shape could be readily correlated with specific alterations in the parameters of our model producing similar alterations; the next section discusses the implications of this assumption in detail. Here, we wish simply to emphasize that it is likely that various kinds of depression involve more than one causative factor, and that both acetylcholine and/or monoamine abnormalities may be present. The availability of quantitative predictions about the effects of each may be of use in specifying subtypes of depression and in classifying other pathological syndromes with REM abnormalities.

PHASE–RESPONSE CURVE PREDICTIONS

Predicting the Phase Response Curve during the REM Sleep Cycle to Acetylcholine Agonist Administration

Studies by several groups of investigators have indicated that the administration of acetylcholine agonists such as physostigmine or arecoline can hasten the onset of the next REM episode in humans (Sitaram, et al., 1980b and 1982; and Gillin, Sitaram and Mendelson, 1982). This data is consistent with the more extensive, direct evidence in animal experiments that direct intrabrainstem administration of acetylcholine agonists, including neostigmine, into the pontine reticular formation (but not bulbar or midbrain reticular formation) can produce a syndrome with all of the signs of REM sleep (Baghdoyan, et al., 1984 a,b; and earlier studies reviewed in McCarley, 1982).

Since a model is most usefully and most easily tested by its predictions, we thought it would be helpful to sketch here, well in advance of any empirical tests that we know of, the phase response curve predicted by the limit cycle model for the administration of an acetylcholine agonist, such as physostigmine, or a similar agent producing a decrement in the rate in which acetylcholine is hydrolyzed. In our model (see Figure 1), this can be described as raising the level of "a" during the effective duration of the acetylcholinesterase blocker; "a" is the term indicating the strength of positive feedback in the excitatory population and thus presumably the strength of cholinergic activity. As a first approximation to the experimental conditions our simulations doubled the strength of "a" (cholinergic feedback) for 10.7 min (step function). These values produced clear–cut effects but did not severely distort the time curves, and produced a phase advance of the REM episode of roughly the same order of magnitude as the single time point experiment of Sitaram and Gillin.

Figure 7 illustrates the basic paradigm for the pharmacological simulation studies. We used the modeling parameters used for normal entrained subjects (as in Figure 2) and modeled the effects as occurring after the second REM episode to avoid confusion with circadian initial conditions at sleep onset. The top portion of Figure 7 shows the effect of transient increase in "a" lasting from 7 to 17 min after the end of the second REM episode. It will be seen that the subsequent REM episode is advanced by a time period indicated by the shading. However, the REM latency decrease is much more pronounced when, in this simulation, the "drug" producing a transient increase in the model constant "a" is applied later, from 41 to 51 min after the onset of the second REM episode. These differential effects can be understood as REM being much easier to induce when the X

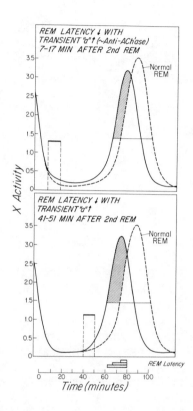

Figure 7   Examples of REM latency shortening by an increase in the model parameter "a", simulating anti–acetylcholinesterase administration. The shaded area shows degree of phase advance; note that the administration at 41 min (bottom) has a greater effect than at 7 min after REM 2 ends (top). See text for further description.

population is on the rising rather than in the falling phase of the sleep cycle. This has to do with both an ease of tipping the X population into an exponential growth phase and also the absence of Y inhibition later in the cycle.

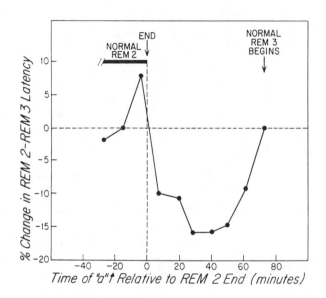

Figure 8   Predicted   phase   response   curve   to
anti–acetylcholinesterase   administration.   Each   point
was generated by a simulation like that described for
the points 7 and 41 min in Figure 7. See text for
further description.

Figure 8 shows a complete phase response curve for the
simulated application of a drug producing an increase in the model
parameter "a" for 10.7 min beginning at various times near the end
of REM 2 episode and in the period between the end of REM 2 and
REM 3. Dots indicate onset times of the treatment. Note that
there is a time near the end of REM 2 when increasing "a" prolongs
the latency of the subsequent REM episode, due to an increase in
the duration of the second REM episode. The phase of the response
then changes rapidly; a shortening of the REM latency of the order
of 10% occurs on administrations starting after the end of the
second REM episode; an increase to maximal effect (17% latency
reduction) occurs with administrations about 25 to 50 min after the

end of the second REM episode. Following this there is relatively less effect, due to the fact that the third REM episode normally occurs very soon thereafter, and thus there is very little room left for shortening. We note that this predicted phase response curve can be used to test the dynamics of the model both in humans and in animals and is, we believe, the first example of such a phase response prediction for REM sleep.

ACKNOWLEDGMENTS

We thank Drs. K. Ito, R. Lydic and H. Baghdoyan for helpful comments on earlier versions of this paper. Supported by grants from the Veterans Administration, NIMH RO1 39,683, RSDA MH 280 to RWM, the Licha Lopez Fund award to SGM, the Milton Fund of Harvard University, and the Burroughs–Wellcome Fund. We thank the American Physiological Society for permission to reproduce figures and text from McCarley and Massaquoi, Am J Physiol, 1986.

REFERENCES

Akerstedt, T. and M. Gillberg. 1981. The circadian variation of experimentally displaced sleep. Sleep 4:159–169.

Baghdoyan, H.A., M.L. Rodrigo–Angulo, R.W. McCarley and J.A. Hobson. 1984a. Site–specific enhancement and suppression of desynchronized sleep signs following cholinergic stimulation of three brainstem regions. Brain Res 306:39–52.

Baghdoyan, H.A., A.P. Monaco, M.L. Rodrigo–Angulo, F. Assens, R.W. McCarley and J.A. Hobson. 1984b. Microinjection of neostigmine into the pontine reticular formation of cats enhances desynchronized sleep signs. J Pharmacol Exp Ther 231:173–180.

Beersma, D.G.M., R.H. van den Hoofdakker, S. Daan, and J.W.B.M. van Berkestijn. 1983a. REM sleep and depression. In Sleep 1982 (Proceedings of the Sixth European Congress on Sleep Research, Zurich, 1982), Koella, W.P. (ed.). Basel: S. Karger, A.G., pp. 349–351.

Beersma, D.G.M., S. Daan and R.H. van den Hoofdakker. 1984b. Distribution of REM latencies and other sleep phenomena in depression as explained by a single ultradian rhythm disturbance. Sleep 7:126–136.

Blier, P. and C. De Montigny. 1983b. Electrophysiological investigations on the effect of repeated zimelidine administration on serotonergic neurotransmission in the rat. J Neurosci 3:1270–1278.

Bloom, F.E. 1975. The role of cyclic nucleotides in central synaptic function. Rev Physiol Biochem Pharmacol 74:1–103.

Borbély, A.A. 1982a. A two–process model of sleep regulation. Hum Neurobiol 1:195–204.

Caille, E.J. and J.L. Bassano. 1975. Approche du processus hypnique: analyse, fonctions temporelles, valeur fonctionnelle. Psychol Méd 7:317–352.

Coble, P., F.G. Foster and D.J. Kupfer. 1976. Electroencephalographic sleep diagnosis of primary depression. Arch Gen Psychiatr
33:1124–1127.

Czeisler, C.A., J.C. Zimmerman, J.M. Ronda, M.C. Moore–Ede and
E.D. Weitzman. 1980. Timing of REM sleep is coupled to the
circadian rhythm of body temperature in man. Sleep 2:329–346.

Daan, S., D.G.M. Beersma and A.A. Borbély. 1984. Timing of
human sleep: recovery process gated by a circadian pacemaker.
Am J Physiol 246:R161–R178.

Endo, S., T. Kobayashi, T. Yamamoto, H. Fukuda, M. Sasaki and
T. Ohta. 1981. Persistence of the circadian rhythm of REM sleep:
a variety of experimental manipulations of the sleep–wake cycle.
Sleep 4:319–328.

Feinberg, I., R.L. Koresko and N. Heller. 1967. EEG sleep
patterns as a function of normal and pathological aging in man. J
Psychiatr Res 5:107–144.

Foster, F.G., D.J. Kupfer, P. Coble and R.J. McPartland. 1976.
Rapid eye movement sleep density. An objective indicator in
severe medical–depressive syndromes. Arch Gen Psychiatr
33:1119–1123.

Gillin, J.C., N. Sitaram and W.B. Mendelson. 1982. Acetylcholine,
sleep, and depression. Hum Neurobiol 1:211–219.

Hobson, J.A., R.W. McCarley, R.T. Pivik and R. Freedman. 1974a.
Selective firing by cat pontine brain stem neurons in desynchronized sleep. J Neurophysiol 37:497–511.

Hobson, J.A., R.W. McCarley, R. Freedman and R.T. Pivik. 1974b.
Time course of discharge rate changes by cat pontine brain stem
neurons during sleep cycle. J Neurophysiol 37:1297–1309.

Hobson, J.A., R.W. McCarley and J.P. Nelson. 1983. Location and
spike–train characteristics of cells in anterodorsal pons having
selective decreases in firing rate during desynchronized sleep.
J Neurophysiol 50:770–783.

Ito, K. and R.W. McCarley. 1984. Alterations in membrane potential and excitability of cat medial pontine reticular formation neurons during changes in naturally occurring sleep–wake states. Brain Res 292:169–175.

Kripke, D.F., D.J. Mullaney, M. Atkinson and S. Wolf. 1978. Circadian rhythm disorders in manic–depressives. Biol Psychiatr 13:335–351.

Kronauer, R.E., C.A. Czeisler, S.F. Pilato, M.C. Moore–Ede and E.D. Weitzman. 1982. Mathematical model of the human circadian system with two interacting oscillators. Am J Physiol 242:R3–R17.

Kupfer, D.J., D.G. Spiker, P.A. Coble, J.F. Neil, R. Ulrich and D.H. Shaw. 1981a. Sleep and treatment prediction in endogenous depression. Am J Psychiatr 138:429–434.

Kupfer, D.J., J.C. Gillin, P.A. Coble, D.G. Spiker, D. Shaw and B. Holzer. 1981b. REM sleep, naps, and depression. Psychiatr Res 5:195–203.

Lotka, A. Elements of Physical Biology. 1956. New York: Dover Press.

Lydic, R., R.W. McCarley and J.A. Hobson. 1983a. The time–course of dorsal raphe discharge, PGO waves, and muscle tone averaged across multiple sleep cycles. Brain Res 274:365–370.

Lydic, R., R.W. McCarley and J.A. Hobson. 1983b. Enhancement of dorsal raphe discharge by medial pontine reticular formation stimulation depends on behavioral state. Neurosci Lett 38:35–40.

Lydic, R., R.W. McCarley and J.A. Hobson. 1984. Forced activity alters sleep cycle periodicity and dorsal raphe discharge rhythm. Am J Physiol 247 (1 Pt 2):R135–R145.

Massaquoi, S.G. 1983. Refinement of the extension of the McCarley–Hobson reciprocal interaction model of REM sleep control. (Unpublished thesis, Harvard Medical School and Division of Health Sciences and Technology, Massachusetts Institute of Technology.)

Massaquoi, S.G. and R.W. McCarley. 1982. Extension of the reciprocal interaction sleep stage control model: a "Karma" control model. Sleep Res 11:216.

McCarley, R.W. 1978. Control of sleep–waking state alteration in Felix domesticus. In Society for Neuroscience Symposia, Volume III: Aspects of Behavioral Neurobiology (Papers Presented at Two Symposia during the Seventh Annual Meeting of the Society for Neuroscience, California, 1977), Ferrendelli, J.A. (ed.). Maryland: Society for Neuroscience, pp. 90–128.

McCarley, R.W. 1980. Mechanisms and models of behavioral state control (chairman's overview of part V). In The Reticular Formation Revisited: Specifying Function for a Nonspecific System (International Brain Research Organization Monograph Series, Volume 6; Papers from a Symposium Sponsored by the International Brain Research Organization and the Society for Neuroscience, Saint Louis, Missouri, 1978), Hobson, J.A. and M.A.B. Brazier (eds.). New York: Raven Press, pp. 375–403.

McCarley, R.W. 1981. Pontine brainstem neuronal activity and REM sleep control mechanisms. In Regulatory Functions of the CNS, Principles of Motion and Organization (Proceedings of the 28th International Congress of Physiological Sciences; Budapest, 1980): Advances in Physiological Science, Volume 1), Szentagothai, M., M. Palkovits and J. Hamori (eds). New York: Pergamon Press, pp. 293–299.

McCarley, R.W. 1982. REM sleep and depression: common neurobiological control mechanisms. Am J Psychiatr 139:565–570.

McCarley, R.W. and J.A. Hobson. 1975. Neuronal excitability modulation over the sleep cycle: a structural and mathematical model. Science 189:58–60.

McCarley, R.W. and S.G. Massaquoi. 1985a. The rapid eye movement sleep ultradian rhythm: a limit cycle mathematical model. In Ultradian Rhythms in Physiology and Behavior (Experimental Brain Research, Supplementum 12), Schulz, H. and P. Lavie (eds.). Berlin: Springer–Verlag, pp. 288–308.

McCarley, R.W. and K. Tio. 1985b. Desynchronized sleep–specific changes in membrane potential and excitability in medial pontine reticular formation neurons: implications for concepts and mechanisms of behavioral state control. In Brain Mechanisms of Sleep, McGinty, D.J., R. Drucker–Colin, A. Morrison and P.L. Parmeggiani (eds.). New York: Raven Press.

McCarley, R.W. and S.G. Massaquoi. 1986. A limit cycle mathematical model of the REM sleep oscillator system. Am J Physiol 251:R1011–R–1029.

Mogilnicka, E., S. Arbilla, H. Depoortere and S.Z. Langer. 1980. Rapid–eye– movement sleep deprivation decreases the density of ³H–dihydroalprenolol and ³H–imipramine binding sites in the rat cerebral cortex. Eur J Pharmacol 65:289–292.

Nelson, J.P., R.W. McCarley and J.A. Hobson. 1983. REM–sleep burst neurons, PGO waves, and eye–movement information. J Neurophysiol 50:784–797.

Pivik, R.T., R.W. McCarley and J.A. Hobson. 1977. Eye movement–associated discharge in brain stem neurons during desynchronized sleep. Brain Res 121:59–76.

Schulz, H., R. Lund, C. Cording and G. Dirlich. 1979. Bimodal distribution of REM sleep latencies in depression. Biol Psychiatr 14:595–600.

Schulz, H., J. Zulley and G. Dirlich. 1984. Statistical properties of the REM–NREM sleep cycle. Unpublished manuscript.

Sitaram, N., J.I. Nurnberger, Jr., E.S. Gershon and J.C. Gillin. 1980b. Faster cholinergic REM sleep induction in euthymic patients with primary affective illness. Science 208:200–202.

Sitaram, N., J.I. Nurnberger, Jr., E.S. Gershon and J.C. Gillin. 1982. Cholinergic regulation of mood and REM sleep: potential model and marker of vulnerability to affective disorder. Am J Psychiatr 139:571–576.

Vogel, G.W., F. Vogel, R.S. McAbee and A.J. Thurmond. 1980. Improvement of depression by REM sleep deprivation. New findings and a theory. Arch Gen Psychiatr 37:247-253.

Volterra, V. 1931. Leçons sur la Théorie Mathématique de la Lutte pour la Vie. Paris: Gauthier-Villars et Cie.

Wehr, T.A., A. Wirz-Justice, F.K. Goodwin, W. Duncan and J.C. Gillin. 1979b. Phase advance of the circadian sleep-wake cycle as an antidepressant. Science 206:710-713.

Wever, R.A. 1982. Behavioral aspects of circadian rhythmicity. In Rhythmic Aspects of Behavior, Brown, F.M. and R.C. Graeber (eds.). Hillsdale, New Jersey: L. Erlbaum Associates, pp. 105-171.

Williams, R.L., I. Karacan and C.J. Hursch. 1974. EEG of Human Sleep: Clinical Applications. New York: J. Wiley & Sons.

Zulley, J. 1979. Der Einfluß von Zeitgebern auf den Schlaf des Menschen. (Doctoral dissertation, Universitat Tübingen.) Frankfurt am Main: Rita Fischer-Verlag.

Zulley, J. 1980. Distribution of REM sleep in entrained 24 hour and free-running sleep-wake cycles. Sleep 2:377-389.

Zulley, J., R. Wever and J. Aschoff. 1981. The dependence of onset and duration of sleep on the circadian rhythm of rectal temperature. Pflugers Arch 391:314-318.

5

PHYSIOLOGICAL BASIS OF CIRCADIAN RHYTHMICITY

Gerard A. Groos

ENDOGENOUS RHYTHMS, ENTRAINMENT AND PACEMAKERS

In man, the state of wakefulness is interrupted periodically by a major episode of sleep. Usually, the distribution of wakefulness and sleep in the course of the day is very regular. It is therefore appropriate to refer to the daily alternation of these states as the sleep–wake rhythm. This rhythm — although the most observable — is only one of a wide variety of daily rhythms. In fact, 24–hour rhythms are a fundamental characteristic of virtually all physiological, biochemical and psychological functions in man as well as in animals (Aschoff, 1981; and Wever, 1979a). Under normal conditions, each of these rhythms follows a typical time course. As a result the different rhythms (e.g., the sleep–wake and the temperature rhythms), maintain fixed temporal relations with respect to each other. Thus, the behavioral, mental and physiological activities of an individual show coordinated and predictable cycles from one day to the next (Richter, 1965; and Wever, 1979a).

The environmental periodicities that result from the rotation of the earth correspond exactly to the 24–hour period of the daily biological rhythms. This raises the question whether biological rhythms are mere physiological responses to these periodic changes in the external milieu. For the majority of 24–hour rhythms this is not the case. There is compelling evidence that biological 24–hour rhythms are endogenous. They are produced by cyclic processes within the organism and can be independently sustained by the

121

body. It is customary to refer to such endogenous 24–hour rhythms as circadian rhythms. The most prominent empirical argument implying an endogenous origin of circadian rhythms is the phenomenon of free–running rhythmicity (Aschoff, 1981).

Free–running rhythms occur when an animal — or a human subject (Wever, 1979a) — is individually isolated under stringently controlled, constant environmental conditions. In such an aperiodic environment, the experimental subject continues to show circadian rhythms. Since, in such an experiment, the rhythms can no longer be assumed to be driven by external cycles, they are called "free–running". In general, the period of the persisting free–running rhythms deviates somewhat from exactly 24 hours. Thus, there is a discrepancy between the period of the circadian rhythms in isolation experiments and the 24–hour rotation cycle of the earth. This observation indicates that free–running circadian rhythms do not reflect any periodic exogenous stimulation. The endogenous nature of circadian rhythms is further demonstrated by the fact that they are innate and susceptible to genetic manipulation (Davis, 1981; Fuchs and Moore, 1980; Konopka, 1979; and Richter, 1971). Furthermore, several neural and neuroendocrine structures that function as pacemakers (or "clocks") for circadian rhythmicity have been identified in animals. These pacemaker studies will be given separate attention below.

Circadian rhythms do not free–run in the normal (i.e., the daily) varying environment. Under such conditions, rhythms maintain synchrony with the external day. The process through which synchronization is established and maintained is known as "entrainment". During steady–state entrainment, circadian rhythms exhibit a precise average period of 24 hours and keep a characteristic, stable phase relation with the environmental cycle. Entrainment studies in various animal species as well as in man have established that the foremost entraining agent in the environment is the light–dark (LD) cycle (Aschoff, Daan and Honma, 1982; Rusak and Zucker, 1979; and Wever, Polasek and Wildgruber, 1983). Using experimental light (L) and dark (D) signals, the dynamic and steady–state properties of LD entrainment have been extensively documented and elegantly interpreted (Pittendrigh, 1981). Similarly, physiological studies have revealed important details of the mechanisms of entrainment. Thus, it has been established that the perception of the entraining LD cycle in mammals is exclusively mediated by the retina and its projection to the hypothalamus (Rusak and Zucker, 1979; and Underwood and Groos, 1982).

From this experimental information, the simple notion of a circadian pacemaker emerges. A circadian pacemaker is thought to be a biological structure

(1) capable of independently generating free–running circadian rhythms;

(2) connected with photoreceptive structures (viz., the retina, in mammals) to receive relevant information about the external LD cycle;

(3) entraining its intrinsic cycle to the LD cycle, and

(4) rhythmically controlling those other biological processes that exhibit and subserve physiological, behavioral or biochemical circadian rhythms.

This pacemaker concept contains two non–trivial elements. From the free–running phenomenon and LD–entrainment experiments, it is obvious that rhythms are generated within the organism and entrain via photoreceptors. It is by no means necessary, however, to assume that a pacemaker "structure" can be functionally distinguished from other tissues or organs. Nor is it obvious that those biological and mental processes that exhibit rhythmicity are anatomically and functionally separate from this pacemaker. The experimental identification and delineation of circadian pacemakers is therefore extremely important for any circadian pacemaker theory. The demonstration that pacemakers actually exist represents critical support for such theories. Before discussing the suprachiasmatic nuclei (SCN), a major pacemaker in mammals, it is worthwhile to review the discovery of pacemaker structures in non–mammalian species. Such a brief excursion will be helpful in establishing the criteria for pacemaker identification, as well as the general biological principles of pacemaker organization.

CIRCADIAN PACEMAKERS IN INVERTEBRATES
AND SUBMAMMALIAN VERTEBRATES

Among the first animal species in which a circadian pace-maker was identified is the marine gastropod, Aplysia california (Takahashi and Zatz, 1982). When explanted and kept in suitable culture conditions, the eyes of Aplysia maintain a circadian rhythm in the spontaneous electrical activity of the optic nerve. In constant chemical and physical conditions, the in vitro rhythm free-runs for periods exceeding one week. This shows that the isolated eye of Aplysia can sustain a circadian rhythm independent of periodic variation in the environment or in other parts of the organism. This observation is considered sufficient evidence that the eye of Aplysia contains a self-sustaining circadian oscillator driving the rhythm of optic nerve activity. For the in vitro Aplysia eye it has also been demonstrated that its retinal oscillator can be entrained to an environmental illumination cycle.

Another example of successful pacemaker identification is found in silk moths (Truman, 1972). These insects complete their development in pupae from which they then emerge. The moment of pupal eclosion is precisely timed. Emergence occurs at a fixed time of day which may be different between silk moth species. For example, the moth Hyalophora cecropia emerges early in the morning, while another species, Anthereae pernyi, emerges in the late afternoon. Eclosion, in other words, exhibits a circadian rhythm. The pacemaker timing the eclosion rhythm has been located in the central nervous system in both species. If the brains are removed in pupal animals, eclosion is no longer timed with respect to the external day, but occurs at random times. However, when the brains are immediately re-implanted into the abdomen, the moth Hyalophora will still emerge in the morning and Anthereae in the evening. In an even more compelling experiment, brains of Hyalophora were transplanted into the abdomen of brainless Anthereae. As a result, Anthereae emerges in the morning instead of in the evening. The opposite result is obtained when Anthereae brains are transplanted into arrhythmic Hyalophora. The brains of these insects presumably rhythmically produce a hormone which induces emergence at a characteristic time of day for the species.

In invertebrates, two techniques, the in vitro explant (Aplysia) and the transplantation of tissue (silk moth), have been useful in the identification of pacemaker structures. In many vertebrate classes, the pineal gland has been studied as a potential pacemaker. Most information is available for birds. When, in a sparrow, the pineal is removed, the locomotor activity rhythm is abolished. Transplantation of the pineal gland from a rhythmic donor bird to a pinealectomized, arrhythmic host re-establishes a locomotor rhythm with a period and phase corresponding to those of the donor (Menaker and Binkley, 1981b). In recent years, several investigators have been able to study the melatonin synthesis of the avian pineal in vitro (Takahashi and Zatz, 1982). In explanted pineal glands melatonin production also occurs rhythmically, even in constant conditions. The pineal rhythm, moreover, is entrainable by LD cycles (Takahashi and Zatz, 1982). Therefore, both the transplantation and the in vitro experiments confirm that the avian pineal complex contains a circadian pacemaker.

In studies attempting to identify circadian pacemakers there is one major complicating factor. It is not only theoretically possible but it in fact occurs that a rhythmic function is driven by more than one single oscillator. For instance, the locomotor activity rhythm of several avian species is not completely abolished by pinealectomy (Gwinner, 1978). In these birds, the SCN in the anterior hypothalamus have been presented as a candidate for additional — perhaps even a major — activity rhythm pacemaker. Consequently, it is extremely difficult to use the transplantation experiment as sufficient evidence that the pineal of a particular bird species is a pacemaker. On the other hand, an in vitro study showing the rhythmicity of their pineal will indicate that it contains a pacemaker for the melatonin rhythm but, by itself, cannot definitively prove that this pacemaker drives the locomotor activity rhythm. It is generally the case that the complete demonstration that a structure is indeed a pacemaker will require multiple types of evidence.

THE SCN OF MAMMALS

Early investigations demonstrated that the pineal gland of mammals is not a circadian pacemaker (Rusak and Zucker, 1979).

Removal of the pineal in the rat, for instance, does not affect the phase, period or steady-state entrainment of various circadian rhythms, with the exception of the melatonin rhythm, which is obviously abolished by pinealectomy. Thus, the pineal gland, a major circadian pacemaker structure in submammalian species, does not fulfill a similar function in mammals. The SCN, of some importance in the circadian system of birds, have been proposed as the predominant circadian pacemaker in mammals.

The SCN are located ventromedially in the anterior hypothalamus, just dorsal to the optic chiasm adjacent to the third ventricle. These nuclei receive afferent nerve fibers, most importantly from the retina (Groos, 1982). A major serotonergic input reaches the SCN from the midbrain raphe nuclei. Multiple efferent projections connect the SCN with the medio-basal hypothalamus, the paraventricular diencephalon and the periaqueductal region of the brain stem (Rusak and Zucker, 1979). Histologically and anatomically, the SCN have common features in all mammals. Most recently, they have also been described in the human hypothalamus (Lydic, et al., 1980).

As a neural structure with various efferent connections, loosely embedded in the surrounding hypotalamic tissue, the SCN have considerable experimental drawbacks compared to the pineal gland. Dissection and subsequent transplantation, on the one hand, or in vitro studies, on the other, are extremely difficult to accomplish with the SCN. Consequently it has so far been impossible to produce direct experimental evidence for the pacemaker function of the SCN. Fortunately, it has been possible to construct a consistent picture for the function of the SCN from various independent types of experiments.

In the 1960s, Richter reported the results of an extensive experimental program in which he had attempted to localize the pacemaker for the rat activity, eating and drinking rhythms (Richter, 1965). He had either placed large lesions in various brain regions or extirpated endocrine organs. Only following lesions of the ventromedian hypothalamic region did he observe elimination of circadian rhythmicity. These studies were the first indication that the hypothalamus might contain a circadian pacemaker. Not much later a direct neural pathway from the retina to the SCN was described (Rusak and Zucker, 1979). This retino–hypothalamic projection (RHP) was subsequently found to be an important pathway mediating the entrainment of circadian rhythms by LD cycles. This could be concluded from the observation that damage to the optic pathways central to the retino–suprachiasmatic projection (RSP) does not interfere with LD entrainment. Within a few years after these results were obtained, it was further established that complete, bilateral lesions of the SCN in rodents produce total, irreversible arrhythmicity in a wide variety of normally cyclic functions (Rusak and Groos, 1982). On this basis, the simple and appealing hypothesis was formulated that the SCN are the "master" circadian pacemaker, the entrainment of which is mediated by its afferent RHP. Although this notion is entirely consistent with each of the findings described above, in the form stated, it is actually a highly selective interpretation of the experimental observations. For instance, it is conceivable that SCN lesions interrupt the efferent fibers of a pacemaker located elsewhere in the brain. In this case, destruction of the SCN would also lead to arrhythmicity, but not because of direct damage to the pacemaker. Clearly, circadian arrhythmicity produced by SCN lesions does not present sufficient evidence that the SCN contain a pacemaker, neither does this result imply that the SCN are a "master" pacemaker, ultimately controlling the full spectrum of rhythms in the body. As soon as one rhythmic process is measured that preserves its rhythmicity in the SCN–lesioned animal, the master pacemaker hypothesis of the SCN is falsified.

Nevertheless, the conclusion that the SCN are a circadian pacemaker entrained via the RH pathway seems inescapable. We can distinguish four lines of support for this notion:

(1)   in addition to lesions placed in the SCN, interruption of SCN efferents also leads to arrhythmicity. On the other hand, lesions of SCN afferents do not affect circadian rhythms in an essential way. For example, cutting the superior cervical sympathetic nerve trunks, which are part of the efferent pathway through which the SCN controls the biosynthetic activity of the pineal gland, produces arrhythmic pineal melatonin levels. In contrast, lesions of the midbrain raphe nuclei, which project numerous serotonergic fibers to the SCN, do not abolish circadian rhythms (Rusak and Zucker, 1979). Similar studies, involving other

afferent or efferent pathways, have produced consistent results.
Therefore, it seems permissible to conclude that the SCN — and
not their neural inputs — generate the pacemaker cycle that
controls peripheral rhythms;

(2) mild electrical stimulation of the SCN — but not
stimulation of regions in their vicinity — in intact rats and
hamsters shifts the phase of the animal's free-running rhythm in a
fashion very similar to that of entraining light stimuli (Rusak and
Groos, 1982). Thus, interference with the ongoing electrical
activity of SCN neurons puts the pacemaker at a different position
(phase) of its intrinsic cycle. Similar results were obtained with
another non-destructive technique of local SCN manipulation.
Stimulating or blocking nicotinic cholinergic receptors on SCN
cells using carbachol or α-bungarotoxin mimics or prevents the
effects of light on the circadian system (Groos, Mason and Meijer,
1983). The fact that local stimulation of the SCN selectively
alters such a fundamental pacemaker characteristic as its phase is
strong evidence that the SCN indeed comprise a pacemaker;

(3) a different and very compelling type of experiment
involves the long-term recording of electrical activity in the SCN
of a conscious animal. Stable rhythms of neuronal discharge occur
in the rat SCN even when these nuclei are surgically isolated from
the rest of the brain by a complete circular knife cut (Inouye and
Kawamura, 1979). While behaviorally and physiologically the rat is
arrhythmic after SCN isolation, the SCN themselves maintain
circadian rhythms that display all the characteristics of a true
pacemaker (Inouye and Kawamura, 1982). Obviously, to exhibit
periodic discharge, the SCN do not require any neural input.
However, the possibility that the SCN are humorally controlled by
a pacemaker outside the suprachiasmatic area is not excluded in
such experiments. Absolute neural isolation of the SCN has
recently been accomplished in in vitro studies of SCN explants
(Groos and Hendriks, 1982). Even under these conditions, the
electrical activity of the SCN behaves rhythmically, at least during
the short duration (approximately 30 hours) of these experiments.
Although incomplete, these electro-physiological investigations
support the view that the SCN are capable of intrinsic, i.e.,
independent, generation of electrical excitability rhythms; and

(4)   it was mentioned earlier that the SCN receive direct innervation from the retina. When this projection is left intact, while all central visual pathways are surgically interrupted, entrainment by LD cycles still readily occurs. This indicates that the optic synapses of the RHP supply the SCN with information about the external illumination cycle. Electrical recordings have confirmed that, even in the absence of the more central visual pathways, a considerable number of SCN cells respond specifically to the luminance level of the environment as well as to gradual changes in illumination (Groos, 1982). Such observations demonstrate the existence of a functionally specialized entrainment input to the SCN.

On the basis of all these findings, a strong case can be built — at least for rodents — that the SCN function as an important circadian pacemaker. Relatively little direct information is available on the interactions between the SCN pacemaker and the periodic functions that it controls. In the case of food and water intake, it could be demonstrated that SCN lesions selectively eliminate circadian rhythmicity but not the regulatory nature of these functions. Thus, the SCN–lesioned rat will maintain a normal caloric balance and regulate its body weight. Similarly, the daily amounts of wakefulness, rapid eye movement (REM) and non–rapid-eye–movement (NREM) sleep produced by an arrhythmic SCN–lesioned rat is comparable to those in normal animals (Ibuka, Inouye and Kawamura, 1977). A lesioned rat is still capable, moreover, of compensating for the effects of sleep deprivation by a sleep rebound (Tobler, Borbély and Groos, 1984). The SCN seem to play a highly specific role in the control of these functions. While both short–term and long–term regulatory responses do not require the SCN, circadian rhythmicity is critically dependent on these nuclei. The function of the SCN is schematically summarized in Figure 1. In this diagram, the SCN exclusively functions as a pacemaker with an intrinsic circadian period and phase. The SCN are entrained by the environmental LD cycle, which is transduced by retinal photoreceptors and transmitted to the SCN by way of the RHP. Via efferent neural and/or neurohumoral pathways, the SCN impose circadian rhythmicity on a variety of functions. These are themselves subject to long– and short–term regulatory processes independent of circadian control.

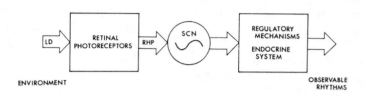

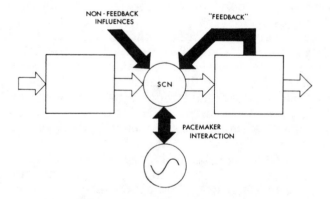

Figure 1 Schematic diagram of the mammalian circadian system. The upper diagram shows a single pacemaker system with the SCN entrained to LD cycles through retinal photoreceptors and the RHP. The lower diagram illustrates how the complex circadian system, which incorporates "feedback" influences from rhythmic (endocrine and other) processes, influences originating in other systems (non–feedback influences) and multi–pacemaker interaction.

THE COMPLEX STRUCTURE OF THE CIRCADIAN SYSTEM

In the foregoing discussion, the position of the SCN within the circadian system of the body has been relatively simple. The pacemaker appears extremely sovereign in its control over the rhythmic processes of the body. The sole influence on the SCN originates in the outside world where the day–night cycle entrains the organism. The question can justly be raised whether the SCN are in fact independent of all kinds of ongoing bodily processes. Moreover, the possibility must be considered that, in addition to the SCN, other pacemakers are part of the mammalian circadian system.

Traditionally, circadian pacemakers of mammals were thought to be extremely resistant to the influence of endogenous biochemical variables. The current view is drastically different. There is extensive documentation that the period and phase of the pacemaker controlling the rest–activity (sleep–wakefulness) rhythm, i.e., the SCN, can be readily altered by hormonal or pharmacological manipulation. Moreover, processes similar to some of these experimentally induced changes are likely to take place spontaneously in the intact animal. Thus, gonadal hormones alter the free–running period and light responsiveness of the activity rhythm in rodents (Davis, Darrow and Menaker, 1983; and Turek and Gwinner, 1982). In intact female animals, these steroid hormones change their level in synchrony with the ovulation cycle. Not surprisingly, the phase of the circadian activity and sleep–wake rhythms changes systematically with the day of the estrous cycle. On the day of pro–estrous, particularly, activity onset occurs earlier than on the other days of the ovulatory cycle (Campbell and Turek, 1981). The control of the pacemaker by sex hormones is paralleled by a sexual differentiation of functional pacemaker properties (Davis, Darrow and Menaker, 1983; and Zucker, Fitzgerald and Morin, 1980), as well as the histological characteristics of the suprachiasmatic region (Gorski, et al., 1978).

The specific mechanisms by which the functional state of the gonads hormonally controls SCN function are unknown. Turek and Gwinner (1982) distinguish two broad possibilities. On the one hand, steroid hormones may directly or indirectly — through other hormones, for example — affect neurons in the suprachiasmatic area and thus alter SCN function. On the other hand, these hormones may change the general state of arousal of the organism. Through some of the accompanying physiological changes, arousal then influences the pacemaker. Unfortunately, substantial evidence relating to either of these proposed mechanisms is lacking.

It is of special interest that the estrous cycle and its endo-crine influences on the SCN pacemaker is itself dependent on pacemaker control. The duration of the estrous cycle in female rodents is a precise integral multiple (e.g., a factor of 4 in hamsters) of the circadian period. Thus, the entrained pacemaker regulates the estrous cycle to 96 hours in the hamster, while the circadian pacemaker free–running with a 26–hour period regulates it to 104 hours. That the SCN is involved in the control of the ovulation cycle is directly demonstrated by the fact that SCN lesions result in severely disrupted estrous cyclicity (Rusak and Zucker, 1979). The case of the estrous cycle is a clear instance that the SCN pacemaker can be under control of physiological processes that, in turn, are controlled by the SCN (Figure 1). There are indications showing that complex "feedback" of the pacemaker on itself may occur more generally than merely in the reproductive system (see, e.g., Groos, 1982; and Menaker, 1981a).

As was mentioned earlier, in the description of the avian circadian system, there may well be more than one circadian pacemaker within the organism. There have been two main ways in which the possible existence of multiple pacemakers was studied. Experimental conditions have been imposed on intact experimental animals and human subjects under which dissociation of different circadian rhythms was observed. In humans, the phenomenon of internal desynchronization illustrates such a dissociation. During internal desynchronization, the sleep–wake rhythm and the body temperature rhythm free–run with apparently different periods (Wever, 1979a). In rodents, similar desynchronization has never been reported, while in monkeys, a convincing demonstration that it can occur is still lacking. Rhythm dissociation of this kind has traditionally been interpreted as showing that distinct pacemakers underlie each pair of dissociated rhythms. However, more recently model studies have produced clear instances of rhythm dissociation in single pacemaker systems (Daan, Beersma and Borbély, 1984). Therefore, it cannot simply be assumed that rhythm dissociation generally implies the existence of more than a single pacemaker. The second type of evidence for multi-pacemaker organization involves lesioning of one known pacemaker and observing arrhythmicity in the function that the pacemaker drives, but the persistence of a rhythm in at least one other function. This approach has been successfully used in the rat and in monkeys. In the rat, all circadian rhythms that have been studied to date are abolished by SCN lesions, with the exception of the rhythmic anticipation of feeding schedules (Stephan, 1982). In monkeys, SCN lesions disrupt behavioral and the pineal melatonin rhythms, but do not eliminate cortisol and body temperature rhythmicity (Albers, et al., 1981; Fuller, et al., 1981; Reppert, et al., 1981; and Spies, Norman and Buhl, 1979). These findings demonstrate that the SCN is not the sole pacemaker in the mammalian circadian system. In the entrained and in most free-running situations, rhythms that are controlled by different pacemakers in primates are mutually stably synchronized. This implies that substantial interaction must occur between the constituent pacemakers of the circadian system. Therefore, in addition to physiological "feedbacks" on circadian pacemakers, mutual interactions between circadian pacemakers must be incorporated in the diagram of Figure 1.

THE CIRCADIAN SYSTEM AND AFFECTIVE ILLNESS

Various authors have described circadian rhythm disturbances accompanying severe mood disorder. The reported abnormalities include changes in waveform, alterations in the daily distribution of sleep (rest) and wakefulness (activity) — particularly around switches between depression and mania in bipolar patients, and internal desynchronization (for reviews, see Wehr and Goodwin, 1981b; and Wehr, Gillin and Goodwin, 1983c). Of these, the periodically perturbed sleep-wakefulness distribution in bipolar patients is perhaps the most consistent rhythm phenomenon in affective disorder (Wehr, Gillin and Goodwin, 1983c). Two essentially different interpretations can be offered for the rhythm disturbances found in patients:

(1)   inherent physiological abnormalities in the circadian system result in the mood disturbance. Thus, circadian dysfunction would underlie, rather than merely reflect, affective illness; and

(2)   affective illness has its origin outside the circadian system but, as one of its many physiological consequences, alters circadian rhythmicity.

If either of these "pure cases" is to be successfully investigated further, then more specific hypotheses should be formulated. A few hypotheses have indeed been put forward. On the basis of the foregoing discussion of the mammalian circadian system, it is conceivable to explore some of the possible ideas relating mood to circadian rhythmicity.

Inherent Abnormalities of the Circadian System

The complex circadian system (Figure 1, lower diagram) can inherently malfunction in each or several of its components. Thus, the entrainment pathway may be super- or subsensitive to the LD cycle resulting in entrainment abnormalities, such as early awakening. The possibility of altered sensitivity to entraining agents in the depressed patient has been suggested by Lewy after he observed a relative reduction in threshold for nocturnal melatonin suppression by light in depressed patients (Lewy, et al., 1981). Further downstream, the circadian system may be different due to an increased (fast) or decreased (slow) cycle time of the constituent pacemaker(s). If this occurs to a different extent in each pacemaker, then deviations will occur in the mutual phase relation between rhythms driven by these pacemakers. The phase-advance hypothesis proposed by Wehr and his co-workers (Wehr and Goodwin, 1981b) exemplifies this line of thought. In a more extreme case, the deviation of a pacemaker's period from normal may be so large that stable mutual synchronization between pacemakers no longer occurs and internal desynchronization between, for instance, the sleep-wake cycle and the temperature rhythm may result (Kripke, et al., 1978).

To test this type of hypothesis, however, is extremely difficult because behavior similar to that resulting from a length-ened (shortened) pacemaker period can also be brought about in a number of different ways. If, for example, the strength of the mutual interactions between pacemakers weakens, internal phase changes or even internal desynchronization will also occur. Thus, if the circadian system consists of at least two interacting pacemakers, the multitude of possible disturbances within the system is virtually prohibitive to develop testable hypotheses as to which abnormality occurs in affective illness. Electronic model simulations (see, e.g., Ypey, et al., 1980) suggest even more such possibilities than those mentioned above. Without further extensive documentation of the exact nature of the rhythm disruptions which are typical of affective disorder, it will therefore be difficult to single out those hypotheses that are worthy of experimental study. A problem quite separate from defining the dysfunctions of the circadian system is to formulate how and why such abnormalities result in pronounced mood alterations. Unfortunately, this problem has received no serious attention thusfar.

Rhythm Disturbances as an Epiphenomenon

As an extreme alternative to the notion that inherent circadian system dysfunction underlies mood disorders, it is conceivable that the pacemaker system is not causally involved. In this case, the observed disturbances in circadian rhythmicity in the depressed patient are thought to be an epiphenomenon of a more fundamental process. Circadian rhythm abnormalities can then be taken as symptoms of affective illness. Figure 1 shows that the most likely way in which rhythms can be affected is through the feedback and non-feedback processes that act on the pacemaker. In addition, the waveform of the rhythm may be changed by a disturbance at the level of the regulatory and endocrine systems. For instance, if the mood disorder involves altered steroid hormone levels, then it should be expected that, through hormonal effects on the pacemaker, rhythmicity in patients will be abnormal. According to the suggestion of Turek and Gwinner (1982), the dramatic shifts in activity and arousal levels that occur between the depressed and (hypo-)manic states may also have a differential influence on the circadian system. A promising approach to this problem is discussed by Daan, Beersma and Borbély (1984). These authors have recently presented a model which combines the circadian pacemaker and the regulatory mechanisms into one interacting system. Using this concept, various possibilities of dysfunctions, either in the circadian or in the regulatory components of this compound system, can be explored. Systematic model studies will then reveal disturbances that might occur in depressed patients (cf., Borbély, this volume).

Animal physiologists have extensively studied the localization and function of circadian pacemakers in various animals. This work has led to the currently accepted view that animals as well as man are endowed with one or more circadian pacemakers in the central nervous and endocrine systems. Unfortunately, the precise nature of the pacemaker(s), their mutual interactions and their interactions with other physiological processes is largely unexplored, particularly in primates. What has emerged from this work, however, is the notion that the circadian system is a closely integrated, interacting system. Therefore, its role in affective illness — whether it be causative or symptomatic — is difficult to determine at this time. By careful formulation of specific ideas, relating mood disorder to circadian physiology, step–wise progress will be ensured.

REFERENCES

Albers, H.E., R. Lydic, P.H. Gander and M.C. Moore–Ede. 1981. Gradual decay of circadian drinking organization following lesions of the suprachiasmatic nuclei in primates. Neurosci Lett 27:119–124.

Aschoff, J. 1981. Handbook of Behavioral Neurobiology (Volume 4, Biological Rhythms). New York: Plenum Press.

Aschoff, J., S. Daan and K.I. Honma. 1982. Zeitgebers, entrainment and masking: some unsettled questions. In Vertebrate Circadian Systems: Structure and Physiology (Papers Presented at a Meeting Held in October 1980 at Schloss Ringberg), Aschoff, J., S. Daan and G.A. Groos (eds.). Berlin: Springer–Verlag, pp. 13–24.

Campbell, C.S. and F.W. Turek. 1981. Cyclic function of the mammalian ovary. In Handbook of Behavioral Neurobiology (Volume 4, Biological Rhythms), Aschoff, J. (ed.). New York: Plenum Press, pp. 523–545.

Daan, S., D.G.M. Beersma and A.A. Borbély. 1984. Timing of human sleep: recovery process gated by a circadian pacemaker. Am J Physiol 246:R161–R178.

Davis, F.C. 1981. Ontogeny of circadian rhythms. In Handbook of Behavioral Neurobiology (Volume 4, Biological Rhythms), Aschoff, J. (ed.). New York: Plenum Press, pp. 257–274.

Davis, F.C., J.M. Darrow and M. Menaker. 1983. Sex differences in the circadian control of hamster wheel–running activity. Am J Physiol 244:R93–R105.

Fuchs, J.L. and R.Y. Moore. 1980. Development of circadian rhythmicity and light responsiveness in the rat suprachiasmatic nucleus: a study using the 2–deoxy[1–^{14}C]glucose method. Proc Natl Acad Sci USA 77:1204–1208.

Fuller, C.A., R. Lydic, F.M. Sulzman, H.E. Albers, B. Tepper and
M.C. Moore–Ede. 1981. Circadian rhythm of body temperature
persists after suprachiasmatic lesions in the squirrel monkey. Am
J Physiol 241:R385–R391.

Gorski, R.A., J.H. Gordon, J.E. Shryne and A.M. Southam. 1978.
Evidence for a morphological sex difference within the medial
preoptic area of the rat brain. Brain Res 148:333–346.

Groos, G. 1982. The neurophysiology of the mammalian
suprachiasmatic nucleus and its visual afferents. In Vertebrate
Circadian Systems: Structure and Physiology (Papers Presented at
a Meeting Held in October 1980 at Schloss Ringberg), Aschoff, J.,
S. Daan and G.A. Groos (eds.). Berlin: Springer–Verlag, pp. 96–105.

Groos, G. and J. Hendriks. 1982. Circadian rhythms in electrical
discharge of rat suprachiasmatic neurones recorded in vitro.
Neurosci Lett 34:283–288.

Groos, G., R. Mason and J.H. Meijer. 1983. Electrical and
pharmacological properties of the suprachiasmatic nuclei. Fed
Proc, Fed Am Soc Exp Biol 42:2790–2795.

Gwinner, E. 1978. Effects of pinealectomy on circadian locomotor
activity rhythms in European starlings (Sturnus vulgaris). J Comp
Physiol 126:123–129.

Ibuka, N., S.I. Inouye and H. Kawamura. 1977. Analysis of
sleep–wakefulness rhythms in male rats after suprachiasmatic
nucleus lesions and ocular enucleation. Brain Res 122:33–47.

Inouye, S.T. and H. Kawamura. 1979. Persistence of circadian
rhythmicity in a mammalian hypothalamic "island" containing the
suprachiasmatic nucleus. Proc Natl Acad Sci USA 76:5962–5966.

Inouye, S.T. and H. Kawamura. 1982. Characteristics of a
circadian pacemaker in the suprachiasmatic nucleus. J Comp
Physiol 146:153–160.

Konopka, R.J. 1979. Genetic dissection of the Drosophila
circadian system. Fed Proc, Fed Am Soc Exp Biol 38:2602–2605.

Kripke, D.F., D.J. Mullaney, M. Atkinson and S. Wolf. 1978. Circadian rhythm disorders in manic–depressives. Biol Psychiatr 13:335–351.

Lewy, A.J., T.A. Wehr, F.K. Goodwin, D.A. Newsome, and N.E. Rosenthal. 1981. Manic–depressive patients may be supersensitive to light. Lancet 1:383–384.

Lydic, R., W.C. Schoene, C.A. Czeisler and M.C. Moore–Ede. 1980. Suprachiasmatic region of the human hypothalamus: homolog to the primate circadian pacemaker. Sleep 2:255–261.

Menaker, M. 1981a. The search for principles of physiological organization in vertebrate circadian systems. In Vertebrate Circadian Systems: Structure and Physiology (Papers Presented at a Meeting Held in October 1980 at Schloss Ringberg), Aschoff, J., S. Daan and G.A. Groos (eds.). Berlin: Springer–Verlag, pp. 1–12.

Menaker, M. and S. Binkley. 1981b. Neural and endocrine control of circadian rhythms in the vertebrates. In Handbook of Behavioral Neurobiology (Volume 4, Biological Rhythms), Aschoff, J. (ed.). New York: Plenum Press, pp. 243–255.

Moore, R.Y. 1978. Central neural control of circadian rhythms. In Frontiers in Neuroendocrinology (Volume 5), Ganong, W. F. and L. Martini (eds.). New York: Raven Press, pp. 185–206.

Pittendrigh, C.S. 1981. Circadian systems: entrainment. In Handbook of Behavioral Neurobiology (Volume 4, Biological Rhythms), Aschoff, J. (ed.). New York: Plenum Press, pp. 95–124.

Reppert, S.M., M.J. Perlow, L.H. Ungerleider, M. Mishkin, L. Tamarkin, D.G. Orloff, H.J. Hoffman and D.C. Klein. 1981. Effects of damage to the suprachiasmatic area of the anterior hypothalamus on the daily melatonin and cortisol rhythms in the rhesus monkey. J Neurosci 1:1414–1425.

Richter, C.P. 1965. Biological Clocks in Medicine and Psychiatry. Springfield: C.C. Thomas.

Richter, C.P. 1971. Inborn nature of the rat's 24 hour clock. J Comp Physiol Psychol 75:1–4.

Rusak, B. and I. Zucker. 1979. Neural regulation of circadian rhythms. Physiol Rev 59:449–526.

Rusak, B. and G. Groos. 1982. Suprachiasmatic stimulation phase shifts rodent circadian rhythms. Science 215:1407–1409.

Spies, H.G., R.L. Norman and A.E. Buhl. 1979. Twenty–four–hour patterns in serum prolactin and cortisol after partial and complete isolation of the hypothalamic–pituitary unit in rhesus monkeys. Endocrinology 105:1361–1368.

Stephan, F.K. 1982. Limits of entrainment to periodic feeding in rats with suprachiasmatic lesions. In Vertebrate Circadian Systems: Structure and Physiology (Papers Presented at a Meeting Held in October 1980 at Schloss Ringberg), Aschoff, J., S. Daan and G.A. Groos (eds.). Berlin: Springer–Verlag, pp. 120–128.

Takahashi, J.S. and M. Zatz. 1982. Regulation of circadian rhythmicity. Science 217:1104–1111.

Tobler, I., A.A. Borbély and G. Groos. 1984. The effect of sleep deprivation on sleep in rats with suprachiasmatic lesions. Neurosci Lett 42:49–54.

Truman, J.W. 1972. Circadian rhythms and physiology with special reference to neuroendocrine processes in insects. In Circadian Rhythmicity: Proceedings of the International Symposium on Circadian Rhythmicity (Wageningen, The Netherlands, April 1971), Bierhuizen, J.F. (ed.). Wageningen, The Netherlands: Centre for Agricultural Publishing and Documentation, pp. 111–135.

Turek, F.W. and E. Gwinner. 1982. Role of hormones in the circadian organization of vertebrates. In Vertebrate Circadian Systems: Structure and Physiology (Papers Presented at a Meeting Held in October 1980 at Schloss Ringberg), Aschoff, J., S. Daan and G.A. Groos (eds.). Berlin: Springer–Verlag, pp. 173–182.

Underwood, H. and G. Groos. 1982. Vertebrate circadian rhythms: retinal and extraretinal photoreception. Experientia 38:1013–1021.

Wehr. T.A. and F.K. Goodwin. 1981b. Biological rhythms and psychiatry. In American Handbook of Psychiatry, Second Edition (Volume VII), Arieti, S. and H.K.H. Brodie (eds.). New York: Basic Books, Inc., pp. 46–74.

Wehr, T.A., J.C. Gillin and F.K. Goodwin. 1983c. Sleep and circadian rhythms in depression. In Sleep Disorders: Basic and Clinical Research (Advances in Sleep Research, Volume 8), Chase, M.H. and Weitzman, E.D. (eds.). New York: S.P. Medical and Scientific Books.

Wever, R.A. 1979a. The Circadian System of Man: Results of Experiments Under Temporal Isolation. New York: Springer–Verlag.

Wever, R.A., J. Polasek and C.M. Wildgruber. 1983. Bright light affects human circadian rhythms. Pflugers Arch 396:85–87.

Ypey, D.L., W.P.M. Van Meerwijk, C. Ince and G. Groos. 1980. Mutual entrainment of two pacemaker cells. A study with an electronic parallel conductance model. J Theor Biol 86:731–755.

Zucker, I., K.M. Fitzgerald and L.P. Morin. 1980. Sex differentiation of the circadian system in the golden hamster. Am J Physiol 238:R97–R101.

6

SLEEP AND BIOLOGICAL RHYTHMS IN AFFECTIVE ILLNESS

Thomas A. Wehr

INTRODUCTION

Disturbances in the duration, timing and continuity of sleep are cardinal symptoms of depression and mania. When patients are depressed, they often have difficulty falling asleep, have frequent arousals during the night, and awaken early in the morning. In some cases (especially in manic depression) patients sleep excessively but do not feel rested by their sleep (Detre, et al., 1972; Kupfer, et al., 1972; Taub, Hawkins and van de Castle, 1978; Garvey, Mungas and Tollefson, 1984; and Rosenthal, et al., 1985a). During mania, patients sleep little or not at all, and seem not to require a normal amount of sleep. Clinicians have long been interested in the changes in sleep that accompany depression and mania because these can be sensitive indicators of the patient's condition and are often a focus of the patient's concerns. In fact, some patients experience depression primarily as a sleep disorder.

Results of clinical research during the past two decades have provided additional reasons for patients and their physicians to be interested in sleep. First, sleep researchers have identified abnormalities in the polygraphically–recorded sleep of depressives, and have proposed that they could be used as an aid in the diagnosis of depression. Second, these abnormalities have led to several hypotheses about possible biological causes of depression. Finally, it has been found that deprivation of sleep, or of certain portions of sleep, can induce temporary remissions in depression and

143

sometimes switches into mania, and that recovery sleep after sleep deprivation can induce relapses into depression. These findings seem to indicate that changes in sleep during depression and mania are not merely symptoms, but may play an important role in the mechanisms that cause these abnormal states. Consequently, these findings have led to an increased interest in the mechanisms that control sleep and in the physiological and biochemical effects of sleep, with the hope of better understanding the causes of depression and mania and devising new types of treatment. During the past decade, sleep researchers have increasingly recognized that biological rhythms are intimately involved in both the mechanisms and effects of sleep. In this chapter, the author reviews evidence concerning abnormalities of sleep in the affective disorders, results of experimental manipulations of sleep, and hypotheses that have been proposed to explain them, with particular attention to the possible role of biological rhythms in these disorders.

THE RHYTHMIC NATURE OF SLEEP

Sleep is a remarkably rhythmic process. The daily cycle of sleeping and waking is not simply a passive response to the daily cycle of changes in the social and physical environment, but is an internally–generated, self–sustaining biological rhythm. The self–sustaining property of the sleep–wake cycle can be observed when persons live in experimental conditions from which all information about time of day has been excluded (see Wever, this volume). In these circumstances, they continue to go to sleep and to wake up approximately once every 25 hours, demonstrating that the rhythm of the sleep–wake cycle persists in the absence of environmental input with an intrinsic frequency that is actually slightly slower than one cycle per day. In a normal environment, the internal 25–hour rhythm of the sleep–wake cycle is modified by the effects of environmental stimuli that function as time cues, so that it becomes synchronized in an appropriate phase relationship with the external 24–hour day–night cycle. Thus, the daily cycle of sleeping and waking is generated by a biological clock or pacemaker mechanism, and its oscillations are coupled to environmental cycles by a second, entrainment mechanism. The neural substrates of these mechanisms have been identified in animals: the suprachiasmatic nucleus (SCN) of the hypothalamus functions as a circadian pacemaker, and the retino–hypothalamic tract (RHT) serves as an entrainment pathway for the phase-resetting properties of visual time cues such as dawn and dusk.

The processes that occur within sleep are also remarkably rhythmic. Stages of non–rapid–eye–movement (NREM) sleep alternate with rapid eye movement (REM) sleep in a cyclical manner every 90 minutes or so. Individual sleep stages, in turn, are characterized by higher frequency oscillations. During stages three and four, the electrical activity of the brain exhibits high amplitude, 2–to–4–cycles–per–second waves. In REM sleep, bursts of quasi–cyclical, high–amplitude, conjugate lateral eye movements occur.

Within the sleep period, the temporal distribution of REM sleep is partly controlled by a circadian pacemaker. The circadian rhythm of REM sleep propensity is such that REM sleep is least likely to occur in the evening just before habitual bedtime and is most likely to occur at dawn just before habitual wake–up time (Weitzman, et al., 1974). Within sleep, the temporal distribution of slow–wave sleep (SWS) shows less evidence of the influence of a circadian pacemaker and is triggered by sleep onset. Most SWS occurs in the first hours of sleep and declines exponentially, regardless of its phase position relative to the circadian pacemaker (Borbély, 1982a).

There is general agreement that at least two types of process appear to be responsible for the behavior of the daily sleep–wake cycle (Wever, 1979a; Borbély, 1982a). The propensity to sleep or awaken is partly related to a homeostatic process corresponding to the intuitive idea that a person becomes increasingly drowsy the longer he remains awake and less drowsy the longer he sleeps. The propensity to sleep or wake is also related to a circadian process. A biological clock in the brain makes a person more sleepy at certain times of day than at others, regardless of the duration of prior wakefulness. The amount of SWS during sleep, as previously mentioned, is mainly a function of the duration of prior wakefulness, and has therefore been identified with the homeostatic process.

The oscillations of the circadian pacemaker cannot be measured directly, but only indirectly, in circadian rhythms exhibited by systems that are under its control (Wever, 1979a). For example, core body temperature exhibits a circadian rhythm, with a maximum late in the day and a minimum late at night. The activity of several neuroendocrine systems is regulated by the circadian pacemaker. These systems include the hypothalamic–pituitary–thyroid (H–P–T) axis, the hypothalamic–pituitary–adrenal (H–P–A) axis, and the hypothalamic–pineal axis, and also, the hypothalamic–pituitary axis which controls prolactin (PRL) secretion. The temporal programming of secretory activity is similar in all of these systems and occurs mainly at night. The paraventricular nucleus (PVN) of the hypothalamus, which includes cell bodies of neurons that secrete the thyrotropin–releasing hormone (TRH) and the corticotropin–releasing hormone (CRH), is a key waystation and branchpoint in the efferent pathways from the SCN that control all of these systems.

THE MEASUREMENT OF SLEEP AND OF CIRCADIAN RHYTHMS

Sleep has generally been measured using electrical recordings of brain, eye muscle, and facial muscle activity. Typically, these recordings are divided into sleep stages on the basis of manual scoring using the criteria of Rechtshaffen and Kales (1968). Certain methodological problems arise when sleep recording techniques are applied in the clinical setting. The sleep recording schedule (11:00 p.m. to 6:00 a.m. in some laboratories) is a Procrustean bed into which the natural sleep patterns of patients and controls are squeezed. Depressed patients, left to themselves, may prefer to sleep longer than the time allotted, or at different times of day. Some patients may habitually nap in the daytime or evening. These naps are never recorded, and patients are usually instructed to avoid them. One suspects that patients sometimes sleep during the daytime despite these prohibitions, and such naps are likely to alter nighttime sleep patterns (by reducing SWS, for example). Manic patients may prefer to sleep very little or not at all. The expectation that the patient will sleep during the seven- to eight–hour recording period, however, may lead him to alter his behavior in this regard.

Less intrusive, more naturalistic methods of sleep monitoring have been employed in some instances. For example, patients living in unstructured environments have worn recording electrodes 24 hours a day and been instructed to sleep whenever they pleased. One patient in this type of experiment slept only three hours a day when she was manic and 12 hours a day when she was depressed (Wehr, et al., 1985b). Continuous motor activity recordings can easily be obtained from ambulatory patients and may reflect natural sleep patterns more accurately than polysomnograms recorded in the laboratory (Wehr, et al., 1982a). Another difficulty arises from the fact that sleep stages in depressed patients cannot always be scored strictly according to conventional sleep–stage criteria. It may not be valid to compare amounts of different sleep stages in depressives and controls when the sleep stages themselves are not normal in depressives.

The behavior of the circadian pacemaker, as reflected in its various overt rhythms, is often masked to some extent by other influences, such as meals, activity, sleep, posture, light and other factors, that directly affect the output of these systems. Masking effects can make it difficult or impossible to accurately measure the behavior of the circadian pacemaker and constitute an important methodological problem in chronobiological investigations of sleep in human subjects. One approach to this problem has been to study subjects while they adhere to a constant routine in which they remain awake at bedrest and eat isocaloric meals every hour. The results of these investigations will be discussed later in the chapter.

SLEEP ELECTROENCEPHALOGRAPHY (EEG) IN AFFECTIVE ILLNESS

The discovery of REM sleep, and its association with dreaming, occurred at a time when psychoanalysis was the dominant influence in psychiatry. Perceptual and cognitive distortions in dreams have been a focus of interest in psychoanalytic theories, and have been compared to psychotic states. From this perspective, polysomnography was viewed as a new method that might make it possible to study the physiology of dreaming. The analogy between psychosis and dreams led to a series of studies of sleep patterns, especially REM sleep patterns, in psychotic patients. At this time, there was also great interest in the possible psychosis–inducing effects of REM sleep deprivation, based on the idea that a blockade of dreaming might lead to the intrusion of dream–like cognitive and perceptual distortions into waking life. Today, these theories have been largely discredited. Ironically, the only clinically significant consequence of REM sleep deprivation that has been reported is that it improves the condition of depressed patients (Vogel, et al., 1980). Studies inspired by these ideas, however, led to an accumulation of data concerning the electroencephalographic (EEG) sleep patterns of affectively ill patients.

Over the years, several different abnormalities in the sleep of these patients have been described (Gresham, Agnew, Jr. and Williams, 1965; Hawkins and Mendels, 1966; Hawkins, et al., 1967; Hartmann, 1968; Kupfer and Foster, 1972c; Snyder, 1972; and Kupfer, Foster and Detre, 1973). In many depressed patients, sleep is fragmented and reduced. Patients take a long time to fall asleep (increased sleep latency), awaken frequently during the night, and wake up early in the morning. There are abnormally frequent transitions between sleep stages. SWS is reduced, and REM sleep occurs abnormally early after sleep onset (decreased REM latency). First REM sleep episodes may be abnormally long. The number of eye movements per minute of REM sleep (REM density) is abnormally high, especially during the first REM period.

On the basis of these findings, Kupfer and colleagues proposed that short REM latency or a constellation of sleep abnormalties could be used as a diagnostic marker for primary depression or endogenous depression (Kupfer and Foster, 1972c). With the passage of time, however, it has become clear that the abnormalities found in depression are almost certainly not specific to that syndrome, but occur in many other syndromes and diseases. Furthermore, there is no convincing evidence that a constellation of abnormalities is specific for depression. Short REM latency has been reported to occur in schizophrenia (Stern, et al., 1969; Jus, et al., 1973; Benson and Zarcone, Jr., 1985a,b; and Hiatt, et al., 1985); anxiety disorders (Foster, et al., 1977); obsessive–compulsive disorder (Insel, et al., 1982); alcoholism (Spiker, et al., 1977);

Korsakoff's syndrome and Alzheimer's disease (Martin, et al., 1986); impotence (Schmidt and Shy, 1986); narcolepsy, borderline personality disorder (Lahmeyer, et al., 1985; and Reynolds, et al., 1985c); anorexia nervosa (Neil, et al., 1980); mania (Mendels and Hawkins, 1967; and Gillin, et al., 1977); insomnia (Schmidt, et al., 1986); and sleep apnea (Reynolds, et al., 1984).

At the same time, there have been a number of studies reporting normal REM latencies in depressed patients, especially in younger patients, including children, and in patients with hypersomnia or typical depressions, as occur frequently in manic–depressive illness (Jovanovic, 1977; Taub, Hawkins and van de Castle, 1978; Puig–Antich, et al., 1982; Linkowski, et al., 1985; Jernajczyk, 1986; Mendelson, et al., 1986; Sack, et al., 1986a; and Thase, et al., 1986a). Short REM latency is more likely to be found in older, psychotic, hospitalized patients. While sleep characteristics are not abnormal in any specific way, or even necessarily abnormal at all, in depressed patients, changes in these characteristics do appear to reflect alterations in the clinical state of patients who have been studied longitudinally (Hawkins, et al., 1967; Hartmann, 1968; Bunney, Jr., et al., 1972b; Wehr, 1977; and Wehr and Goodwin, 1983b).

In some sleep EEG studies of depression, the frequency distribution of REM latency has been found to be bimodal (Schulz, et al., 1979; and Coble, Kupfer and Shaw, 1981). One mode is similar to the frequency distribution seen in normal subjects. The second mode results from a large number of very short REM latencies, associated with sleep–onset REM periods (SOREMP). The existence of this type of bimodal distribution of REM latencies is a novel prediction of one of the models that has been developed to describe sleep EEG abnormalities in depression (McCarley, 1982; and van den Hoofdakker and Beersma, 1985a), a model based on the McCarley–Hobson reciprocal interaction model of the REM–non–REM ultradian sleep cycle (see McCarley and Massaquoi, this volume). The existence of a bimodal distribution of REM latencies has been called into question, however, by recent studies of large numbers of patients (Thase, Kupfer and Spiker, 1984). Bimodal distributions due to SOREMP may be limited to older, psychotic, inpatient samples, and may not be characteristic of most depressed patients.

It has long been recognized that reduced SWS is also a relatively non-specific finding; it has been reported to occur in schizophrenia and many other disorders (Benson and Zarcone, 1985a,b; and Guazzelli, et al., 1985). Nevertheless, deficiency of SWS has become the focus of one model of depressive sleep disturbances (see Borbély, this volume). According to this model, reduced SWS reflects a deficiency in the rate of increase in a process, S, during wakefulness. Process S is a homeostatic process that decreases exponentially during sleep and is postulated to be partly responsible for sleep propensity, the amount of SWS, and the duration of sleep. In the model, S interacts with a circadian process, C, that regulates thresholds for sleeping and waking. The level of S, identified with power density of the sleep EEG, is hypothesized to be deficient in depression. Contrary to this prediction, two recent studies reported normal power densities in depressives, despite reduced levels of manually-scored SWS (van den Hoofdakker and Beersma, 1985; and Mendelson, et al., 1986).

Clearly, abnormalities in polygraphically-monitored sleep in depression are not pathognomonic and do not seem likely to be very helpful in the diagnosis of depression. They are akin to symptoms of depression, such as diurnal variation in mood, that may or may not be present in any given case, and that, by themselves, are not critical for the diagnosis of the syndrome. From a practical point of view, symptoms are easier and less expensive to measure than electrical activity during sleep, and there does not seem to be any advantage to using the latter instead of the former as an aid to diagnosis. In fact, the sleep centers that have proliferated during the past decade are used mainly to assist in the diagnosis of neurological and respiratory diseases.

In light of the foregoing discussion, it could be argued at the outset that sleep abnormalities do not provide a very suitable basis for the development of models of pathophysiology or pathogenesis of depression because of their lack of specificity and their inconstancy. Lack of specificity need not be a major stumbling block, however, because there are many indications that the various separate syndromes in psychiatry are actually closely related to one another in terms of genetic factors, symptomatology, pathophysiology and treatment. The fact that sleep EEG abnormalities are not consistently present in depression, however, does seem to indicate that they are not an essential or core feature of the syndrome.

EFFECTS OF SLEEP MANIPULATIONS ON MOOD

A better argument for the relevance of sleep physiology to the fundamental causes of depression and mania is the observation that deprivation of sleep is capable of inducing switches out of depression, and sometimes switches into mania, and that sleep is capable of inducing switches into depression in patients who have responded to sleep deprivation. These experimental observations show that mood–regulating mechanisms are extraordinarily sensitive to sleep– and/or wakefulness–dependent processes. They also suggest that changes in the timing and duration of sleep which occur spontaneously in the course of affective episodes are not merely symptoms, but almost certainly play a role in pathogenesis.

Responses to total sleep deprivation have been studied in over 1,000 depressed patients (Gillin, 1983b). Seventy percent of depressed bipolar patients, 60% of endogenously depressed unipolar patients, and 40% of reactive or neurotically depressed unipolar patients respond to the procedure. Many bipolar patients switch into mania after total sleep deprivation (Wehr, et al., 1982a). Responses to sleep deprivation are typically short–lived. Most patients relapse into depression after recovery sleep. Mania following sleep deprivation may persist after recovery sleep, perhaps because insomnia secondary to mania creates a vicious cycle in which the effects of sleep loss and mania are mutually reinforcing. In fact, many factors that are believed to be capable of precipitating mania could act through their capacity to cause loss of sleep (Wehr, et al., 1987). These factors include insomnia caused by emotional responses to events or persons, such as grief, rage, fear, and infatuation. They also include insomnia associated with drugs or withdrawal from drugs, and disruptions in sleep schedules related to travel, social activities, work, and various types of emergencies. The sleep deprivation paradigm is based on extensive experimental observations and provides a plausible final common pathway for diverse factors thought to be involved in the genesis of mania in real–life situations.

The sleep deprivation procedure seems to be a simple intervention, but actually involves many potentionally separate simultaneous interventions, including deprivation of sleep, exposure to light, loss of body heat, and changes in posture, physical activity and social stimuli. The search for the mechanism of action of sleep deprivation could be expected to lead to increased understanding of the causes of depression and mania, and to new types of treatment. This search could be conducted more efficiently if the essential element(s) of the sleep deprivation procedure could be identified, and extraneous elements eliminated. Some progress has been made in this direction. Exposure to light is not a necessary condition for the therapeutic effect of sleep deprivation (Wehr, et al., 1985a). Total sleep deprivation is not necessary; partial sleep deprivation in the second half of the night is as effective an antidepressant as total sleep deprivation (Schilgen and Tölle, 1980). Furthermore, there are indications that partial sleep deprivation in the second half of the night is more effective than partial sleep deprivation in the first half of the night (Goetze and Tölle, 1981). This last finding indicates that the timing of sleeping and waking relative to phase intervals of circadian rhythms may be a critical factor in the response. This possibility receives further support from uncontrolled experiments which show that shifting the timing of the sleep period six hours earlier, from its usual 11:00 p.m. to 7:00 a.m. time to a new 5:00 p.m. to 1:00 a.m. time, without curtailing sleep, is capable of inducing remissions in depressed patients (Wehr, et al., 1979b; and Sack, et al., 1985).

Experiments designed to investigate the role of the timing of sleep in antidepressant responses to sleep deprivation are plagued by methodological problems. In order to conduct a controlled experiment patients must sleep on at least two different schedules (e.g., early vs. late). Because of circadian variations in sleep propensity, patients sleep easily on certain schedules (e.g., late at night) and with difficulty on others (e.g., early in the evening). Thus, it is technically difficult to balance sleep durations on the different schedules in order to prevent effects of the timing of sleep being confounded with effects of the duration of sleep. One approach to this problem is to reduce the duration of sleep by equal amounts on each schedule (partial sleep deprivation) to enhance the likelihood that sleep durations will be balanced. Unfortunately, when this approach was used in one study, it was not successful in preventing patients from sleeping slightly less during an evening sleep schedule compared with a morning sleep schedule (Sack, et al., 1986b). Another problem with this type of experiment is that the effects of sleeping at different times are confounded with the possible effects of varying durations of prior wakefulness, a factor that may influence patients' responses to sleep schedule changes. A possible solution to this problem is to carry out such experiments for several days in succession, in the hope that effects of differing durations of prior wakefulness during the first day will have washed out by the end of the experiment. For the present it cannot be said with certainty that the timing of sleep is a critical variable in patients responses to sleep manipulations; neither has this possibility been eliminated.

INTERACTIONS OF SLEEP AND CIRCADIAN RHYTHMS IN DEPRESSION

If the timing of sleep is an important variable in patients' responses to sleep manipulations, then interactions between sleep and circadian rhythms may be involved in the responses. In the search for possible mechanisms of action of sleep deprivation therapy, systems that are regulated by the circadian pacemaker and that also respond to sleeping and waking must be considered. Some interactions of this type have been investigated. For example, as mentioned previously, the amount of REM sleep within the sleep period is partly governed by a circadian process that controls REM sleep propensity. REM sleep propensity is lowest in the evening and highest near dawn. Thus, sleep that occurs early in the evening contains 50% less REM sleep than sleep late in the night (Sack, et al., 1986b). The greater antidepressant efficacy of early evening sleep schedules compared with late night sleep schedules could be due to differential effects of the schedules on REM sleep. This hypothesis is supported by earlier work of Vogel and co-workers (1980), who found that selective REM sleep deprivation was more effective than selective NREM sleep deprivation in inducing remissions in depressed patients. It is also supported by recent work of Wiegand and colleagues (1986), who found that patients responding to total sleep deprivation, taking midday naps, relapsed if REM sleep occurred during the naps, but did not relapse if REM sleep did not occur during the naps.

Several neuroendocrine systems are regulated by the circadian pacemaker and are also strongly influenced by sleeping and waking. Therefore, these systems provide material for other hypotheses about the mechanism of action of sleep deprivation therapy. The secretion of the thyrotropin–stimulating hormone (TSH) exhibits a nocturnal surge resulting in a broad peak in hormone levels from early evening to late morning (Parker, Pekary and Hershman, 1976). The nocturnal surge in TSH secretion is thought to result from a corresponding surge in TRH secretion originating in cell bodies located in the PVN of the hypothalamus. Tumors impinging on this structure can eliminate the nocturnal surge in TSH and produce hypothyroidism (Caron, et al., 1986). The nocturnal surge of TSH is suppressed to some extent by sleep and augmented by sleep deprivation (Parker, Pekary and Hershman, 1976; and Sack, et al., 1986a).

Several investigators have reported that the nocturnal surge of TSH (and presumably TRH) secretion is deficient in depressed unipolar and bipolar patients (Weeke and Weeke, 1978; Golstein, et al., 1980; Kijne, et al., 1982; Kjellman, et al., 1984; and Sack, et al., 1986a). In these patients, sleep deprivation augments TSH secretion and restores its nocturnal surge to normal levels (Sack, et al., 1986b). Thus, it can be hypothesized that the mechanism of action of sleep deprivation depends on its capacity to stimulate nocturnal secretion of TSH (and TRH), which is deficient in depressed patients. This hypothesis can be tested in several ways. TRH administered at night during sleep might be expected to mimic the effects of sleep deprivation. Heat loss is thought to be responsible for the stimulation of TSH secretion associated with sleep deprivation (O'Malley, et al., 1984). Prevention of heat loss during sleep deprivation might be expected to block the antide–pressant effects of the procedure. Any sleep schedule that displaces sleep so that it no longer coincides with the nocturnal peak of TSH secretion might be expected to have antidepressant effects, even when the duration of sleep is not reduced.

PRL secretion also exhibits a nocturnal surge similar to that of TSH (Parker, Rossman and Vanderlan, 1974). In fact, the nocturnal surge of TRH may be responsible for the temporal pattern of secretion of both TSH and PRL. In contrast to TSH, PRL secretion is augmented by sleep and diminished by sleep deprivation. Thus, reduction of PRL secretion could be involved in the mechanism of action of sleep deprivation therapy. The nightly surge of PRL secretion depends on sleep, regardless of when sleep occurs. Thus, shifts in the timing of the sleep period have little effect on the total amount of PRL secreted, and, according to this model, should have little effect on mood.

The adrenocorticotrophic hormone (ACTH) and CRH are secreted most actively in the latter part of the night (Weitzman, et al., 1968). The first three to four hours of sleep suppress ACTH (and presumably CRH) secretion (Weitzman, et al., 1981a). Ordinarily, the first hours of sleep coincide with the quiescent interval of the circadian rhythm of ACTH secretion, so that little effect of sleep on ACTH secretion occurs. Therefore, if the phase position of the circadian rhythm of H–P–A axis secretory activity is normal, its output is little affected by sleep deprivation and is therefore not likely to be involved in the mechanism of action of therapeutic sleep deprivation. However, the phase position of the daily onset of the H–P–A axis circadian rhythm may be advanced several hours earlier than normal in depressed patients (Doig, et al., 1966; Conroy, Hughes and Mills, 1968; Fullerton, et al., 1968; Yamaguchi, Maeda and Kuromaru, 1978; Sherman, Pfohl and Winokur, 1984; Linkowski, et al., 1985; and Sack and Wehr, 1986c; see, however, Sachar, et al., 1973; von Zerssen, et al., 1985; and Sack, et al., 1986a). In this case, the period when H–P–A axis secretory activity is greatest would coincide with the first portion of the sleep period when the inhibitory influence of sleep is also greatest; in this situation, in contrast to the normal situation, sleep deprivation could be expected to significantly augment H–P–A axis secretory activity. Disinhibition of H–P–A axis function by sleep deprivation is less intuitively appealing as a possible mechanism of its antidepressant effect, however, because it would exacerbate, rather than correct, the functional disturbance reported to exist in this system in depression.

The foregoing discussion illustrates how abnormalities in circadian rhythms could play a central role in the mechanism of action of sleep deprivation therapy. In the example of TSH secretion, the amplitude of the H–P–T axis circadian rhythm is lost, and this deficiency is corrected by sleep deprivation. With regard to cortisol secretion, when the nadir of the H–P–A axis circadian rhythm is phase–advanced, sleep deprivation has a secretion–augmenting effect that it does not have when the phase relationship between the H–P–A rhythm and the sleep period is normal. Thus, identification of circadian rhythm amplitude and/or phase disturbances may be essential for understanding the mechanism of sleep deprivation therapy.

Circadian Rhythm Amplitude Disturbances in Depression

Reduction of the amplitude of circadian rhythms in depression has been reported for TSH, as already described, and for core body temperature and cortisol. The reduction in amplitude of the TSH rhythm is due to the absence of a normal nocturnal surge in secretion of this hormone; daytime TSH levels are nearly normal (this abnormality would escape detection by standard clinical procedures in which blood is sampled in the morning). There are several reports indicating that the amplitude of body temperature is also reduced in depression, primarily because the nocturnal minimum is elevated (Avery, Wildschiodtz and Rafaelsen, 1982; Schulz and Lund, 1983, 1985; and van den Hoofdakker and Beersma, 1985a). Amplitude disturbances in the TSH and core temperature circadian rhythms may be interrelated. Both abnormalities occur at night, and both systems are involved in thermoregulation. In fact, the amplitude of the nocturnal surge of TSH secretion is strongly influenced by heat loss, and heat–loss–induced augmentation of TSH secretion may be involved in the mechanism of sleep deprivation therapy, as previously described. Sleep, by modifying exposure to environmental conditions, also may have a thermoregulatory function. The pattern of human sleep, with nighttime sleep periods and afternoon naps, effectively insulates the organism from temperature extremes in the environment and may be a form of behavioral thermoregulation. In this model, depression and antidepressant effects of sleep manipulations arise from interactions between different components of a thermoregulatory system controlling sleep, body temperature, the H–P–T axis, and mood. The amplitude of the circadian cortisol rhythm has been reported to be reduced in some depressed patients, primarily because of increased secretory activity at night during what is normally called the quiescent phase (Sachar, et al., 1973).

Reports of reduced amplitude of circadian rhythms can be misleading. In many published studies, results of measurements of circadian rhythms are reported only as group means of values at different times of day. With this type of presentation of data effects of changes in amplitude are confounded with effects of changes in phase. If individuals' circadian rhythm amplitudes were completely normal, the amplitude of the group mean circadian rhythm would nevertheless be reduced if interindividual variation in phase position of the rhythm were increased (with phase dispersion of the individuals' rhythms, peaks and troughs of the individuals' rhythms tend to cancel one another out in the averaging of data for the different times of day). Thus, it is essential to evaluate amplitudes of circadian rhythms in the individuals of which a group is composed. Amplitudes of individuals' circadian rhythms in TSH (Sack, et al., 1986a) and core temperature (Schulz and Lund, 1985) have been found to be reduced in some studies of depressed patients.

Circadian Rhythm Phase Disturbances in Depression

Results of investigations of possible phase disturbances in circadian rhythms in depression are inconsistent. The majority of studies of adrenocorticosteroid (ACS) circadian rhythms indicate that the nadir and the daily onset of secretion are advanced several hours earlier than normal, but that the peak occurs at a normal time (Conroy, Hughes and Mills, 1968; Fullerton, et al., 1968; Yamaguchi, Maeda and Kuromaru, 1978; Sherman, Pfohl and Winokur, 1984; Linkowski, et al., 1985; and Sack and Wehr, 1986c). Thus the waveform of the rhythm is abnormal. Strictly speaking, it is not possible to compare phases of rhythms that have different waveforms (there are no equivalent states of the two rhythms). However, it is possible that AC secretory activity is controlled by two rhythmic processes, and that different components of the waveform of its circadian rhythm behave differently. A similar situation arises when normal people are permitted to free-run in isolation from external time cues (Weitzman, et al., 1982a) or when they cross several time zones during westward flight (Desir, et al., 1981); the minimum of the cortisol circadian rhythm becomes advanced several hours relative to its maximum. The fact that the phase–relationship between the minimum and maximum can change in this way may indicate that their times of occurrence are controlled by two potentially separate rhythmic processes (the maximum is closely related to the sleep–wake transition of the sleep–wake cycle in depressed patients and in normal people during jet–lag or temporal isolation experiments). Evidence regarding the phase position of the core temperature circadian rhythm is also inconsistent (for a review, see Wehr and Goodwin, 1983b, and Sack, et al., 1986d). There are some indications that circadian rhythms are more likely to be phase–advanced in unipolar than in bipolar patients, just as REM sleep abnormalities are more likely to be found in these patients (Linkowski, et al., 1985; and Sack, et al., 1986a,c). Changes in the phase of circadian rhythms are partly related to age; with increasing age, for example, the nadir of cortisol secretion is increasingly phase–advanced (Linkowski, et al., 1985). REM sleep changes are similarly related to age; with increasing age, REM latency decreases (Gillin, et al., 1981). Thus, changes in the cortisol circadian rhythm and in REM sleep seen in some depressives resemble those seen in old age.

REM sleep abnormalities in depression could be related to circadian rhythm phase disturbances. As previously described, REM sleep propensity exhibits a circadian rhythm, with a minimum in the evening and a maximum near dawn. In cases where the circadian rhythms of core temperature and/or AC secretory activity are phase–advanced, short REM latencies and longer first REM periods could be caused by a corresponding phase advance in the circadian rhythm of REM sleep propensity. In a longitudinal study of sleep EEG and temperature in a rapidly cycling manic-depressive patient, Wehr and Goodwin (1983b) found an apparent relationship between changes in the temporal distribution of REM sleep, changes in the phase position of the temperature rhythm, and clinical state.

If circadian rhythms are abnormally phase–advanced relative to the timing of sleep in depression, and if this internal phase disturbance plays a role in its pathogenesis, then patients could be treated by shifting the timing of the sleep period sufficiently early to correct the abnormal phase relationship between sleep and circadian rhythms. As previously described, this type of phase-advance treatment has been reported to induce remission in some depressed patients in uncontrolled studies. In a kind of mirror-image experiment the sleep period of normal subjects has been shifted later than usual in order to simulate the phase disturbance hypothesized to exist in depression. In a recent experiment of this type normal subjects developed short REM latencies and early awakening, and they experienced depressive mood changes (Knowles and MacLean, 1986).

THE PROBLEM OF MASKING

Circadian rhythms are not the only factors that govern body temperature or other variables that are measured in chronobiological studies. Changes in physiological state are also evoked by stress, physical activity, meals, interactions with other people, and many other influences. Some of these influences are external and strongly reflect the time structure of the social and physical environment. The evoked physiological responses are superimposed on and may even obscure changes related to the circadian rhythm, making its parameters difficult to measure. Distortion of circadian rhythms by evoked responses is called "masking". Another form of masking occurs when one circadian rhythm affects the expression of another (internal masking). For example, sleep lowers body temperature and activity raises it; therefore, the timing of the sleep–wake cycle relative to the temperature rhythm will partly determine the waveform of the temperature rhythm that is measured. The problem of masking highlights the fact that an overt rhythm is only an indirect measure of the oscillator that drives it. In clinical studies of circadian rhythms, one must assume that an abnormality in the phase position of a circadian rhythm, if present, will be masked to some extent by sleep schedules and other influences emanating from the temporal structure of the environment.

One approach to the problem of masking is to remove, or alternatively, to evenly distribute masking influences by placing subjects on a constant routine while circadian rhythm measurements are obtained. In this type of study, individuals remain constantly awake at bedrest, at 45° elevation, and eat isocaloric liquid meals every hour for more than 24 hours. Sack and Wehr (1986c) have recently completed such a study involving depressed unipolar patients and age and sex-matched controls. Melatonin (MT) circadian rhythms were essentially identical in the two groups. The nadir of the cortisol circadian rhythm and the maxima and minima of the rectal temperature rhythm were phase-advanced in depressed patients compared with controls, as previously reported by some investigators.

The findings with regard to phase-advanced circadian rhythms in depression are rather similar to those with REM latency. Phase-advanced circadian rhythms and short REM latency are partly related to age. Thus, they are more likely to be found in older patients. Also, they are more commonly found in unipolar than in bipolar patients. It has not been determined whether circadian rhythm phase abnormalities are specific to depression. The analogy with REM latency suggests that this is not likely to be so.

The results of longitudinal studies indicate that the phase position of circadian rhythms in depressed patients is abnormally unstable, that it shifts dramatically earlier or later from day to day (Pflug, Erikson and Johnsson, 1976). Thus, in an individual patient, the phase might appear normal on one night and phase-advanced on another. In a group of depressed patients, there would always be some patients with phase-advanced rhythms and some with normal rhythms on any given day, but the composition of these subgroups would change from day to day. Obviously, a single day's measurements would be insufficient to detect this kind of phase instability and would give the false impression that circadian rhythms in some patients with unstable phases were normal. Averaging data from several days measurements for the individuals or for the group would "smear" the profile of the rhythm and obscure the phase instability. These findings indicate that, in studies of depressed patients, circadian rhythms should be measured for several days, and that data for each day should be analyzed separately.

CONCLUSIONS AND SPECULATIONS

Sleep EEG abnormalities in depression are inconsistent and non-specific; thus, they are probably not useful as an aid to diagnosis, and they do not seem to be a promising point of departure for the development of pathogenetic models of the illness. What is really important about sleep in depression is that when it is not permitted to occur, patients remit or become manic, and when it is permitted to occur, they relapse. Knowledge of the mechanisms of these effects of sleeping and waking on the illness seems likely to lead to increased understanding of the causes of the illness and to the development of new types of treatment. In considering possible mechanisms of action of sleep deprivation therapy, I have focused on REM sleep and on neuroendocrine systems that are known to respond to sleep manipulations. With increasing knowledge of the biological effects of sleep, other systems may need to be considered.

The neuroendocrine systems under consideration have implications concerning possible neural substrates of the mechanisms that are involved in depression and sleep deprivation therapy. TRH, which appears to be responsible for the nocturnal surge of TSH and PRL secretion, and CRH, which appears to be responsible for the nightly onset of ACTH and cortisol secretion, both originate in cell bodies of the PVN of the hypothalamus. The clock mechanism that signals the PVN to begin its nocturnal secretory activity resides in the SCN of the hypothalamus. The PVN also lies along the pathway through which the SCN triggers the nocturnal surge in MT secretion by the pineal gland. Thus, under the temporal control of the SCN, the PVN stimulates a surge of nocturnal secretory activity in several different neuroendocrine systems, which are relatively quiescent in the daytime. The central role of the SCN–PVN axis in the regulation of these systems may explain the similarity of 24–hour profiles of TSH, PRL and MT levels.

Of the various possible neuroendocrine mechanisms of sleep deprivation, augmentation of TSH (and TRH) secretion is the most intuitively appealing, because it appears to correct a deficiency in the nocturnal secretion of this hormone in depression. Since this effect of sleep deprivation on TSH secretion is due to heat loss, it implicates thermoregulatory mechanisms in depression and its response to sleep deprivation. These considerations raise the possibility that the sleep–wake cycle, itself, may be a form of behavioral thermoregulation that protects the organism from extremes of environmental temperature in the middle of the afternoon and late at night. During sleep, REM sleep may serve a special thermoregulatory function as a mechanism for periodic sampling of environmental light and temperature conditions.

In the environment there are not only daily, but also seasonal challenges to energy regulation. Interestingly, the SCN–PVN axis is also involved in the regulation of annual rhythms in behavior and physiology that are adaptations to seasonal changes in the environment; lesions of the SCN or the PVN in animals abolish some of these seasonal rhythms. The timing of seasonal and circadian rhythms is regulated by changes in environmental light, acting on the SCN via the RHT.

There are also marked seasonal influences on the incidence of mania and depression. Certain patients regularly become depressed or manic at certain times of year, and light has been shown to be an effective treatment in these cases. Patients' responses to phototherapy and sleep deprivation therapy have a similar time course, and some patients respond to both types of treatment. Depression and its treatment may involve perturbations of a hypothalamic energy–regulating system involving the eyes, SCN, PVN and H–P–T axis. This system is highly attuned to changes in environmental light and temperature, and it regulates appetite, weight, metabolism, sleep and behavior. The PVN, a central component of this system, may be part of the final common pathway of the antidepressant effects of light and sleep deprivation (or heat–loss) therapy.

REFERENCES

Akiskal, H.S., T.L. Rosenthal, R.F. Haykal, H. Lemmi, R.H. Rosenthal and A. Scott–Strauss. 1980. Characterological depressions. Clinical and sleep EEG findings separating "subaffective dysthymias" from "character spectrum disorders". Arch Gen Psychiatr 37:777–783.

Ansseau, M., R. Machowski, G. Franck and M. Timsit–Berthier. 1985. REM sleep latency and contingent negative variation in endogenous depression. Suggestion for a common cholinergic mechanism. Biol Psychiatr 20:1303–1307.

Aschoff, J. 1981. Annual rhythms in man. In Handbook of Behavioral Neurobiology (Volume 4, Biological Rhythms), Aschoff, J. (ed.). New York: Plenum Press, pp. 475–487.

Avery, D.H., G. Wildschiodtz and O. Rafaelsen. 1982. REM latency and temperature in affective disorder before and after treatment. Biol Psychiatr 17:463–470.

Beersma, D.G.M., S. Daan and R.H. van den Hoofdakker. 1984b. Distribution of REM latencies and other sleep phenomena in depression as explained by a single ultradian rhythm disturbance. Sleep 7:126–136.

Benson, K.L. and V.P. Zarcone, Jr. 1985a. Testing the REM sleep phasic event intrusion hypothesis of schizophrenia. Psychiatr Res 15:163–173.

Benson, K.L. and V.P. Zarcone, Jr. 1985b. Low REM latency in schizophrenia. Sleep Res 14:124.

Borbély, A.A. 1982a. A two–process model of sleep regulation. Hum Neurobiol 1:195–204.

Borbély, A.A. and A. Wirz–Justice. 1982b. Sleep, sleep deprivation, and depression. A hypothesis derived from a model of sleep regulation. Hum Neurobiol 1:205–210.

Borbély, A.A., I. Tobler, M. Loepfe, D.J. Kupfer, R.F. Ulrich, V. Grochocinski, J. Doman and G. Matthews. 1984. All-night spectral analysis of the sleep EEG in untreated depressives and normal controls. Psychiatr Res 12:27–33.

Bunney, Jr., W.E., F.K. Goodwin, D.L. Murphy, K.M. House and E.K. Gordon. 1972b. The "switch process" in manic–depressive illness. II. Relationship to catecholamines, REM sleep and drugs. Arch Gen Psychiatr 27:304–309.

Caron, P.J., L.K. Nieman, S.R. Rose and B.C. Nisula. 1986. Deficient nocturnal surge of thyrotropin in central hypothyroidism. J Clin Endocrinol Metab 62:960–964.

Cartwright, R.D., S. Lloyd, L. Paul and K. Stephenson. 1980. Pressure to dream during a major life crisis. Sleep Res 9:131.

Coble, P., F.G. Foster and D.J. Kupfer. 1976. Electroencephalographic sleep diagnosis of primary depression. Arch Gen Psychiatr 33:1124–1127.

Coble, P.A., D.J. Kupfer and D.H. Shaw. 1981. Distribution of REM latency in depression. Biol Psychiatr 16:453–466.

Conroy, R.T.W.L., B.D. Hughes and J.N. Mills. 1968. Circadian rhythm of plasma 11–hydroxy corticosteroid in psychiatric disorders. Br Med J 3:405–407.

Désir, D., E. van Cauter, V.S. Fang, E. Martino, C. Jadot, J.P. Spire, P. Noël, S. Refetoff, G. Copinschi and J. Golstein. 1981. Effects of "jet–lag" on hormonal patterns. I. Procedures, variations in total plasma proteins, and disruption of adrenocortico-tropin–cortisol periodicity. J Clin Endocrinol Metab 52:628–641.

Detre, T., J. Himmelhoch, M. Swartzburg, C.M. Anderson, R. Byck and D.J. Kupfer. 1972. Hypersomnia and manic–depressive disease. Am J Psychiatr 128:1303–1305.

Doig, R.J., R.V. Mummery, M.R. Wills and A. Eikes. 1966. Plasma cortisol levels in depression. Br J Psychiatr 112:1263–1267.

Duncan, W.C., K.D. Pettigrew and J.C. Gillin. 1979. REM architecture changes in bipolar and unipolar depression. Am J Psychiatr 136:1424–1427.

Elsenga, S. and R.H. van den Hoofdakker. 1982–1983. Clinical effects of sleep deprivation and clomipramine in endogenous depression. J Psychiatr Res 17:361–374.

Feinberg, M., J.C. Gillin, B.J. Carroll, J.F. Greden and A.P. Zis. 1982. EEG studies of sleep in the diagnosis of depression. Biol Psychiatr 17:305–316.

Foster, F.G., T. Grau, D.G. Spiker, D. Love, P. Coble and D.J. Kupfer. 1977. EEG sleep in generalized anxiety disorder. Sleep Res 6:145.

Fullerton, D.T., F.J. Wenzel, F.N. Lohrenz and H. Fahs. 1968. Circadian rhythm of adrenal cortical activity in depression. I. A comparison of depressed patients with normal subjects. Arch Gen Psychiatr 19:674–681.

Garvey, M.J., D. Mungas and G.D. Tollefson. 1984. Hypersomnia in major depressive disorders. J Affect Disord 6:283–286.

Giles, D.E., H.P. Roffwarg, M.A. Schlesser and A.J. Rush. 1986. Which endogenous depressive symptoms relate to REM latency reduction? Biol Psychiatr 21:473–482.

Gillin, J.C. 1983b. The sleep therapies of depression. Prog Neuropsychopharmacol Biol Psychiatr 7:351–364.

Gillin, J.C., C. Mazure, R.M. Post, D. Jimerson and W.E. Bunney, Jr. 1977a. An EEG sleep study of a bipolar (manic–depressive) patient with a nocturnal switch process. Biol Psychiatr 12:711–718.

Gillin, J.C., W. Duncan, K.D. Pettigrew, B.L. Frankel and F. Snyder. 1979a. Successful separation of depressed, normal, and insomniac subjects by EEG sleep data. Arch Gen Psychiatr 36:85–90.

Gillin, J.C., W.C. Duncan, D.L. Murphy, R.M. Post, T.A. Wehr, F.K. Goodwin, R.J. Wyatt and W.E. Bunney, Jr. 1981. Age–related changes in sleep in depressed and normal subjects. Psychiatr Res 4:73–78.

Gillin, J.C., N. Sitaram, T.A. Wehr, W. Duncan, R.M. Post, D.L. Murphy, W.B. Mendelson, R.J. Wyatt and W.E. Bunney, Jr. 1984. Sleep and affective illness. In Neurobiology of Mood Disorders (Frontiers of Clinical Neuroscience, Volume 1), Post, R.M. and J.C. Ballenger (eds.). Baltimore: Williams & Wilkins, pp. 157–189.

Goetze, U. and R. Tölle. 1981. Antidepressive Wirkung des partiellen Schlafentzuges während der 1. Hälfte der Nacht. Psychiatr Clin (Basel) 14:129–149.

Golstein, J., E. van Cauter, P. Linkowski, L. Vanhaelst and J. Mendlewicz. 1980. Thyrotropin nyctohemeral pattern in primary depression: differences between unipolar and bipolar women. Life Sci 27:1695–1703.

Gresham, S.C., H.W. Agnew, Jr. and R.L. Williams. 1965. The sleep of depressed patients. An EEG and eye movement study. Arch Gen Psychiatr 13:503–507.

Guazzelli, M., C. Maggini, G. Landini, T.C. Floyd and I. Feinberg. 1985. Similarity of non–REM abnormalities in schizophrenia and depression. Arch Gen Psychiatr 42:834–835.

Hartmann, E. 1968. Longitudinal studies of sleep and dream patterns in manic–depressive patients. Arch Gen Psychiatr 19:312–329.

Hawkins, D.R. and J. Mendels. 1966. Sleep disturbance in depressive syndromes. Am J Psychiatr 123:682–690.

Hawkins, D.R., J. Mendels, J. Scott, G. Bensch and W. Teachey. 1967. The psychophysiology of sleep in psychotic depression: a longitudinal study. Psychosom Med 29:329–344.

Hiatt, J.F., T.C. Floyd, P.H. Katz and I. Feinberg. 1985. Further evidence of abnormal non–rapid–eye–movement sleep in schizophrenia. Arch Gen Psychiatr 42:797–802.

Hobson, J.A., R.W. McCarley and P.W. Wyzinski. 1975. Sleep cycle oscillation reciprocal discharge by two brainstem neuronal groups. Science 189:55-58.

Hoffmann, K. 1981. Photoperiodism in vertebrates. In Handbook of Behavioral Neurobiology (Volume 4, Biological Rhythms), Aschoff, J. (ed.). New York: Plenum Press, pp. 449-473.

Insel, T.R., J.C. Gillin, A. Moore, W.B. Mendelson, R.J. Loewenstein and D.L. Murphy. 1982. The sleep of patients with obsessive-compulsive disorder. Arch Gen Psychiatr 39:1372-1377.

Jernajczyk, W. 1986. Latency of eye movement and other REM sleep parameters in bipolar depression. Biol Psychiatr 21:465-472.

Jovanovic, U.J. 1977. The sleep profile in manic-depressive patients in the depressive phase. Waking Sleeping 1:199-210.

Jus, K., M. Bouchard, A.K. Jus, A. Villeneuve and R. Lachance. 1973. Sleep EEG studies in untreated, long-term schizophrenic patients. Arch Gen Psychiatr 29:386-390.

Kerkhofs, M., G. Hoffmann, V. De Martelaere, P. Linkowski and J. Mendlewicz. 1985. Sleep EEG recordings in depressive disorders. J Affect Disord 9:47-537.

Kijne, B., H. Aggernaes, F. Fog-Moller, H.H. Andersen, J. Nissen, C. Kirkegaard and N. Bjorum. 1982. Circadian variation of serum thyrotropin in endogenous depression. Psychiatr Res 6:277-282.

Kjellman, B.F., J. Beck-Friis, J.G. Ljunggren and L. Wetterberg. 1984. Twenty-four-hour serum levels of TSH in affective disorders. Acta Psychiatr Scand 69:491-502.

Knowles, J.B. and A.W. MacLean. 1986. A critical evaluation of models of depression. In Biological Psychiatry, 1985: Proceedings of the IVth World Congress of Biological Psychiatry (September 8-13, 1985; Philadelphia, Pennsylvania), Shagass, C., R.C. Josiassen, W.H. Pridter, K.J. Weiss, D. Stoff and G.M. Simpson (eds.). New York: Elsevier Science Publishing Company, pp. 943-948.

Kupfer, D.J., J.M. Himmelhoch, M. Schwartzberg, C. Anderson, R. Byck and T.P. Detre. 1972b. Hypersomnia in manic–depressive disease (a preliminary report). Dis Nerv Syst 33:720–724.

Kupfer, D.J. and F.G. Foster. 1972c. Interval between onset of sleep and rapid eye movement sleep as an indicator of depression. Lancet 2:684.

Kupfer, D.J., F.G. Foster and T.P. Detre. 1973. Sleep continuity changes in depression. Dis Nerv Syst 34:192–195.

Kupfer, D.J., R.F. Ulrich, P.A. Coble, D.B. Jarrett, V. Grochocinski, J. Doman, G. Matthews and A.A. Borbély. 1984. Application of automated REM and slow wave sleep analysis: II. Testing the assumptions of the two–process model of sleep regulation in normal and depressed subjects. Psychiatr Res 13:335–343.

Kupfer, D.J., C.F. Reynolds 3d, V.J. Grochocinski, R.F. Ulrich and A. McEachran. 1986a. Aspects of short REM latency in affective states: a revisit. Psychiatr Res 17:49–59.

Lahmeyer, H.W., E. Val, M. Gaviria and B.R. Prasad. 1985. EEG sleep in borderline personality disorder. Sleep Res 14:133.

Lewy, A.J., H.A. Kern, N.E. Rosenthal and T.A. Wehr. 1982. Bright artificial light treatment of a manic–depressive patient with a seasonal mood cycle. Am J Psychiatr 139:1496–1498.

Linkowski, P., J. Mendlewicz, R. LeClercq, M. Brasseur, P. Hubain, J. Golstein, G. Copinschi and E. van Cauter. 1985. The 24–hour profile of adrenocorticotropin and cortisol in major depressive illness. J Clin Endocrinol Metab 61:429–438.

Martin, P.R., R.J. Loewenstein, W.H. Kaye, M.H. Ebert, H. Weingartner and J.C. Gillin. 1986. Sleep EEG in Korsakoff's psychosis and Alzheimer's disease. Neurology 36:411–414.

McCarley, R.W. 1982. REM sleep and depression: common neurobiological control mechanisms. Am J Psychiatr 139:565–570.

McCarley, R.W. and S.G. Massaquoi. 1985a. The rapid eye movement sleep ultradian rhythm: a limit cycle mathematical model. In Ultradian Rhythms in Physiology and Behavior (Experimental Brain Research, Supplementum 12), Schulz, H. and P. Lavie (eds.). Berlin: Springer–Verlag, pp. 288–308.

McNamara, E., C.F. Reynolds 3d, P.H. Soloff, R. Mathias, A. Rossi, D. Spiker, P.A. Coble and D.J. Kupfer. 1984. EEG sleep evaluation of depression in borderline patients. Am J Psychiatr 141:182–186.

Mendels, J. and D.R. Hawkins. 1967a. Sleep and depression. A controlled EEG study. Arch Gen Psychiatr 16:344–354.

Mendelson, W.B., J.V. Martin, R. Wagner, J.G. Milton, S.P. James, D.A. Sack, N.E. Rosenthal and T.A. Wehr. 1986. Do depressed patients have decreased delta power in the sleep EEG? Sleep Res 15:146.

Neil, J.F., J.R. Merikanges, F.G. Foster, K.R. Merikanges, D.G. Spiker and D.J. Kupfer. 1980. Waking and all–night sleep EEGs in anorexia nervosa. Clin Electroencephalogr 11:9–15.

O'Malley, B.P., A. Richardson, N. Cook, S. Swart and F.D. Rosenthal. 1984. Circadian rhythms of serum thyrotropin and body temperature in euthyroid individuals and their responses to warming. Clin Sci 67:433–437.

Papousek, M. 1975. Chronobiologische aspekte der Zyklothymie. Fortschr Neurol Psychiatr 43:381–440.

Parker, D.C., L.G. Rossman and E.F. Vanderlan. 1974. Relation of sleep–entrained human prolactin release to REM–nonREM cycles. J Clin Endocrinol Metab 38:646–651.

Parker, D.C., A.E. Pekary and J.M. Hershman. 1976. Effect of normal and reversed sleep–wake cycles upon nyctohemeral rhythmicity of plasma thyrotropin: evidence suggestive of an inhibitory influence in sleep. J Clin Endocrinol Metab 43:318–329.

Pflug, B. and R. Tölle. 1971. Disturbance of the 24–hour rhythm in endogenous depression and the treatment of endogenous depression by sleep deprivation. Int Pharmacopsychiatr 6:187–196.

Pflug, B., R. Erikson and A. Johnsson. 1976. Depression and daily temperature. A long–term study. Acta Psychiatr Scand 54:254–266.

Post, R.M., F.J. Stoddard, J.C. Gillin, M. Buchsbaum, D.C. Runkle, K. Black and W.E. Bunney, Jr. 1977. Alterations in motor activity, sleep, and biochemistry in a cycling manic–depressive patient. Arch Gen Psychiatr 34:470–477.

Puig–Antich, J., R. Goetz, C. Hanlon, M. Davies, J. Thompson, W.J. Chambers, M.A. Tabrizi and E.D. Weitzman. 1982. Sleep architecture and REM sleep measures in prepubertal children with major depression: a controlled study. Arch Gen Psychiatr 39:932–939.

Quitkin, F.M., D. Schwartz, M.R. Liebowitz, J.R. Stewart, P.J. McGrath, F. Halpern, J. Puig–Antich, E. Tricamo, E.J. Sachar and D.F. Klein. 1982. Atypical depressives: a preliminary report of antidepressant response and sleep patterns. Psychopharmacol Bull 18:78–80.

Rapoport, J., R. Elkins, D.H. Langer, W. Sceery, M.S. Buchsbaum, J.C. Gillin, D.L. Murphy, T.P. Zahn, R. Lake, C. Ludlow and W. Mendelson. 1981. Childhood obsessive–compulsive disorder. Am J Psychiatr 138:1545–1554.

Rechtschaffen, A. and A. Kales. 1968. A Manual of Standardized Terminology, Techniques and Scoring System for Sleep Stages of Human Subjects (Publication No. 204). Washington, D.C.: National Institutes of Health.

Reynolds 3d, C.F., D.J. Kupfer, A.B. McEachran, L.S. Taska, D.E. Sewitch and P.A. Coble. 1984. Depressive psychopathology in male sleep apneics. J Clin Psychiatr 45:287–290.

Reynolds 3d, C.F., P.H. Soloff, D.J. Kupfer, L.S. Taska, K. Restifo, P.A. Coble and M.E. McNamara. 1985c. Depression in borderline patients: a prospective EEG sleep study. Psychiatr Res 14:1–15.

Rosenthal, N.E., D.A. Sack and T.A. Wehr. 1983. Seasonal variation in affective disorders. In Circadian Rhythms in Psychiatry, Wehr, T.A. and F.K. Goodwin (eds.), pp. 185–201. Pacific Grove: Boxwood Press.

Rosenthal, N.E., D.A. Sack, C.J. Carpenter, B.L. Parry, W.B. Mendelson and T.A. Wehr. 1985a. Antidepressant effects of light in seasonal affective disorder. Am J Psychiatr 142:163–170.

Sachar, E.J., L. Hellman, H.P. Roffwarg, F.S. Halpern, D.K. Fukushima and T.F. Gallagher. 1973. Disrupted 24–hour patterns of cortisol secretion in psychotic depression. Arch Gen Psychiatr 28:19–24.

Sack, D.A., J.I. Nurnberger, Jr., N.E. Rosenthal, E. Ashburn and T.A. Wehr. 1985. Potentiation of antidepressant medications by phase advance of the sleep–wake cycle. Am J Psychiatr 142:606–608.

Sack, D.A., S.P. James, N.E. Rosenthal, et al.. 1986a. TSH is low at night during sleep and sleep deprivation in rapid cycling manic–depressives. Submitted.

Sack, D.A., N.E. Rosenthal, W.C. Duncan, et al.. 1986b. Early versus late partial sleep deprivation therapy of depression. Submitted.

Sack, D.A. and T.A. Wehr. 1986c. Circadian rhythms in depressed patients and normal controls measured on a constant routine. Submitted.

Sack, D.A., N.E. Rosenthal, B.L. Parry and T.A. Wehr. 1986d. Biological rhythms in psychiatry. In Psychopharmacology: The Third Generation of Progress, Meltzer, H.Y. (ed.). New York: Raven Press, pp. 669–685.

Schilgen, B. and R. Tölle. 1980. Partial sleep deprivation as therapy for depression. Arch Gen Psychiatr 37:267–271.

Schmidt, H.S. and K. Shy. 1986. Short-REM latency in impotence without depression. In New Research Program and Abstracts (Proceedings of the 139th Annual Meeting of the American Psychiatric Association). Washington, D.C.: American Psychiatric Association, p. 139.

Schulz, H., R. Lund, C. Cording and G. Dirlich. 1979. Bimodal distribution of REM sleep latencies in depression. Biol Psychiatr 14:595-600.

Schulz, H. and R. Lund. 1983. Sleep onset REM episodes are associated with circadian parameters of body temperature. A study in depressed patients and normal controls. Biol Psychiatr 18:1411-1426.

Schulz, H. and R. Lund. 1985. On the origin of early REM episodes in the sleep of depressed patients: a comparison of three hypotheses. Psychiatr Res 16:65-77.

Sherman, B., B. Pfohl and G. Winokur. 1984. Circadian analysis of plasma cortisol levels before and after dexamethasone administration in depressed patients. Arch Gen Psychiatr 41:271-275.

Silberman, E.K. and R.M. Post. 1982. Atypicality in primary depressive illness: a preliminary survey. Biol Psychiatr 17:285-304.

Snyder, F. 1972. NIH studies of EEG sleep in affective illness. In Recent Advances in the Psychobiology of the Depressive Illness (Proceedings of a Workshop Sponsored by the Clinical Research Branch Division of Extramural Research Programs, National Institute of Mental Health, Virginia, April-May 1969), Williams, T.A., M.M. Katz and J.A. Shield (eds.). Washington, D.C.: U.S. Government Printing Office, pp. 171-192.

Spiker, D.G., F.G. Foster, P.A. Coble, D. Love and D.J. Kupfer. 1977. The sleep disorder in depressed alcoholics. Sleep Res 6:161.

Stern, M., D. Fram, R.J. Wyatt, L. Grinspoon and B. Tursky. 1969. All-night sleep studies of acute schizophrenics. Arch Gen Psychiatr 20:470-477.

Taub, J.M., D.R. Hawkins and R.L. van de Castle. 1978. Electrographic analysis of the sleep cycle in young depressed patients. Biol Psychol 7:203-216.

Thase, M.E., D.J. Kupfer and D.G. Spiker. 1984. Electroencephalographic sleep in secondary depression: a revisit. Biol Psychiatr 19:805-814.

Thase, M.E., J.M. Himmelhoch, A.G. Mallinger, D.B. Jarrett and D.J. Kupfer. 1986a. Sleep and cortisol in anergic bipolar depression. In New Research Program and Abstracts (Proceedings of the 139th Annual Meeting of the American Psychiatric Association). Washington, D.C.: American Psychiatric Association, p. 79.

van den Hoofdakker, R.H. 1986. Effects of total sleep deprivation on mood and chronophysiology in depression. In Biological Psychiatry, 1985: Proceedings of the IVth World Congress of Biological Psychiatry (September 8-13, 1985; Philadelphia, Pennsylvania), Shagass, C., R.C. Josiassen, W.H. Pridter, K.J. Weiss, D. Stoff and G.M. Simpson (eds.). New York: Elsevier Science Publishing Company, pp. 969-971.

van den Hoofdakker, R.H. and D.G.M. Beersma. 1985a. On the explanation of short REM latencies in depression. Psychiatr Res 16:155-163.

Vogel, G.W., F. Vogel, R.S. McAbee and A.J. Thurmond. 1980. Improvement of depression by REM sleep deprivation. New findings and a theory. Arch Gen Psychiatr 37:247-253.

von Zerssen, D., H. Barthelmes, G. Dirlich, P. Doerr, H.M. Emrich, L. von Lindern, R. Lund and K.M. Pirke. 1985. Circadian rhythms in endogenous depression. Psychiatr Res 16:51-63.

Weeke, A. and J. Weeke. 1978. Disturbed circadian variation of serum thyrotropin in patients with endogenous depression. Acta Psychiatrica Scand 57:281-289.

Wehr, T.A. 1977. Phase and biorhythm studies of affective illness in the switch process in manic–depressive psychosis, pp. 321–324, In The switch process in manic–depressive psychosis, Bunney, Jr., W.E., Moderator (Transcription of a Combined Clinical Staff Conference, National Institute of Mental Health, Bethesda, Maryland, February 1976). Ann Intern Med 87:319–335.

Wehr, T.A., A. Wirz–Justice, F.K. Goodwin, W. Duncan and J.C. Gillin. 1979b. Phase advance of the circadian sleep–wake cycle as an antidepressant. Science 206:710–713.

Wehr, T.A. and F.K. Goodwin. 1981b. Biological rhythms and psychiatry. In American Handbook of Psychiatry, Second Edition (Volume VII), Arieti, S. and H.K.H. Brodie (eds.). New York: Basic Books, Inc., pp. 46–74.

Wehr, T.A., F.K. Goodwin, A. Wirz–Justice, J. Breitmaier and C. Craig. 1982a. 48–hour sleep–wake cycles in manic–depressive illness: naturalistic observations and sleep deprivation experiments. Arch Gen Psychiatr 39:559–565.

Wehr, T.A. and A. Wirz–Justice. 1982b. Circadian rhythm mechanisms in affective illness and in antidepressant drug action. Pharmacopsychiatria 15:31–39.

Wehr, T.A. and F.K. Goodwin. 1983a. Introduction. In Circadian Rhythms in Psychiatry, Wehr, T.A. and F.K. Goodwin (eds.). Pacific Grove: Boxwood Press, pp. 1–15.

Wehr, T.A. and F.K. Goodwin. 1983b. Biological rhythms and manic–depressive illness. In Circadian Rhythms in Psychiatry, Wehr, T.A. and F.K. Goodwin (eds.). Pacific Grove: Boxwood Press, pp. 129–184.

Wehr, T.A., N.E. Rosenthal, D.A. Sack and J.C. Gillin. 1985a. Antidepressant effects of sleep deprivation in bright and dim light. Acta Psychiatr Scand 72:161–165.

Wehr, T.A., D.A. Sack, W.C. Duncan, W.B. Mendelson, N.E. Rosenthal, J.C. Gillin and F.K. Goodwin. 1985b. Sleep and circadian rhythms in affective patients isolated from external time cues. Psychiatr Res 15:327–339.

Wehr, T.A., D.A. Sack and N.E. Rosenthal. 1987. Sleep reduction as a final common pathway in the genesis of mania. Am J Psychiatr 144:201–204.

Weitzman, E.D. 1982a. Chronobiology of man. Sleep, temperature and neuroendocrine rhythms. Hum Neurobiol 1:173–183.

Weitzman, E.D., D. Goldmacher, D. Kripke, P. MacGregor, J. Kream and L. Hellman. 1968. Reversal of sleep–waking cycle: effect on sleep stage pattern and certain neuroendocrine rhythms. Trans Am Neurol Assoc 93:153–157.

Weitzman, E.D., C. Nogeire, M. Perlow, D. Fukushima, J. Sassin, P. MacGregor, T.F. Gallagher and L. Hellman. 1974. Effects of a prolonged 3–hour sleep–wake cycle on sleep stages, plasma cortisol, growth hormone and body temperature in man. J Clin Endocrinol Metab 38:1018–1030.

Weitzman, E.D., C.A. Czeisler, J.C. Zimmerman and J.M. Ronda. 1981a. The sleep–wake pattern of cortisol and growth hormone secretion during nonentrained (free–running) conditions in man. In Human Pituitary Hormones: Circadian and Episodic Variations (A Workshop Symposium held in Brussels, Belgium, November 29–30, 1979; Sponsored by the Commission of the European Communities, as advised by the Committee on Medical and Public Health Research) [Developments in Endocrinology, Volume 1], van Cauter, E. and G. Copinschi (eds.). The Hague: Martinus Nijhoff, pp. 29–41.

Wever, R.A. 1979a. The Circadian System of Man: Results of Experiments Under Temporal Isolation. New York: Springer–Verlag.

Wiegand, M., M. Berger, J. Zulley, C. Lauer and D. von Zerssen. 1986. The influence of daytime naps on the therapeutic effect of sleep deprivation. Biol Psychiatr 22:389–392.

Yamaguchi, N., K. Maeda and S. Kuromaru. 1978. The effects of sleep deprivation on the circadian rhythm of plasma cortisol levels in depressive patients. Folia Psychiatr Neurol Jpn 32:479–487.

7

ABNORMALITIES IN CIRCADIAN PERIODICITY IN DEPRESSION

Dorothy T. Krieger

Abnormalities in the function of the hypothalamic–pituitary–adrenal (H–P–A) axis have been described in a substantial percentage of patients with endogenous depression. Such abnormalities are those of excessive cortisol secretion, resistance to normal feedback inhibition and possible disturbances in the pattern of plasma corticosteroid secretion. There is a considerable amount of information available concerning factors involved in regulation of these parameters in normal subjects. If the abnormalities in H–P–A function in depressed subjects are secondary to altered regulation of this axis, the question arises whether such alterations are responsible for both the endocrine and psychiatric disturbances present in these patients. In view of the topic of this volume, this review will consider factors involved in one aspect of these abnormalities, i.e., circadian periodicity. Normal regulation of such periodicity will first be considered, then abnormalities of such periodicity encountered in disease states other than psychiatric disease, and the abnormalities encountered in depressed patients, including abnormalities of circadian variation of other hormonal parameters.

CHARACTERIZATION OF CIRCADIAN PERIODICITY OF THE H–P–A AXIS

This has been investigated, for the most part, because of its ease of measurement, by study of changes in plasma or adrenal corticosteroid concentrations, although there have been studies in

177

which plasma adrenocorticotrophic hormone (ACTH) concentrations were measured as well. Until recently, studies of corticotropin–releasing factor (CRF) periodicity have depended on indirect bioassays; the isolation of CRF (Vale, et al., 1981) and the expected availability of immunoassays for this in the near future should facilitate studies in this regard.

The circadian pattern of both plasma corticosteroid and ACTH concentrations has been characterized as one in which peak concentrations occur prior to or at the time of awakening, with a decline during the remainder of the 24–hour period. Such peak concentrations are seen in the early morning hours in human subjects and in the early evening in nocturnal animals. The pattern is not dependent on activity, and undergoes reversal with reversed light–dark or reversed sleep–wake conditions (Perkoff, et al., 1959). A similar pattern of human plasma ACTH concentrations has also been demonstrated (Krieger, et al., 1971; and Gallagher, et al., 1973). Lastly, a rhythm of hypothalamic CRF bioactivity has been demonstrated in the hypothalamus of several species (David–Nelson and Brodish, 1969; Hiroshige, Sakakura and Itoh, 1969; Hiroshige and Sato, 1970; Takebe, Sakakura and Mashimo, 1972; Sato and George, 1973; and Ixart, et al., 1977). In all of these studies, the phase of the CRF rhythm preceded that of plasma corticosterone, whereas there was no phase difference between the rhythms of plasma ACTH and corticosteroid concentrations. Over the last decade, it has become evident from studies utilizing half–hourly or more frequent sampling (Krieger, et al., 1971; and Gallagher, et al., 1973) that, in addition to the above–noted circadian periodicity of plasma ACTH and corticosteroid concentrations, episodic, relatively synchronous, ultradian peaks of plasma ACTH and corticosteroid concentrations are superimposed on such a circadian pattern. Such episodic peaks occur with a variable frequency. In human subjects, the majority of such episodic peaks occur in the period from 0300 to 0900 (at the time of the circadian rise), with other bursts of episodic secretion seen most frequently in relation to mealtimes. In normal subjects, there appears to be six to nine major secretory episodes over 24 hours. The source of such episodic secretion, whether at a hypothalamic or a pituitary level, still remains to be explored.

Although studies have indicated that an endogenous periodicity may exist at all levels of the H–P–A axis, it would appear that the primary modulator of periodic release resides within the central nervous system (CNS). There is controversy as to whether there is a circadian periodicity in the secretion of cultured adrenal glands (Shiotsuka, Jovanovich and Jovanovich, 1974; and O'Hare and Hornsby, 1975) or whether adrenal corticosteroid periodicity persists in hypophysectomized animals (Meier, 1976). A circadian rhythm in adrenal sensitivity to ACTH has been reported in both animal and human studies (Perkoff, et al., 1959; Ungar and Halberg, 1962; and Dallman, Engeland and Shinsako, 1976). Such variation in responsiveness may be explained in part by the lack of adrenal priming by endogenous ACTH prior to the less responsive phase. In human subjects, such decreased responsiveness, seen when ACTH is administered at 2300 (the time of lowest endogenous ACTH concentrations), becomes normal if a submaximal injection of ACTH is given prior to its administration at 2300 (Perkoff, et al., 1959). The constant slow infusion of small amounts of ACTH over a 24–hour period is accompanied by a constant level of plasma corticosteroid concentrations, further indicating no inherent periodicity in adrenal responsiveness to ACTH (Nugent, et al., 1960).

There also appears to be a circadian rhythm of responsiveness of corticosteroid concentrations to stress (Takebe, Setaishi and Hirama, 1966; and Dunn, Scheving and Millet, 1972). In the human, this is evidenced by a greater responsiveness of plasma corticosteroid concentrations following an evening, in contrast to a morning, injection of pyrogen (Takebe, Setaishi and Hirama, 1966) or evening administration of metyrapone (Martin and Hellman, 1964; and Takebe, Setaishi and Hirama, 1966). This can be interpreted as reflecting the presence of enhanced pituitary stores of ACTH prior to their depletion at the time of the circadian rise, though it is obvious that other factors, viz., potentiators of ACTH release or removal of inhibitory factors, also need be considered. There is also increased sensitivity in the human to feedback suppression of the pituitary adrenal axis following PM vs. AM corticosteroid administration (Nichols, Nugent and Tyler, 1963).

Although the above data suggest that there may be limited circadian periodicity of adrenal secretion, and perhaps of adrenal responsiveness to ACTH, it is apparent that a circadian variation of plasma ACTH concentrations is present in the absence of the adrenal glands, with, however, higher plasma ACTH concentrations present than under normal conditions because of the lack of adrenocorticosteroid feedback (Graber, et al., 1965; Cheifetz, Gaffud and Dingan, 1968; and Krieger and Gewirtz, 1974). [Since ACTH is derived from a precursor molecule (Mains, Eipper and Ling, 1977; and Roberts and Herbert, 1977) which, in human anterior pituitary, also serves as a precursor to ß–lipotropin, some of which may be further processed, to a small extent, to ß–endorphin, it is not surprising that a similar circadian variation of these percursor–derived peptides is also present (Petraglia, et al., 1983).] There is limited available evidence with regard to circadian variation of pituitary responsiveness to CRF–like substances, and none with regard to CRF itself.

The findings noted in the adrenalectomized subjects indicate that ACTH periodicity is not dependent on adrenal corticosteroid feedback. The circadian periodicity of the H–P–A axis can be abolished by corticosteroid administration. These studies have utilized the artificial steroid, dexamethasone, rather than the endogenous steroid, although suppression can be seen in either instance. The locus of such feedback may be either at the hypothalamic or pituitary level. The sensitivity of this aspect of ACTH secretion and feedback inhibition has formed the basis of the dexamethasone suppression test, which is employed both in pituitary hypersecretory states and in depressive subjects. Dexamethasone, a synthetic glucocorticoid, is used clinically to evaluate the suppressibility of the H–P–A axis, since the plasma corticosteroid levels, rather than those of ACTH (which is technically more difficult to determine), can be monitored. Whether use of such a synthetic glucocorticoid is physiologically relevant is somewhat open to question, in that glucocorticoid receptors in different parts of the CNS and pituitary vary with regard to their relative avidity for dexamethasone and endogenous glucocorticoids. The pituitary also contains steroid–binding proteins, in addition to classical receptors, which would bind endogenous steroids but not dexamethasone. The test is commonly performed by administering dexamethasone in the late evening, utilizing the known greater circadian sensitivity of the H–P–A axis to such suppression at this time (Nichols, Nugent and Tyler, 1963; and Krieger, et al., 1971).

Periodicity in hypothalamic CRF content, which is also present in hypophysectomized animals, has been reported

(Hiroshige, Sakakura and Itoh, 1969; and Hiroshige and Sakakura, 1971). There is also a circadian periodicity in CNS content of a number of neurotransmitters believed to be involved in ACTH regulation (Krieger, 1983), i.e., of acetylcholine (Hanin, Massarelli and Costa, 1970), serotonin (Reis, Corvelli and Conners, 1969), and dopamine (Reis, Weinbren and Corvelli, 1968). This may be correlated with other evidence of circadian rhythmicity of neuronal activity; i.e., there are circadian morphological changes in neurons of the supraoptic and paraventricular nuclei (PVN) (Armstrong and Hatton, 1976), the latter being an area in which CRF-containing cell bodies have been demonstrated (Swanson, et al., 1983). There is a circadian rhythm in the frequency of firing of neurons in the ventromedial nuclei and lateral hypothalamic area (Koizuma and Nishino, 1976), and there is a circadian rhythm in spontaneous, compound action potential in the isolated Aplysia ganglion (Eskin, 1981). Additional evidence of neuronal involvement in the regulation of circadian periodicity of ACTH-corticosteroid concentrations may be obtained from developmental studies. Such periodicity is not present either in animals (Allen and Kendall, 1967; Hiroshige and Sato, 1970; and Johnson and Levine, 1973) or in humans (Franks, 1967) until the mid-prepubertal period. In the experimental animal, the age of the appearance of such periodicity is correlated with appearance of evidence of CNS maturation, such as eyelid opening, development of the retinal-hypothalamic tract (RHT) to the suprachiasmatic nucleus (SCN) (see below), and the appearance of periodicity of hypothalamic CRF levels (Hiroshige and Sato, 1970). Once circadian periodicity is attained, this persists unchanged in the presence of normal CNS function; normal periodicity has been seen in humans through the eighth decade (Silverberg, Rizzo and Krieger, 1968).

The anatomical locus believed to generate such periodicity is the SCN (Stephan and Nunez, 1977). Lesions of this area (Moore and Eichler, 1972) are reported to result in obliteration of corticosteroid periodicity and of circadian drinking and activity patterns in the rat (Stephan and Zucker, 1972). A circadian rhythm in the electric discharge of rat suprachiasmatic neurons has been recorded in vitro (Groos and Hendriks, 1982). Circadian variation of SCN multi-unit activity has also been observed in vivo in animals in whom surgical isolation of the SCN has been performed (Inouye and Kawamura, 1979). There is a circadian rhythm in metabolic activity in the SCN (as evidenced in studies utilizing the 2–deoxyglucose methodology), with higher activity during the light period of a light–dark cycle. This rhythm free–runs in constant darkness; it is the only brain area examined in which such a rhythm has been found (Schwartz and Gainer, 1977). Neuronal activity recorded from single SCN neurons in vitro (Shibata, et al., 1982) indicated that the time of peak activity changed in correspondence to the environmental light–dark cycle. Electrical stimulation of the SCN alters both the phase and periodicity of free–running circadian rhythms in experimental animals (Rusak and Groos, 1982). These findings are interpreted as strong evidence that the SCN is a major circadian pacemaker in the mammalian brain. The nature of the efferent and afferent projections subserving such SCN input or of the neurotransmitters involved is still unclear. The SCN appears to exhibit a functional organization with regard to the areas therein receiving specific neurotransmitter inputs, as well as with regard to neuropeptide distribution throughout this nucleus. Retinal projections are observed mainly to the ventral and lateral component of the caudal portion of the nucleus. The vasoactive intestinal peptide (VIP), vasopressin, and somatostatin are localized to distinct and consistent subfields within this nucleus. Serotonergic, cholinergic, avian pancreatic polypeptide– and Substance–P–containing afferent projections, with characteristic distributions, are present (Moore and Lenn, 1972; and Gamlin, Reiner and Karten, 1982). The major efferent relationships are with nearby hypothalmic areas. The SCN has no long ascending or descending projections, so that major processing of SCN output appears to take place at the hypothalmic level (Stephan, Berkley and Moss, 1981).

Experimental evidence indicates that, in the animal and human species, cholinergic and serotonergic mechanisms play a major role in regulation of circadian rhythmicity of plasma ACTH and corticosteroid concentrations (Krieger, et al., 1968; Krieger and Rizzo, 1969; Scapagnini, et al., 1971; Chihara, et al., 1976; and Ferrari, et al., 1977).

Evidence to date indicates that the rhythmicity of the H–P–A axis is an endogenous one. Implicit in the definition of an endogenous circadian rhythm is that, under constant conditions (viz., in the absence of temporal and environmental cues), such a rhythm will free-run, i.e., maintain its own innate periodicity, the synchronization to the 24-hour periodicity of the environment serving as an entraining stimulus or Zeitgeber. There has not, however, been a rigorous demonstration of a free-running rhythm in animal and human subjects. Such a free-running rhythm has been observed in adult blinded animals (Wilson, Rice and Critchlow, 1976) and in blind human subjects (Orth, King and Nicholson, 1975). Additional studies in which human subjects were maintained for prolonged periods in constant light (Krieger, Kreutzer and Rizzo, 1969), constant dark (Orth, Island and Liddle, 1969; and Aschoff, et al., 1971), with an altered day-length schedule (Orth, Island and Liddle, 1967), in light-dark reversal without sleep-wake reversal, or subjected to prolongation of the dark interval beyond the period of morning awakening (Orth, Island and Liddle, 1969), would indicate the presence of an endogenous 24-hour periodicity of corticosteroid concentrations more related to sleep-wake changes, in which light acts either as a co-existing entraining agent or independently causes elevation of corticosteroid concentrations in a noncircadian manner. Further support for the endogenous nature of this rhythm is apparent in the length of time required for a phase-shift of this rhythm to occur in the presence of reversed light-dark and sleep-wake conditions (approximately one week). In most animal and human studies in which phase-shifting has been performed, not only has light-dark been inverted but also sleep-wake and the time of feeding, each of which may possibly serve as a Zeitgeber (Kreiger, 1974). Sleep-wake may not be an important Zeitgeber, as evidenced by persistence of normal circadian rhythms during sleep deprivation, as well as the presence of such normal rhythms in narcolepsy (Takahashi, et al., 1975; and Besset, et al., 1976). The phasing effect of light is believed to be transmitted to the SCN via the retinal hypothalamic pathway (RHP) (Moore and Lenn, 1972).

CIRCADIAN PERIODICITY OF PLASMA ACTH AND CORTICOSTEROID LEVELS IN NONPSYCHIATRIC DISEASE

Abnormal periodicity of such levels is seen in adrenal disease (autonomous hypersecretion of corticosteroids with resultant suppression of plasma ACTH concentrations), disease of organs involved in metabolizing corticosteroids, resulting in altered metabolic clearance, viz., as in patients with liver disease (Tucci, Albacete and Martin, 1966), patients with chronic congestive failure (Knapp, Keane and Wright, 1967), and instances of tumor that ectopically secrete ACTH. More pertinent to the considerations of this chapter are abnormalities seen in patients with organic CNS disease. It was initially reported that patients with acute or chronic diffuse CNS disease, who showed disturbance of consciousness, demonstrated absence or alteration of periodicity of plasma corticosterid concentrations. It has subsequently been shown that over 53 percent of patients with disease localized radiographically and clinically to the hypothalamic or limbic system have altered circadian periodicity of both plasma ACTH and corticosteroid concentrations (Krieger and Krieger, 1966; and Apfelbaum, et al., 1974), in contrast to the incidence of five percent abnormality in patients with localized CNS disease not involving these areas. The lack of a higher percentage of abnormalities in patients with hypothalamic or limbic system disease may be related to the fact that diagnosis was made on a clinical basis only, so that exact anatomical localization was not possible.

Patients with Cushing's disease (pituitary ACTH hypersecretion), a disease of thusfar undetermined etiology, exhibit excessive corticosteroid and ACTH secretion, resistance to feedback suppressibility, and abnormal circadian periodicity of plasma ACTH and corticosteroid concentrations. It has been suggested that such ACTH hypersecretion may, in some cases, be secondary to local pituitary pathology, and in others, to excessive pituitary stimulation arising from disordered CNS regulatory mechanisms. The latter is suggested by the additional observation of other neuroendocrine abnormalities in these patients, such as absent circadian periodicity of growth hormone and prolactin (PRL) secretion and abnormal sleep EEG patterns which are characterized by a decrease in the percentage of slow−wave sleep (SWS) (Krieger and Glick, 1972, 1974). Additional evidence for the presence of a possible CNS defect in Cushing's disease is the occurrence of remission in the clinical and laboratory manifestations of this disease in approximately 50 percent of patients treated with cyproheptadine, a serotonergic blocking agent (Krieger, Amorosa and Linick, 1975; and Krieger and Condon, 1978). As noted previously, serotonin has been implicated, with regard to the circadian regulation of ACTH release, as well as having a stimulatory role on basal release (Fuller, 1981), although other reports may suggest an inhibitory role. It should be emphasized that other neurotransmitters, such as acetylcholine, gamma–amino–butyric acid (GABA), angiotensin, and histamine have also been suggested as possible regulators in the control of CRF and secondarily of ACTH release (Krieger, 1979). All of these substances, in addition to catecholamines and vasopressin, which have been shown to potentiate CRF–induced ACTH release (Giguere and Labrie, 1982; and Labrie, et al., 1984) are possible candidates for consideration should an abnormality in regulation of the H–P–A axis be demonstrated in patients with depression.

CIRCADIAN ASPECTS OF THE H–P–A AXIS IN DEPRESSION

The use of frequent sampling techniques, as described above in the description of normal circadian periodicity, has produced evidence that a significant number of depressed patients manifest an increased number of cortisol secretory episodes occurring over the 24–hour period. A greater total percentage of the 24–hour period is spent in active secretion, including the nighttime period, in contrast to the lack of such activity during this time in normal subjects. Depressed patients, however, still display a circadian variation in plasma corticosteroid levels, although the magnitude of such variation is blunted, as the evening cortisol concentrations do not decline to the same extent as seen in normals (Sachar, 1975). There have been some reports that depressed patients manifest a phase advance of several hours in the pattern of plasma corticosteroid concentrations (Doig, et al., 1966; and Lohrenz, et al., 1969). Phase advances have also been reported in such patients with regard to the periodicity of motor activity (Foster and Kupfer, 1975) and the sleep–wake cycle (Hawkins and Mendels, 1966). The presence of such phase abnormalities in depressed subjects has led to the suggestion that drugs which may produce a phase delay in neurotransmitter activity may be therapeutically effective in depressed patients. For example, it has been observed that chronic treatment with the tricyclic antidepressant drug, imipramine, delays the peaks in the circadian rhythms of α– and β–adrenergic receptor number in rat brain (Wirz–Justice, et al., 1980).

If there is a phase shift in the time of the circadian activation of the H-P-A axis, it is possible that the overnight dexamethasone suppression test as commonly performed (i.e., dexamethasone administration at 2300) might result in dexamethasone administration at an inappropriate time of the circadian response curve, resulting in an apparent, rather than a real, resistance to feedback suppression, which has been widely reported as an endocrine hallmark of depression. This hypothesis was tested (Pepper, et al., 1983) by administering dexamethasone at either 2300 or 1900 to patients with a major depressive illness. However, no difference in suppressibility or the type of response seen, i.e., nonsuppression, normal suppression, or an early escape response, was evident between these two groups. With the sampling regimen employed, no phase shift of basal circadian periodicity was evident in the patients, raising the possiblity that those with phase-advance of the H-P-A axis could comprise a subgroup of depressive patients.

The similarity of some of the abnormalities of the H-P-A axis in depression compared to those present in patients with Cushing's disease has led to attempts to understand the pathophysiology of the former in the framework of what is postulated with regard to the latter, most specifically with the hypothesis that such abnormalities are secondary to alterations in neurotransmitter function. There is a large literature consistent with altered serotonergic, cholinergic and catecholaminergic function in depression, any of which would be compatible with the evidence of altered function of the H-P-A axis in depression. These findings would suggest that both the psychiatric symptomatology and the neuroendocrine abnormalities stem from a similar neurobiological etiology. The heterogeneity of neuroendocrine abnormalities in depressed patients may indicate the presence of biochemical subgroups within this diagnostic category, so that further studies based on more clearly defining such subgroups may be of aid in establishing possible etiological factors.

REFERENCES

Allen, C. and J.W. Kendall. 1967. Maturation of the circadian rhythm of plasma corticosterone in the rat. Endocrinology 80:926–930.

Apfelbaum, M., J.S. Bishop, D. Cressy, G. Davies, R. Does, F.C. Goetz, F. Halberg, E. Haus, K. Kramm, J. MacDonald, W. Nelson, A. Reinberg, L. Schevin and J. Simpson. 1974. Human or murine endocrine and metabolic rhythms after changes in meal timing with or without a fixed activity schedule. In The Endocrine Society — 56th Annual Meeting, Program and Abstracts. Bethesda, Maryland: The Endocrine Society, p. A–209 (Abstract No. 308).

Armstrong, W.E. and G.I. Hatton. 1976. Morphological changes in hypothalamic neurosecretory neurons during the diurnal cycle. Neurosci Abst 2:643 (Abstract No. 922).

Aschoff, J., M. Fatranska, H. Disdke, P. Doerr, D. Stamm and H. Wisser. 1971. Human circadian rhythms in continuous darkness: entrainment by social cues. Science 171:213–215.

Besset, A., A. Arguner, B. Descomps, M. Billiard, A. Bonnardet, N. Bressot, G. Desch, A. Crastes de Paulet and P. Passouant. 1976. Sécrétion de GH et de cortisol en rapport avec les états de vigilance au cours du nycthémère chez dix narcoleptiques. Rev Electroencephalogr Neurophysiol Clin 6:17–22.

Cheifetz, P., N. Gaffud and J.F. Dingan. 1968. Effects of bilateral adrenalectomy and continuous light on the circadian rhythm of corticotropin in female rats. Endocrinology 82:1117–1124.

Chihara, K., Y. Kato, K. Maeda, S. Matsukura and H. Imura. 1967. Suppression by cyproheptadine of human growth hormone and cortisol secretion during sleep. J Clin Invest 57:1393–1402.

Dallman, M.F., W.C. Engeland and J. Shinsako. 1976. Circadian changes in adrenocortical responses to ACTH. In The Endocrine Society — 58th Annual Meeting, Program and Abstracts. Bethesda, Maryland: The Endocrine Society, p. A–58 (Abstract No. 4).

David–Nelson, G.A. and A. Brodish. 1969. Evidence of diurnal rhythm of corticotropin releasing factor in the hypothalamus. Endocrinology 85:861–866.

Doig, R.J., R.V. Mummery, M.R. Wills and A. Eikes. 1966. Plasma cortisol levels in depression. Br J Psychiatr 112: 1263–1267.

Dunn, J., L. Scheving and P. Millet. 1972. Circadian variation in stress–evoked increases in plasma corticosterone. Am J Physiol 223:402–406.

Eskin, A. 1981. Properties of the aplysia visual system. Z Vgl Physiol 74:353–371.

Ferrari, E., P.A. Bossolo, A. Vailata, I. Martinelli, A. Rea and I. Nosari. 1977. Variations circadiennes des effets d'une substance vagolytique sur le systeme ACTH–sécrétant chez l'homme. Ann Endocrinol (Paris) 38:203–213.

Foster, F.G. and D.J. Kupfer. 1975. Psychomotor activity as a correlate of depression and sleep in acutely disturbed psychiatric inpatients. Am J Psychiatr 132:928–931.

Franks, R. 1967. Diurnal variation of plasma 17–OHCS in children. J Clin Endocrinol Metab 27:75–78.

Fuller, R.W. 1981. Serotonergic stimulation of pituitary adrenocortical function in rats. Neuroendocrinology 32:118–127.

Gallagher, T.F., K. Yoshida, H.D. Roffwarg, D.K. Fukushima, E.D. Weitzman and L. Hellman. 1973. ACTH and cortisol secretory patterns in man. J Clin Endocrinol Metab 36:1058–1073.

Gamlin, P.D.R., A. Reiner and H.J. Karten. 1982. Substance–P–containing neurons of the avian suprachiasmatic nucleus project directly to the nucleus of Edinger–Westphal. Proc Natl Acad Sci USA 79:3891–3895.

Giguere, V. and F. Labrie. 1982. Vasopressin potentiates cyclic AMP accumulation and ACTH release induced by corticotropin releasing factor (CRF) in rat anterior pituitary cells in culture. Endocrinology 111:1752–1754, 1982.

Graber, A.L., J. Givens, W. Nicholson, D.P. Island and G.W. Liddle. 1965. Persistence of diurnal rhythmicity in plasma ACTH concentrations in cortisol deficient patients. J Clin Endocrinol Metab 85:804–807.

Groos, G. and J. Hendriks. 1982. Circadian rhythms in electrical discharge of rat suprachiasmatic neurones recorded in vitro. Neurosci Lett 34:283–288.

Hanin, I., R. Massarelli and E. Costa. 1970. Acetylcholine concentrations in rat brain: diurnal oscillation. Science 170: 341–342.

Hawkins, D.R. and J. Mendels. 1966. Sleep disturbance in depressive syndromes. Am J Psychiatr 123:683–690.

Hiroshige, T. and M. Sakakura. 1971. Circadian rhythm of corticotropin releasing activity in the hypothalamus of normal and adrenalectomized rats. Neuroendocrinology 7:25–36.

Hiroshige, T. and T. Sato. 1970. Postnatal development of circadian rhythm of corticotropin releasing activity in the rat hypothalamus. Endocrinol Jpn 17:1–6.

Hiroshige, T., M. Sakakura and S. Itoh. 1969. Diurnal variation of corticotropin releasing activity in the rat hypothalamus. Endocrinol Jpn 16:465–467.

Inouye, S.T. and H. Kawamura. 1979. Persistence of circadian rhythmicity in a mammalian hypothalamic "island" containing the suprachiasmatic nucleus. Proc Natl Acad Sci USA 76:5962–5966.

Ixart, G., A. Szafarczyk, J. Belougou and I. Assenmacher. 1977. Temporal relationships between the diurnal rhythm of hypothalamic corticotropin releasing factor, pituitary corticotropin and plasma corticosterone in the rat. J Endocrinol 72:113–120.

Johnson, J.T. and S. Levine. 1973. Influence of water deprivation on adrenocortical rhythms. Neuroendocrinology 11:268–273.

Knapp, M.S., P.M. Keane and J.G. Wright. 1967. Circadian rhythm of plasma 17-hydroxycorticosteroids in depressive illness, congestive heart failure, and Cushing's syndrome. Br Med J 2:27-30.

Koizuma, K. and H. Nishino. 1976. Circadian and other rhythmic activity of neurones in the ventromedial nuclei and lateral hypothalamic area. J Physiol 263:331-356.

Krieger, D.T. 1974. Food and water restriction shifts corticosterone, temperature, activity and brain amine periodicity. Endocrinology 95:1195-1201.

Krieger, D.T. 1979. Physiopathology of ACTH secretion. In Clinical Neuroendocrinology—Pathophysiologic Approach, Tolis, G., S. Labrie, J.B. Martin and S. Naftolin (eds.). New York: Raven Press, pp. 261-267.

Krieger, D.T. 1983. Neurotransmitter regulation of ACTH release. Mt Sinai J Med NY 40:302-314.

Krieger, D.T. and H.P. Krieger. 1966. Circadian variation of the plasma 17-OHCS in central nervous system disease. J Clin Endocrinol Metab 26:929-940.

Krieger, D.T., A.I. Silverberg, F. Rizzo and H.P. Krieger. 1968. Abolition of circadian periodicity of plasma 17-OHCS levels in the cat. Am J Physiol 215:959-967.

Krieger, D.T., J. Kreutzer and F. Rizzo. 1969. Constant light: effect on circadian pattern and phase reversal of steroid and electrolyte levels in man. J Clin Endocrinol Metab 29:1634-1638.

Krieger, D.T. and F. Rizzo. 1969. Serotonin mediation of circadian periodicity of plasma 17 hydroxycorticosteroids. Am J Physiol 217:1703-1707.

Krieger, D.T., W. Allen, F. Rizzo and H.P. Krieger. 1971. Characterization of the normal pattern of plasma corticosteroid levels. J Clin Endocrinol Metab 32:266-284.

Krieger, D.T. and S.M. Glick. 1972. Growth hormone and cortisol responsiveness in Cushing's syndrome: relation to a possible central nervous system etiology. Am J Med 52:25-39.

Krieger, D.T. and G.P. Gewirtz. 1974. Recovery of hypothalamic pituitary adrenal function, growth hormone responsiveness and sleep EEG pattern in a patient following removal of an adrenal cortical adenoma. J Clin Endocrinol Metab 38:1075-1082.

Krieger, D.T. and S.M. Glick. 1974. Sleep EEG stages and plasma growth hormone concentration in states of endogenous and exogenous hypercortisolemia on ACTH elevation. J Clin Endocrinol Metab 39:986-1000.

Krieger, D.T., L. Amorosa and F. Linick. 1975. Cyproheptadine induced remission of Cushing's disease. N Engl J Med 293:893-896.

Krieger, D.T. and E.M. Condon. 1978. Cyproheptadine treatment of Nelson's syndrome: restoration of plasma ACTH circadian periodicity and reversal of response to TRF. J Clin Endocrinol Metab 46:349-352.

Labrie, F., L. Proulx, V. Giguere and H. Meunier. 1984. Interactions of catecholamines with CRF and vasopressin in the control of ACTH secretion in the rat. In Stress, The Role of Catecholamines and Other Neurotransmitters: Proceedings of the Third International Symposium on Catecholamines and Other Neurotransmitters in Stress (Smolenice, Czechoslovakia; June 1983), Usdin, E., R. Kvetnansky and J. Axelrod (eds.). New York: Gordon & Breach Science Publishers, pp. 211-224.

Lohrenz, F.N., D.T. Fullerton, F.J. Wenzel, J.J. Chosy, K.B. Dickson and L. Reineke. 1969. Circadian rhythm of adrenal cortical activity in depression. Behav Neuropsychiatr 1:10-13.

Mains, R.E., B.A. Eipper and N. Ling. 1977. Common precursor to corticotropins and endorphins. Proc Natl Acad Sci USA 74:3014-3019.

Martin, M.M. and D.E. Hellman. 1964. Temporal variation in SU-4885 responsiveness in man: evidence in support of circadian variation in ACTH secretion. J Clin Endocrinol Metab 24:253-260.

Meier, A.H. 1976. Daily variation in concentration of plasma corticosteroid in hypophysectomized rats. Endocrinology 98:1475–1479.

Moore, R.Y. and V.B. Eichler. 1972. Loss of a circadian adrenal corticosterone rhythm following suprachiasmatic lesions in the rat. Brain Res 42:201–206.

Moore, R.Y. and N.J. Lenn. 1972. Retinohypothalamic projections in the rat. J Comp Neurol 146:1–4.

Nichols, T., C.A. Nugent and F.H. Tyler. 1963. Diurnal variation in suppression of adrenal function by glucocorticoids. J Clin Endocrinol Metab 25:343–349.

Nugent, C.A., K. Eik–Nes, H.S. Kent, L.T. Samuels and F.J. Tyler. 1960. A possible explanation for Cushing's syndrome associated with adrenal hyperplasia. J Clin Endocrinol Metab 20:1259–1268.

O'Hare, M.J. and P.J. Hornsby. 1975. Absence of a circadian rhythm of corticosterone secretion in monolayer cultures of adult rat adrenocortical cells. Experentia 31:378–380.

Orth, D.N., D.P. Island and G.W. Liddle. 1967. Experimental alteration of the circadian rhythm in plasma cortisol concentration in man. J Clin Endocrinol Metab 27:549–555.

Orth, D.N., D.P. Island and G.W. Liddle. 1969. Light synchronization of the circadian rhythm in plasma cortisol concentration in man. J Clin Endocrinol Metab 29:479–486.

Orth, D.N., P.H. King and W.E. Nicholson. 1975. Free–running circadian plasma cortisol rhythm in a blind human subject. In The Endocrine Society — 57th Annual Meeting, Program and Abstracts. Bethesda, Maryland: The Endocrine Society, p. A–303 (Abstract No. 54).

Pepper, G.M., K.L. Davis, B.M. Davis and D.T. Krieger. 1983. Dexamethasone suppression test in depression is unaffected by altering the clock time of its administration. Psychiatr Res 8:105–109.

Perkoff, G.T., K. Eik-Nes, C.A. Nugent, H.L. Fred, R.A. Nimer, L. Rush, L.T. Samuels and F.H. Tyler. 1959. Studies of the diurnal variation of plasma 17-hydroxycorticosteroids. J Clin Endocrinol Metab 16:432-443.

Petraglia, F., F. Facchinetti, D. Parrini, G. Micieli, S. De Luca and A. Ganazzani. 1983. Simultaneous circadian variations of plasma ACT, beta-lipotropin, beta-endorphin and cortisol. Horm Res 17:147-152.

Reis, D.J., A. Corvelli and J. Conners. 1969. Circadian and ultra-dian rhythms of serotonin regionally in cat brain. J Pharmacol Exp Ther 167:328-333.

Reis, D.J., M. Weinbren and A. Corvelli. 1968. A circadian rhythm of norepinephrine regionally in cat brain: its relationship to environmental lighting and to regional diurnal variations in brain serotonin. J Pharmacol Exp Ther 164:135-145.

Roberts, J. and E. Herbert. 1977. Characterization of a common precursor to corticotropin and ß-lipotropin: cell-free synthesis of the precursor and identification of corticotropin peptides in the molecule. Proc Natl Acad Sci USA 74:4826-4830.

Rusak, B. and G. Groos. 1982. Suprachiasmatic stimulation phase shifts rodent circadian rhythms. Science 215:1407-1409.

Sachar, E.J. 1975. Neuroendocrine abnormalities in depressive illness. In Topics in Psychoendocrinology, Sachar, E.J. (ed.). New York: Grune & Stratton, pp. 135-156.

Sato, T. and J.C. George. 1973. Diurnal rhythm of corticotropin releasing factor activity in the pigeon hypothalamus. Can J Physiol Pharmacol 51:743-747.

Scapagnini, U., G.P. Moberg, G.R. van Loon, J. DeGroot and W.F. Ganong. 1971. Relation of brain 5-hydroxytryptamine content to the diurnal variation in plasma corticosterone in the rat. Neuroendocrinology 7:90-96.

Schwartz, W.J. and H. Gainer. 1977. Suprachiasmatic nucleus: Use of ^{14}C–labeled deoxyglucose uptake as a functional marker. Science 197:1089–1091.

Shibata, S., Y. Oomura, H. Kita and K. Hattori. 1982. Circadian rhythmic changes of neuronal activity in the suprachiasmatic nucleus of the rat hypothalamic slice. Brain Res 247:154–158.

Shiotsuka, R., J. Jovonovich and J.A. Jovonovich. 1974. Circadian and ultradian corticosterone rhythms in adrenal organ cultures. In Chronological Aspects of Endocrinology, Schattauer, F.K. (ed.). New York: Springer–Verlag, pp. 255–267.

Silverberg, A.I., F. Rizzo and D.T. Krieger. 1968. Nyctohemeral periodicity of plasma 17–OHCS levels in elderly subjects. J Clin Endocrinol Metab 28:1661–1663.

Stephan, F.K., K.J. Berkley and R.L. Moss. 1981. Efferent connections of the rat suprachiasmatic nucleus. Neuroscience 6:2625–2641.

Stephan, F.K. and A.A. Nunez. 1977. Elimination of circadian rhythms in drinking activity, sleep and temperature by isolation of the suprachiasmatic nuclei. Behav Biol 20:1–16.

Stephan, R.K. and I. Zucker. 1972. Circadian rhythms in drinking behavior and locomotor activity of rats are eliminated by hypothalamic lesions. Proc Natl Acad Sci USA 69:1583–1586.

Swanson, L.W., P.E. Savchenko, J. Rivier and W.W. Vale. 1983. Organization of ovine corticotropin–releasing factor immunoreactive cells and fibers in the rat brain: an immunohistochemical study. Neuroendocrinology 36:165–186.

Takahashi, Y., K. Takahashi, T. Higuchi, Y. Niimi, A. Miyasita and Y. Ishii. 1975. Pituitary hormone secretions and narcolepsy. In Narcolepsy: Proceedings of the First International Symposium on Narcolepsy (Montpelier, France; July 1975) [Advances in Sleep Research, Volume 3], Guilleminault, C., W.C. Dement and P. Passouant (eds.). New York: Spectrum Publications, pp. 544–563.

Takebe, K., C. Setaishi and M. Hirama. 1966. Effects of a bacterial pyrogen on the pituitary–adrenal axis at various times in the 24 hours. J Clin Endocrinol Metab 26:437–442.

Takebe, T., M. Sakakura and K. Mashimo. 1972. Continuance of diurnal rhythmicity of CRF activity in hypophysectomized rats. Endocrinology 90:1515–1520.

Tucci, J.R., R.A. Albacete and M.M. Martin. 1966. Effect of liver disease upon steroid circadian rhythms in man. Gastroenterology 50:637–644.

Ungar, F. and F. Halberg. 1962. Circadian rhythm in the in vitro response of mouse adrenal to adrenocorticotropic hormone. Science 137:1058–1059.

Vale, W., J. Spiess, C. Rivier and J. Rivier. 1981. Characterization of a 41–residue ovine hypothalamic peptide that stimulates secretion of corticotropin and ß–endorphin. Science 213:1394–1397.

Wilson, M.M., R.W. Rice and V. Critchlow. 1976. Evidence for a free–running circadian rhythm in pituitary–adrenal function in blinded adult female rats. Neuroendocrinology 20:289–295, 1976.

Wirz–Justice, A., M.S. Kafka, D. Naber and T.A. Wehr. 1980. Circadian rhythms in rat brain alpha– and beta–adrenergic receptors are modified by chronic imipramine. Life Sci 27:341–347.

8

INTENSITY, WAVELENGTH AND TIMING: THREE CRITICAL PARAMETERS FOR CHRONOBIOLOGICALLY ACTIVE LIGHT

Alfred J. Lewy
Robert L. Sack

INTRODUCTION

Biological rhythms have long been thought to be related to certain psychiatric disorders (Wehr and Goodwin, 1981b). However, for years, this area was considered to be too complex because of the jargon, mathematical theories and the amount of detail involved in such studies, and because this research area involved methodologies of considerable difficulty, such as long–term recordings and temporal isolation facilities. Research in this area was also considered to be of questionable significance because many circadian rhythms passively follow the sleep–wake cycle and are therefore not considered to be "endogenous".

The use of melatonin (MT) production as a marker for circadian rhythms has helped researchers to overcome some of these difficulties. The production of MT is increased at night and is decreased during the day in both diurnal and nocturnal species. It has a clear–cut circadian rhythm that does not passively follow the sleep–wake cycle (Lewy, 1983a); thus, measuring its timing provides an accurate indication of circadian phase position. Measurement of MT is also important because bright light can suppress nighttime MT production in humans; therefore, bright light can be used as a specific tool for manipulating human biological rhythms (Lewy, et al., 1980b). Human studies are particularly useful, because the sleep–wake cycle can be dissociated from the light–dark (LD) cycle (Lewy, Sack and Singer, 1984a).

VALIDATION OF MT AS A BIOLOGICAL MARKER

Because of the way in which MT production is regulated, measurement of this hormone is a very useful "biological marker" for pineal adrenergic activity, its endogenous circadian pacemaker, and the effects of light. A circadian rhythm of sympathetic stimulation of the pineal is generated in the suprachiasmatic nuclei (SCN) of the hypothalamus. A multisynaptic neural pathway then links the SCN to the intermediolateral nuclei of the spinal cord, which is the origin of preganglionic sympathetic neurons (Klein, et al., 1983; and Pickard and Turek, 1983). These preganglionic neurons synapse in the superior cervical ganglia; the postganglionic neurons re-enter the cranium as the nervi conarii and innervate the pineal (Ariens Kappers, 1960). These neurons release the neurotransmitter, norepinephrine, that stimulates β_1–adrenergic receptors on the pinealocytes (Romero, Zatz and Axelrod, 1975b). The retino–hypothalamic tract (RHT), which extends from the retina to the hypothalamus, conveys photic input to the SCN (Moore and Lenn, 1972).

With the development of accurate assays for plasma MT in humans (Arendt, 1981; Rollag, 1981; Brown, et al., 1983; and Lynch, 1983), this hormone has become a useful biological marker. In 1978, we published our gas chromatographic–negative chemical ionization mass spectrometric (neg CI GC–MS) assay for plasma MT (Lewy and Markey, 1978). In the 1970s, most of the radioimmunoassays (RIAs) did not appear to be very specific, in that the reported levels were significantly higher than those of the neg CI GC–MS assay, a finding that suggested these RIAs were measuring substances in addition to MT.

Using our GC–MS assay for plasma MT, we demonstrated that the pineal gland is the exclusive source for circulating MT in the rat and the human (Lewy, et al., 1980a; and Neuwelt and Lewy, 1983). Using a similar GC–MS assay for 6–hydroxymelatonin (Tetsuo, Markey and Kopin, 1980), Markey has shown that pinealectomy in rats (Markey and Buell, 1982) and monkeys

(Tetsuo, et al., 1982) abolishes levels of the major urinary metabolite of MT. When RIAs were used in similar pinealectomy studies, substantial levels of immunoreactive MT were reported (Ozaki, Lynch and Wurtman, 1976; and Yu, et al., 1981). However, data from recent studies that use more specific RIAs (Brown, et al., 1983) has yielded results that are similar to ours. Exclusive pineal derivation of MT validates the use of MT as a marker for pineal function.

BIOLOGICAL EFFECTS OF LIGHT

Light appears to have at least two or three well-defined effects on biological rhythms: (1) light exposure during the night appears to acutely suppress the production of MT (this effect appears to be unique for MT) (Wurtman, Axelrod and Phillips, 1963); (2) the 24-hour LD cycle appears to entrain (synchronize) the SCN, which regulates MT, and perhaps other, circadian rhythms (Binkley, Muller and Hernandez, 1981); and (3) through a combination of the first two effects of light, the duration of nighttime MT production is greater during the long nights of winter than during the short nights of summer (Illnerova and Vanecek, 1980; and Goldman, et al., 1981). The length of the phototperiod (light period) and the scotoperiod (dark period), whether or not mediated by MT, are important cues for the timing of seasonal rhythms, such as reproduction (seasonal estrus) (Lincoln, 1983).

In constant darkness, circadian rhythms free-run. Some totally blind people have 25-hour rhythms in MT production (Lewy and Newsome, 1983c). One can also demonstrate 25-hour rhythms in sighted people under conditions of temporal isolation; their periods average 25 hours ± 0.5 hours, which is thought to represent the period of the endogenous circadian pacemaker (located in the SCN) no longer entrained to 24-hour time cues (Wever, 1979a).

INTENSITY: THE FIRST CRITICAL PARAMETER FOR CHRONOBIOLOGICALLY ACTIVE LIGHT IN HUMANS

Although the effects of light have been well-documented in a variety of animal species, chronobiologists (Wever, 1979a) and

pineal physiologists (Klein, 1979) had been in general agreement
that light did not have this effect in humans. However, in 1980, we
showed that human nighttime MT production could be suppressed
by exposure to light, providing sufficiently intense light was used
(Figure 1; Lewy, et al., 1980b). Exposure to 500 lux (which is about
the level of normal indoor lighting) had little effect, whereas 1,500
lux partially suppressed, and 2,500 lux totally suppressed, MT
production. (Outdoor ambient light is 10,000 lux to 100,000 lux,
depending on the cloud cover.)

These findings had at least three implications: (1) humans
could have biological rhythms (both circadian and seasonal) that
are cued to the natural LD cycle unperturbed by the use of
ordinary room light; (2) previous studies of biological rhythms in
humans should be repeated using appropriately intense light; and
(3) human biological rhythms could be experimentally (and perhaps
therapeutically) manipulated using bright artificial light.

Our first test of the therapeutic implications was in a
63–year–old man who had a 13–year history of depression that
recurred annually when the days grew shorter and remitted when
day length increased (Lewy, et al., 1982). During Winter 1980, we
exposed him to 2,000 lux Vita–Lite between 0600 and 0900 and
between 1600 and 1900. Within four days, he began to switch out
of his depression, two months before the expected time. In Winter
1981, in a study directed by Dr. Norman Rosenthal, we used the
bright light–dim light paradigm (Lewy, 1981) to include a placebo
control group (Rosenthal, et al., 1984). Nine winter depressive
patients responded to lengthening their winter days with bright
light exposure; there was no statistically significant effect when
dim light exposure at the same times was used as a control.

WAVELENGTH: THE SECOND CRITICAL PARAMETER FOR CHRONOBIOLOGICALLY ACTIVE LIGHT IN HUMANS

Next, we examined the action spectrum for suppression of
human nighttime MT production (Brainard, et al., 1985). The peak

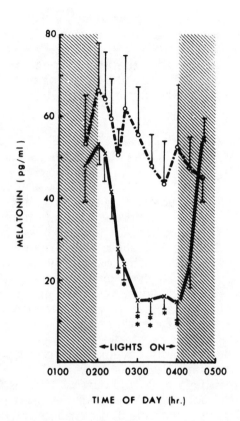

Figure 1   The first critical parameter for light to be
chronobiologically active in humans: intensity.   Six
normal volunteers were awakened between 0200 and
0400. On one night, they were exposed to light of 500
lux (o). On another night, they were exposed to light of
2,500 lux (x). Only the very bright light caused a
consistently robust reduction in plasma MT levels (*,
$p < 0.05$;   **, $p < 0.01$).   Bright   light   is   therefore
considered to be essential for light to have chronobiological activity in humans. (From Lewy, et al., 1980b,
copyright 1980 by the American Association for the
Advancement of Science.)

wavelength appeared to be approximately 509 nM, which is the same peak wavelength for activation of retinal rhodopsin (Figure 2). This is consistent with a rod–mediated response (Wald and Brown, 1958). We assume that the action spectrum for suppression of human MT production is also the action spectrum for the other biological rhythm effects of light in humans.

TIMING THE PHASE–RESPONSE CURVE (PRC): THE THIRD CRITICAL PARAMETER FOR CHRONOBIOLOGICALLY ACTIVE LIGHT IN HUMANS

Having satisfied ourselves with obtaining a rudimentary understanding of the formal properties of light necessary for suppression of MT production in humans, we next turned our attention to how light could shift the circadian MT production rhythm, as well as other circadian rhythms. Animal studies (DeCoursey, 1960; and Pittendrigh and Daan, 1976) of phase–response curves (PRCs) provided us with some important clues, assuming (as we did) that humans would respond in similar ways, providing the light was sufficiently bright.

The PRC was originally developed to describe how free–running animals in constant darkness responded to brief, infrequent light pulses. The PRC is a plotted curve. The abscissa is circadian time, and indicates each time the light pulse is given. The ordinate is the direction (above the line for advance responses, below the line for delay responses) and magnitude of the phase shift. (An advance response is a phase shift to an earlier time; a delay response is a phase shift to a later time.) Because the animals are in constant dark, we denote subjective night for the rest phase and subjective day for the activity phase of diurnal animals (the opposite for nocturnal animals).

Certain features of PRCs seem to be generally true for both diurnal (Hoban and Sulzman, 1985) and nocturnal (DeCoursey 1960; and Pittendrigh and Daan, 1976) species. When the pulse of light occurs during subjective day, there is a minimal shift in the animal's rhythms (Figure 3); when the pulse of light occurs during the first half of subjective night, the animal delays its circadian phase. When the pulse of light occurs during the second half of the

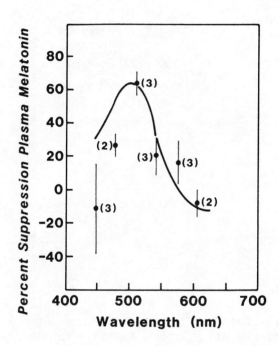

Figure 2   The second critical parameter for light to be chronobiologically active in humans: wavelength. Three male volunteer subjects were exposed to four to five different wavelengths of light. The peak wavelength for this effect appears to be at 509 nM (from Brainard, et al., 1985). This is near the peak for activation of retinal rhodopsin. (The super-imposed curve is from Wald and Brown, 1958.)

night, the animal advances its circadian phase. During the middle of the night, there is an inflection point, when delay responses are separated from advance responses by only a few minutes. The closer to the middle of the night, the greater the magnitude of the phase shift.

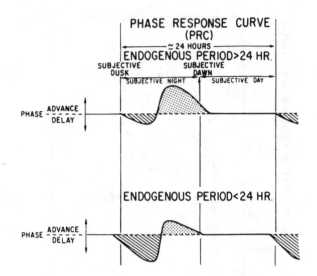

<u>Figure 3</u>   The third critical parameter for light to be chronobiologically active in humans: timing. Exposure during the first part of the night delays circadian rhythms (<u>i.e.</u>, shifts them later). Exposure during the last part of the night advances circadian rhythms (<u>i.e.</u>, shifts them earlier). The closer the light exposure occurs to the normal photoperiod, the less the effect.

Extrapolating from these animal studies, we hypothesized that humans would advance in response to bright light exposure in the morning, and would delay in response to bright light exposure in the evening, even though our human subjects would be essentially entrained to the day–night cycle (Lewy, <u>et al.</u>, 1983d). During Summer 1983, we tested this hypothesis in four normal volunteer subjects (Lewy, Sack and Singer, 1984a). After plasma MT was sampled on a baseline day, "dusk" was advanced from about 2100 to 1600 for one week. "Dawn" was held at the subjects' constant wake–up time of 0600. The next week, dawn, but not wake–up time, was delayed to 0900. As we predicted, advancing dusk caused a gradual advance in the MT production rhythm, and delaying dawn caused a gradual delay in the MT production circadian rhythm. These findings agreed with our hypothesized PRC for humans.

We also found, in agreement with another of our predictions, that the MT onset (but not the offset) shifted significantly earlier the first night of advanced dusk. This finding supported our idea that, during photoperiods of sufficiently long duration, bright light exposure in the evening suppresses the onset of nighttime MT production. Consequently, we now recommend that, to use MT production as a marker for circadian phase position, bright light should be avoided after 1700 or 1800. We call this circadian phase marker the dim light melatonin onset (DLMO). The nighttime secretory onset is probably the most accurate portion of the MT curve for marking circadian phase position, because it is presumably least affected by changes in beta adrenergic receptors, and perhaps because substrate availability could decrease during the night and reduce the amplitude of MT production during the course of the night (Romero and Axelrod, 1975a; Romero, Zatz and Axelrod, 1975a; and Zatz, et al., 1976).

Using the DLMO for marking circadian phase position, we were now ready to apply our hypothesized PRC to the assessment and treatment of biological rhythm disturbances. We initially thought of winter depression as a seasonal rhythm, and this may be the case, certainly with regard to the pattern of recurrence. But we also were aware that these patients had morning hypersomnia, and therefore seemed to be phase–delayed. (We thought that wake–up time would be a more reliable phase marker than sleep onset, because, according to our clock–gate model and our understanding of PRCs for animals with endogenous periods greater than 24 hours, light exposure at dawn seems to be more important than light exposure at dusk). If these patients were truly phase delayed, then they represented a very different type of circadian rhythm disturbance than had been previously hypothesized for depression. [Many patients with major (melancholic) depression have early morning awakening, and are consequently thought to have phase–advanced circadian rhythms (Papousek, 1975; Kripke, et al., 1978; and Wehr and Wirz–Justice, 1981a).]

If most of our winter depressive patients were indeed phase-delayed, and if being phase–delayed was related to their mood disturbance, then according to our hypothesized PRC, bright light exposure should have more antidepressant effects when administered in the morning than in the evening. (Bright light exposure in the morning would reduce a corrective phase advance.) During Winter 1984, we studied 14 patients with winter depression. Baseline determinations of circadian phase position were made during the first and last day of a week of controlled (scheduled) light–dark and sleep–wake conditions. Patients slept between 2200 and 0600 throughout the entire study. They were kept away from sunlight by staying indoors (and by wearing welder's goggles when necessary) between 1700 and 0800. For the second week, half of the group was exposed to bright light in the morning (0600 to 0800) and the other half of the group was exposed to bright light in the evening (2000 to 2200). In the third week, they were crossed over to the other light exposure schedule. For a fourth week, eight patients were exposed to bright light both morning and evening.

According to double–blind Hamilton ratings, as well as other behavioral measures, morning bright light exposure caused a highly statistically significant decrease in depressive symptoms when compared to both the baseline week ratings and the depression ratings after the week of evening light exposure. Morning plus evening bright light (week #4) seemed to be less effective than morning bright light alone. Bright light exposure shifted their circadian rhythms in the predicted directions as reflected in the DLMO, the core body temperature minimum and rapid eye movement (REM) latency: morning light advanced these rhythms and evening light delayed them. Thus, most of the patients with winter depression preferentially responded to morning light exposure. We now recommend that these patients schedule bright light exposure as soon as they get up in the morning.

With regard to delayed sleep phase syndrome, we have reported that this group of patients also responds to morning bright light exposure (Lewy, et al., 1983d; and Lewy, Sack and Singer, 1984a), which provides a corrective phase–advance. They are able to advance their sleep time 30 to 60 minutes per day, providing they are exposed to about one hour of bright light immediately upon awakening. We have treated fewer patients with phase-advanced circadian rhythms; however, this group appears to respond to bright light exposure for one to two hours in the evening (between 2000 and 2200; Lewy, et al., 1985b). Endogenous major (melancholic) depressives with early morning awakening also appear to benefit from evening bright light exposure (avoiding bright light in the morning), which delays circadian phase position and restores the sleep phase to normal (Lewy, Sack and Singer, 1984a, 1985a). Assessment of the remaining symptoms of depression in the endogenous depressives awaits the study of a larger group of patients.

Kripke and co-workers (1978) and Wehr and Goodwin (1981b), among others, have proposed that depressed patients (including rapid cycling manic-depressives in both mood states) have "fast" or phase-advanced circadian rhythms. Based on the work of Wever (1979a), Kronauer and colleagues (1982), and Moore-Ede, Sulzman and Fuller (1982), it has been assumed that one endogenous circadian pacemaker governs the temperature rhythm (or the "strong" oscillator), and a separate endogenous circadian pacemaker governs the sleep-wake cycle (or the "weak" oscillator). It has been proposed that the strong oscillator is phase-advanced with respect to the weak oscillator. Wehr and partners (1979b) have shown that scheduling sleep earlier in a few such patients causes a brief remission in depressive symptoms. He relates this to previous work of Pflug and Tölle (1971) and others, who have shown that sleep deprivation, particularly in the second half of the night, causes a transient decrease in depressive symptoms. Wehr and Wirz-Justice (1981a) have proposed that there is a "critical interval" (the last half of the night) in order for sleep deprivation to be an effective antidepressant. According to their phase-advance hypothesis, this critical interval (which they associate with the strong oscillator) is presumed to be abnormally phase-advanced with respect to sleep. They have further proposed an internal coincidence model which suggests it is the advanced phase of the strong oscillator relative to the weak oscillator that accounts for depression in some individuals, and that advancing sleep presumably advances the weak oscillator, restoring a more normal phase angle between the two presumed oscillators.

Kripke (1984) has modified these ideas for the use of bright light exposure, substituting bright light for sleep deprivation. He

has kept the same critical interval (the second half of the night) as
the essential time for bright light exposure. Accordingly, he has
been treating patients with major depression (whom he presumes to
have a phase–advanced strong oscillator) with bright light exposure
in the morning. At first, Kripke's results showed a modest effect
(Kripke, 1982; and Kripke, Risch and Janowsky, 1983). More recent
studies do not appear to be showing an effect. Most recently, he
has switched to morning–plus–evening bright light, presumably
testing critical intervals of external coincidence for light at both
ends of the scotoperiod.

In contradistinction to Kripke's approach to the treatment of
major (melancholic) depression with bright light, of all of the
animal studies that might suggest human models, we have been
most impressed with studies of the PRC. The PRC animal studies,
and our own work with shifting the human MT circadian rhythm
with bright light exposure according to our hypothesized PRC, have
led us to propose that endogenous depressives with early morning
awakening (and who, therefore, are presumably phase–advanced)
should respond best to bright light exposure in the evening (Lewy,
et al., 1983d; Lewy, Sack and Singer, 1984a; and Lewy, 1984b). As
mentioned above, preliminary results are encouraging (Lewy, Sack
and Singer, 1984a, 1985a).

Our approach also differs from that of Rosenthal and
colleagues with respect to the treatment of winter depression with
bright light. Rosenthal and co–workers (1985) have recently stated
that, in the case of winter depressives, morning light does not
appear to be critical for the antidepressant response. Our results
suggest the opposite: morning light does appear to be critical for
the antidepressant response (Lewy, Sack and Singer, 1984a).
Rosenthal and partners did not test morning light alone, whereas
we specifically compared morning light exposure to evening light
exposure. Furthermore, although their patients were
experimentally exposed only to bright artificial light in the
evening, these patients were free to go outside and be exposed to
sunlight in the morning, thus obtaining bright light exposure at both
times.

We think that it is very important to control for light
exposure in such studies. When testing bright light exposure at a

specific time of the day, bright light shoul[...]
times when it might be effective. Accordi[...]
PRC, morning and evening (as well as th[...]
critical times when bright light can be act[...]
we expose patients to bright light in the m[...]
light after 1700. When they are exposed to bright light in tne
evening, they avoid bright light until after 0800.

PHASE–TYPING OF CHRONOBIOLOGIC SLEEP AND MOOD DISORDERS

We have also been concerned with the possibility that the phase–advance hypothesis of depression has perhaps diverted attention away from the fact that some nonseasonally depressed patients (in addition to winter depressives) may actually have phase–delayed circadian rhythms. Consequently, we have proposed (Lewy, Sack and Singer, 1984a, 1985a) that patients be "phase–typed" on an individual basis, into either the phase–advance type or the phase–delay type, if indeed a chronobiologic abnormality exists.

Phase–typing is particularly useful when scheduling bright light exposure to produce the optimal therapeutic effect. Bright light should be scheduled at the correct time (as indicated by our hypothesized PRC) to produce the desired phase shift and must be avoided at those times that would retard such a shift.

Phase–typing raises several interesting questions. Are some disorders categorically of one phase type or the other? Are some people difficult to phase–type because they are actually free–running? [Free–running individuals have been reported (Kokkoris, et al., 1978; and authors' unpublished data), but such rhythms are extremely rare in sighted people living in society.] Is it possible for a person to be phase–delayed during one episode and phase–advanced during another?

CONCLUSION

The first parameter to be identified for light to be chrono–biologically active in humans is that light has to be sufficiently ght (Figure 1), probably greater than about 2,000 lux, although some people may be more sensitive to light than others (Lewy, 1981; and Lewy, et al., 1985b), and some factors, such as time of the year or time of the day, might influence light sensitivity as well. The second critical parameter is wavelength; the peak for the action spectrum appears to be approximately 509 nM (Figure 2), which is well–represented in most available light sources. Our data on shifting circadian rhythms, as indicated by the DLMO, the core body temperature rhythm and REM latency, as well as our behavioral response data, suggests that the timing of light is a third critical parameter for it to be chronobiologcially active in humans (Figure 3). Thus, we have identified three critical parameters for light to be chronobiologically active in humans: intensity, wavelength and timing. Proper testing of light in experimental studies or therapeutic trials should take these factors into account.

Not every patient with a sleep or mood disorder has a chronobiologic abnormality. However, if one exists, according to our phase–typing hypothesis, it is likely to be either a phase–advance or a phase–delay disturbance. Even if light proves to be therapeutic in some chronobiologic sleep and mood disorders, this does not necessarily mean that the disorder was primarily caused by a chronobiologic abnormality. Light can be associated with a placebo effect, and bright light may have an "activating" effect on some people. Furthermore, a shift in the sleep–wake cycle, for whatever reason, could cause a shift in the other circadian rhythms, because the sleep–wake cycle, to some extent, super-imposes its structure on the experienced LD cycle (through opening and closing of the eyes), which could then shift the other circadian rhythms. Moreover, people do not necessarily become depressed when undergoing a phase–shift, as is the case with most air travelers. What causes these disturbances is not as yet known. However, phase typing individuals and correcting phase position with appropriately timed bright light may make easier the study of other predisposing biological and psychological factors.

REFERENCES

Arendt, J. 1981. Current status of assay methods of melatonin. In Melatonin: Current Status and Perspectives: Proceedings of the International Symposium on Melatonin (September 1980; Bremen, West Germany) [Advances in the Biosciences, Volume 29], Birau, N. and W. Schloot (eds.). Oxford: Pergamon Press, pp. 3-7.

Ariens Kappers, J. 1960. The development, topographical relations and innervation of the epiphysis cerebri in the albino rat. Z Zellforsch Mikrosk Anat 52:163-215.

Binkley, S., G. Muller and T. Hernandez. 1981. Circadian rhythm in pineal N-acetyltransferase activity: phase-shifting by light pulses (I). J Neurochem 37:798-800.

Brainard, G.C., A.J. Lewy, M. Menaker, R.H. Fredrickson, L.S. Miller, R.G. Weleber, V. Cassone and D. Hudson. 1985. Effect of light wavelength on the suppression of nocturnal plasma melatonin in normal volunteers. In The Medical and Biological Effects of Light [Based on the Conference of the Medical and Biological Effects of Light, New York City, October-November 1984 (Annals of the New York Academy of Sciences, Volume 453)], Wurtman, R.J., M.J. Baum and J.T. Potts, Jr. (eds.). New York City: New York Academy of Sciences Press, pp. 376-378.

Brown, G.M., L.J. Grota, O. Pulido, T.G. Burns, L.P. Niles and V. Snieckus. 1983. Application of immunologic techniques to the study of pineal indolealkylamines. In Pineal Research Reviews, Volume 1, Reiter, R.J. (ed.). New York: Alan R. Liss, Inc., pp. 207-246.

De Coursey, P.J. 1960. Daily light sensitivity rhythm in a rodent. Science 131:33-35.

Goldman, B., V. Hall, C. Hollister, S. Reppert, P. Roychoudhury, S. Yellon and L. Tamarkin. 1981. Diurnal changes in pineal melatonin content in four rodent species: relationship to photo-periodism. Biol Reprod 24:778-783.

Hoban, T.M. and F.M. Sulzman. 1985. Light effects on circadian timing system of a diurnal primate, the squirrel monkey. Am J Physiol 249:R274-R280.

Illnerova, H. and J. Vanecek. 1980. Pineal rhythm in N-acetyl-transferase activity in rats under different artificial photoperiods and in natural daylight in the course of a year. Neuroendocrinology 31:321-326.

Klein, D.C. 1979. Circadian rhythms in the pineal gland. In Endocrine Rhythms, Krieger, D.T. (ed.). New York: Raven Press, pp. 203-223.

Klein, D.C., R. Smoot, J.L. Weller, S. Higa, S.P. Markey, G.J. Creed and D.M. Jacobowitz. 1983. Lesions of the paraventricular nucleus areas of the hypothalamus disrupt the suprachiasmatic spinal cord circuit in the melatonin rhythm generating system. Brain Res Bull 10:647-652.

Kokkoris, C.P., E.D. Weitzman, C.P. Pollak, A.J. Spielman, C.A. Czeisler and H. Bradlow. 1978. Long-term ambulatory temperature monitoring in a subject with a hypernycterohemeral sleep-wake cycle disturbance. Sleep 1:177-190.

Kripke, D.F. 1982. Photoperiodic mechanisms for depression and its treatment. In Biological Psychiatry, 1981: Proceedings of the IInd World Congress of Biological Psychiatry, Perris, C., G. Struwe and B. Jansson (eds.). Amsterdam: Elsevier, pp. 1249-1252.

Kripke, D.F. 1984. Critical interval hypothesis for depression. Chronobiol Int 1:73-80.

Kripke, D.F., D.J. Mullaney, M. Atkinson and S. Wolf. 1978. Circadian rhythm disorders in manic-depressives. Biol Psychiatr 13:335-351.

Kripke, D.F., S.C. Risch and D. Janowsky. 1983. Bright white light alleviates depression. Psychiatr Res 10:105-112.

Kronauer, R.E., C.A. Czeisler, S.F. Pilato, M.C. Moore–Ede and E.D. Weitzman. 1982. Mathematical model of the human circadian system with two interacting oscillators. Am J Physiol 242:R3–R17.

Lewy, A.J. 1981. The effects of light in man: melatonin secretion, circadian sleep and affective disorders, and the bright light/dim light paradigm. Sleep Res 10:297.

Lewy, A.J. 1983a. Biochemistry and regulation of mammalian melatonin production. In The Pineal Gland, Current Endocrinology: Basic and Clinical Aspects, Relkin, R.M. (ed.). New York: Elsevier North–Holland Biomedical Press, pp. 77–128.

Lewy, A.J. 1983b. Effects of light on melatonin secretion and the circadian system of man. In Circadian Rhythms in Psychiatry, Wehr, T.A. and F.K. Goodwin (eds.). Pacific Grove: Boxwood Press, pp. 203–219.

Lewy, A.J. 1984b. Human melatonin secretion (II): A marker for the circadian system and the effects of light. In Neurobiology of Mood Disorders (Frontiers of Clinical Neuroscience, Volume 1), Post, R.M. and J.C. Ballenger (eds.). Baltimore: Williams & Wilkins, pp. 215–226.

Lewy A.J. and S.P. Markey. 1978. Analysis of melatonin in human plasma by gas chromatography negative chemical ionization mass spectrometry. Science 201:741–743.

Lewy, A.J., M. Tetsuo, S.P. Markey, F.K. Goodwin and I.J. Kopin. 1980a. Pinealectomy abolishes plasma melatonin in the rat. J Clin Endocrinol Metab 50:204–205.

Lewy, A.J., T.A. Wehr, F.K. Goodwin, D.A. Newsome and S.P. Markey. 1980b. Light suppresses melatonin secretion in humans. Science 210:1267–1269.

Lewy, A.J., H.E. Kern, N.E. Rosenthal and T.A. Wehr. 1982. Bright artificial light treatment of a manic–depressive patient with a seasonal mood cycle. Am J Psychiatr 139:1496–1498.

Lewy, A.J. and D.A. Newsome. 1983c. Different types of melatonin circadian secretory rhythms in some blind subjects. J Clin Endocrinol Metab 56:1103–1107.

Lewy, A.J., R.L. Sack, R.H. Fredrickson, M. Reaves, D.D. Denney and D.R. Zielske. 1983d. The use of bright light in the treatment of chronobiologic sleep and mood disorders: the phase–response curve. Psychopharmacol Bull 19:523–525.

Lewy, A.J., R.L. Sack and C.M. Singer. 1984a. Assessment and treatment of chronobiologic disorders using plasma melatonin levels and bright light exposure: the clock–gate model and the phase response curve. Psychopharmacol Bull 20:561–565.

Lewy, A.J., R.L. Sack and C.M. Singer. 1985a. Treating phase typed chronobiologic sleep and mood disorders using appropriately timed bright artificial light. Psychopharmacol Bull 21:368–372.

Lewy, A.J., J.I. Nurnberger, Jr., T.A. Wehr, D. Pack, L.E. Becker, R.-L. Powell and D.A. Newsome. 1985b. Supersensitivity to light: possible trait marker for manic–depressive illness. Am J Psychiatr 142:725–727.

Lincoln, G. 1983. Melatonin as a seasonal time–cue: a commercial story. Nature 302:755.

Lynch, H.J. 1983. Assay methodology. In The Pineal Gland (Current Endocrinology: Basic and Clinical Aspects), Relkin, R. (ed.). New York: Elsevier Biomedical Press, pp. 129–150.

Markey, S.P. and P.E. Buell. 1982. Pinealectomy abolishes 6–hydroxy–melatonin excretion by male rats. Endocrinology 111:425–426.

Moore, R.Y. and N.J. Lenn. 1972. Retinohypothalamic projection in the rat. J Comp Neurol 146:1–4.

Moore-Ede, M.C., F.M. Sulzman and C.A. Fuller. 1982. The Clocks That Time Us. Cambridge: Harvard University Press.

Neuwelt, E.A. and A.J. Lewy. 1983. Disappearance of plasma melatonin after removal of a neoplastic pineal gland. N Engl J Med 308:1132-1135.

Ozaki, Y., H.J. Lynch and R.J. Wurtman. 1976. Melatonin in rat pineal, plasma and urine: 24-hour rhythmicity and effect of chlorpromazine. Endocrinology 98:1418-1424.

Papousek, M. 1975. Chronobiologische aspekte der Zyklothymie. Fortschr Neurol Psychiatr 43:381-440.

Pflug, B. and R. Tölle. 1971. Disturbance of the 24-hour rhythm in endogenous depression and the treatment of endogenous depression by sleep deprivation. Int Pharmacopsychiatr 6:187-196.

Pickard, G.E. and F. Turek. 1983. The hypothalamic paraventricular nucleus mediates the photoperiodic control of reproduction but not the effects of light on the circadian rhythm of activity. Neurosci Lett 43:67-72.

Pittendrigh, C.S. and S. Daan. 1976. A functional analysis of circadian pacemakers in nocturnal rodents. IV. Entrainment: pacemaker as clock. J Comp Physiol 106:291-331.

Rollag, M.D. 1981. Methods for measuring pineal hormones. In The Pineal Gland, Anatomy and Biochemistry, Volume 1, Reiter, R.J. (ed.). Boca Raton: CRC Press, pp. 273-302.

Romero, J.A. and J. Axelrod. 1975a. Regulation of sensitivity to beta-adrenergic stimulation in induction of pineal N-acetyltransferase. Proc Natl Acad Sci USA 72:1661-1665.

Romero, J.A., M. Zatz and J. Axelrod. 1975b. Beta-adrenergic stimulation of pineal N-acetyltransferase: adenosine 3',5'-cyclic monophosphate stimulates both RNA and protein synthesis. Proc Natl Acad Sci USA 72:2107-2111.

Rosenthal, N.E., D.A. Sack, J.C. Gillin, A.J. Lewy, F.K. Goodwin, Y. Davenport, P.S. Mueller, D.A. Newsome and T.A. Wehr. 1984. Seasonal affective disorder. Arch Gen Psychiatr 41:72-80.

Rosenthal, N.E., D.A. Sack, C.J. Carpenter, B.L. Parry, W.B. Mendelson and T.A. Wehr. 1985. Antidepressant effects of light in seasonal affective disorder. Am J Psychiatr 142:163-170.

Tetsuo, M., S.P. Markey and I.J. Kopin. 1980. Measurement of 6-hydroxy-melatonin in human urine with its diurnal variation. Life Sci 27:105-109.

Tetsuo, M., M.J. Perlow, M. Mishkin and S.P. Markey. 1982. Light exposure reduces and pinealectomy virtually stops urinary excretion of 6-hydroxy-melatonin by Rhesus monkeys. Endocrinology 110:997-1003.

Wald, G.M. and P.K. Brown. 1958. Human rhodopsin. Science 127:222-226.

Wehr, T.A., A. Wirz-Justice, F.K. Goodwin, W. Duncan and J.C. Gillin. 1979b. Phase advance of the sleep-wake cycle as an antidepressant. Science 206:710-713.

Wehr, T.A. and A. Wirz-Justice. 1981a. Internal coincidence model for sleep deprivation and depression. In Sleep 1980: Circadian Rhythms, Dreams, Noise and Sleep, Neurophysiology and Therapy (Proceedings of the Fifth European Congress on Sleep Research, Amsterdam, 1980), Koella, W.P. (ed.). Basel: S. Karger, A.G., pp. 26-33.

Wehr, T.A. and F.K. Goodwin. 1981b. Biological rhythms and psychiatry. In American Handbook of Psychiatry, Second Edition (Volume VII), Arieti, S. and H.K.H. Brodie (eds.). New York: Basic Books, pp. 46-74.

Wever, R.A. 1979a. The Circadian System of Man: Results of Experiments Under Temporal Isolation. New York: Springer-Verlag.

Wurtman, R.J., J. Axelrod and L.S. Phillips. 1963. Melatonin synthesis in the pineal gland: control of light. Science 142:1071-1073.

Yu, H.S., S.F. Pang, P.L. Tang and G.M. Brown. 1981. Persistence of circadian rhythms of melatonin and N–acetylserotonin in the serum of rats after pinealectomy. Neuroendocrinology 32:262–265.

Zatz, M., J.W. Kebabian, J.A. Romero, R.J. Lefkowitz and J. Axelrod. 1976. Pineal adrenergic receptor: Correlation of binding of ^{3}H–alprenolol with stimulation of adenylate cyclase. J Pharmacol Exp Ther 196: 714–722.

9

NEUROENDOCRINE SUBSTRATES OF CIRCANNUAL RHYTHMS

Irving Zucker

INTRODUCTION

Although the ancients suspected a link between seasons and mood disorders, it was not until Esquirol analyzed admission records for the years 1806 through 1814 at the Salpetriere Hospital in Paris that seasonal variations in the onset of mental illness were convincingly documented (Hare, 1980). About a century later, the existence of seasonal mood cycles in individual patients was established (see Rosenthal, Sack and Wehr, 1983 for references). Studies over the past 20 years have revealed clear peaks (acrophases) during some months of the year in the incidence of mania, depression, suicide, hormone secretion, sexual behavior, conception rates and cardiovascular disease (Reinberg, 1974; Reinberg, et al., 1980; Scragg, 1981; Ewing, 1982; Pinatel, Czyba and Souchier, 1982; and Rosenthal, Sack and Wehr, 1983). Many nonhuman mammals also manifest striking seasonal rhythms in behavior and physiology (Sadleir, 1969; Negus and Berger, 1972; Davis, 1976; Mrosovsky, 1978; Zucker, Johnston and Frost, 1980; and Gwinner, 1981a). The degree to which these cycles reflect endogenous versus exogenous control mechanisms differs among animals adapted to distinct habitats. In some desert species, exogenous factors predominate and the occurrence of seasonal behaviors varies substantially from year to year depending on timing of rainfall and growth of vegetation (Reichman and van de Graff, 1975). At the other extreme, several hibernating mammals manifest pronounced, precisely-timed endogenous seasonal rhythms that persist in the absence of variations in the external environment (Figure 1). Rhythms of the latter type have been designated circannual cycles. As used here, this term denotes an annual rhythm that, under constant conditions, persists for one or more cycles with a free-running period that approximates 365 days. Many writers dealing with human rhythms have adopted a less restrictive definition in which any annual cycle, whether endogenous or not, is labelled a circannual rhythm (e.g., Sasaki and Halberg, 1979; and Reinberg, et al., 1980).

The ultimate and proximate factors that contribute to human seasonal cycles remain unspecified. Many of the conditions that led to the evolution of seasonality in humans (e.g., Speth and Davis, 1976), no longer prevail in urban, industrialized societies capable of central heating, air-conditioning, fluorescent lighting, subterranean shopping malls, year-round food availability and other developments that blunt the impact of the external environment. Nevertheless, it is virtually certain that vestigial seasonality remains an important component of psychobiological organization among urban human populations.

Biological psychiatrists seek to develop physiological interventions for the treatment of the several affective disorders and to formulate plausible organic hypotheses for the causation of mental disturbance. Within this context, it is important to determine the extent to which seasonal predispositions to affective malaise reflect endogenous circannual fluctuations in brain chemistry (von Knorring, et al., 1982) or in reactivity to external stimuli (see discussion in Zucker, 1983). Such information is central to conceptualization and management of these conditions. It is unfortunately difficult to implement experiments on human subjects that would elaborate the endogenous nature of seasonal cycles in behavior (Reinberg, 1974). Individuals would have to be isolated from fluctuations in temperature, photoperiod, feeding, contact with conspecifics and innumerable other environmental perturbations for at least two years to establish the endogenous nature of annual rhythms. This is impractical, if not impossible, and even the most heroic isolation experiments (Wever, 1979a) fall short of this requirement. Furthermore, many of the interventions necessary to elaborate neuroendocrine substrates for circannual rhythms cannot be employed on humans. As a conse-

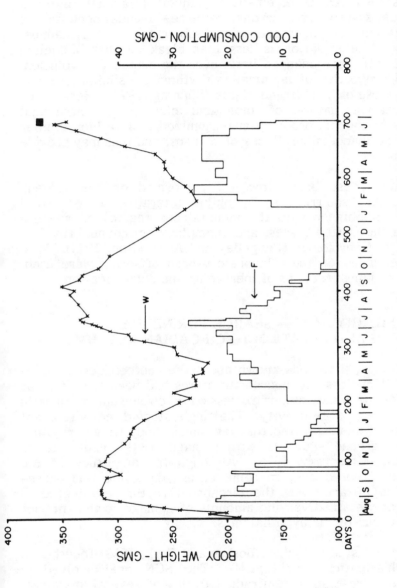

Figure 1   Body weight (W), mean daily food consumption (F), hibernation periods (solid horizontal black bars), and active periods (clear spaces between black bars) of an individual *Spermophilus lateralis* observed daily for two years. Food is consumed during periodic arousal from hibernation during intervals denoted with black bars. (From Pengelley and Asmundson, 1974.)

quence, there is little substantive information concerning central nervous system (CNS) involvement in human circannual rhythms. Animal model systems provide one of the few avenues open for the characterization of neuroendocrine substrates of circannual rhythmicity. The situation is less than bleak because biological clocks appear to have changed little over the course of evolution. The formal properties of mammalian rhythms are similar in many respects to those of insects and plants (Bünning, 1973). Because of the conservative nature of biological clocks, the circannual pacemakers of rodents probably are organized in a fashion similar to that of the inaccessible clocks of humans, and thus may provide a suitable model.

The work described below was performed on the golden–mantled ground squirrel (Spermophilus lateralis), a long–lived diurnal rodent indigenous to the mountainous regions of western Canada and the United States, and exemplar of circannual rhythms in behavior and physiology (Pengelley and Asmundson, 1974). Wild trapped specimens or their laboratory–born offspring were used, thereby minimizing problems of inbreeding and domestication.

CIRCANNUAL RHYTHMS — SEARCH FOR NEURAL OSCILLATORS AND RELATION TO CIRCADIAN RHYTHMS

As of 1978, little was known about the neuroendocrine bases of circannual cycles. No neural structures had been identified as necessary for the generation or expression of circannual rhythms in cellular and behavioral activity. The single study directly relevant to this question demonstrated that circannual body weight rhythms persisted in ground squirrels with damage to the ventromedial hypothalamus (Mrosovsky, 1975). Although the amplitude of the rhythm was affected and, in some cases, the cycle was phase–shifted, in no instance was the circannual rhythm eliminated in squirrels that sustained varying amounts of damage to the anterior and medial nuclei of the hypothalamus.

Our initial study (Zucker, Boshes and Dark, 1983) focused on the suprachiasmatic nuclei (SCN). The SCN are involved in expression of circadian and infradian cycles of several mammals (see review in Rusak and Zucker, 1979), and we conjectured they also might mediate circannual rhythms. One of the major hypotheses for circannual timing posits that annual cycles are derived via frequency demultiplication of circadian rhythms (see Mrosovsky, 1978; Gwinner, 1981 a,b). This is essentially a "counting" hypothesis, in which the occurrence of a certain number of circadian cycles is decoded as one circannual cycle; several physical analogies for such a mechanism have been described (see Gwinner, 1981 a,b). It follows from the demultiplication hypothesis that interventions which interfere with normal circadian organization might be expected to disrupt circannual cycles as well. We anticipated that ablation of the SCN would eliminate circadian rhythms in ground squirrels and enable us to test the validity of the demultiplication hypothesis for circannual cycles. At the same time, we sought to assess whether a common neural substrate mediates circadian and circannual rhythms.

Destruction of the SCN coincided with elimination or disruption of circadian activity rhythms of ground squirrels (Figures 2 and 3). The coherent free-running activity rhythm manifested during preoperative testing was not in evidence during many months of postoperative testing (Figure 2). Lesions of the SCN permitted the emergence of higher frequency rhythms (months of May through July of the first year; Figure 3) similar to those observed after ablation of the SCN in nocturnal hamsters (Rusak, 1977). All 11 squirrels with disrupted activity cycles had extensive damage to their SCN, and only two animals sustaining substantial SCN lesions manifested normal circadian rhythms. The SCN are a significant component of the circadian system mediating behavioral rhythms of diurnal squirrels as well as of nocturnal rats (Stephan and Zucker, 1972) and hamsters (Rusak, 1977).

The effects of SCN ablation on circannual rhythms were more variable. Four of 11 squirrels with disrupted daily activity cycles also had abnormal circannual body weight rhythms. In two animals, the circannual cycle was eliminated (e.g., Figure 4, no. 20); in a third animal, the cycle was phase-shifted, at least temporarily (not illustrated); and in one animal, the circannual rhythm was replaced by three- to five-month body weight cycles (Figure 4, no. 201). The remaining seven animals manifested normal circannual body weight rhythms despite moderate to severe disruption of their circadian activity cycles (Figure 4, no. 380).

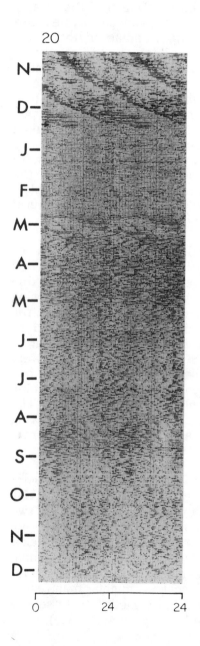

Figure 2 Pre– and postoperative wheel–running activity record of squirrel no. 20 maintained in constant illumination. The activity record is double–plotted to permit visualization of 48 h spans. Arrow at left indicates day on which SCN were ablated. The ordinate indicates months of the year. (From Zucker, Boshes and Dark, 1983.)

37

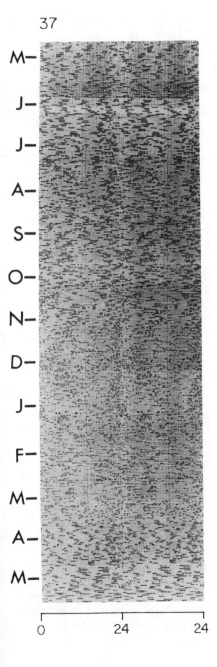

Figure 3 Postoperative wheel–running activity of squirrel no. 37, beginning with the day on which the SCN were lesioned. The animal had a coherent free–running activity rhythm pre–operatively and was maintained in constant illumination throughout. (From Zucker, Boshes and Dark, 1983.)

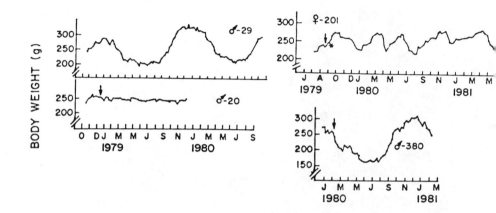

Figure 4   Circannual body weight cycles of an unop-
erated squirrel (no. 29; ♂) and of three squirrels with
complete ablation of the SCN. The body weight rhythm
was eliminated in no. 20 (♂), normal in no. 380 (♂) and
replaced with a three- to five-month cycle in no. 201
(♀). The arrows designate the times at which the
animals sustained SCN lesions. (Modified from Zucker,
Boshes and Dark, 1983.)

    These results suggest that the generation and expression of
circannual rhythms are not dependent upon the integrity of the
circadian system; circannual body weight and reproduction rhythms
persisted in several squirrels whose circadian activity rhythms
were eliminated by lesions of the SCN (Zucker, Boshes and Dark,
1983). We tentatively concluded that circannual cycles are not
derived via frequency demultiplication of circadian rhythms (cf.
Mrosovsky, 1978; Gwinner, 1981b). This conclusion is supported by
a recently completed study (Carmichael and Zucker, 1986), in
which female squirrels were maintained for over two years in
artificial day lengths of 23 h, 24 h or 25 h. Entrainment of each
animal's activity cycle to the appropriate photoperiod was
confirmed by continuous monitoring of wheel-running activity.
The period in real time of the circannual body weight cycle was not

shorter for animals entrained to 23 h as compared to 25 h day lengths, and thus did not support the frequency demultiplication hypothesis.

It also appears that separable neural substrates generate circadian and circannual rhythms in squirrels. Some brain lesions that eliminated circadian rhythm expression spared circannual rhythms, whereas other neural insults disrupted circannual but not circadian cycles. The extent to which the two systems overlap is in need of specification.

The elimination or phase-shifting of circannual rhythms and the emergence in one animal of three- to five-month body weight cycles after ablation of the SCN, may indicate a weakened coupling postoperatively among circannual oscillators. We do not understand why SCN lesions have far more variable effects on circannual than on circadian organization. Certainly the SCN are not "master" circannual clocks; the majority of squirrels with ablated SCN continue to manifest normal circannual rhythms (Zucker, Boshes and Dark, 1983).

Subsequent experiments (Dark, Pickard and Zucker, 1985) reveal that the effects of SCN ablation on circannual rhythms do not depend on the stage of the circannual cycle in which the lesions are sustained; furthermore, when individual animals were moni-tored for two or more postoperative cycles, the effects of SCN ablation observed during the first postoperative cycle were predictive of subsequent circannual patterns. The results to date suggest that the SCN may be part of a neural network that regulates endogenous cycles of body weight and reproduction in golden-mantled ground squirrels.

CIRCANNUAL INFLUENCES ON CIRCADIAN ORGANIZATION

The period of the circadian activity rhythm varies with the phase of the circannual cycle in neurologically intact squirrels maintained under constant conditions for over a year. This relation was first reported for a single male squirrel (Mrosovsky, et al., 1976), and has since been observed in several female squirrels (e.g., Figure 5). The period of the circadian rhythm is shorter than 24 h

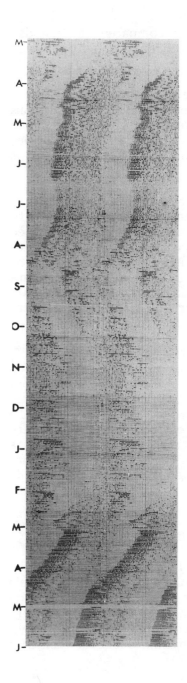

Figure 5 Continuous activity record of an intact female squirrel. Record begins 133 days after the animal was placed in constant illumination.

and activity levels are increased beginning about the time the animal enters reproductive condition (between April and June of the first year, and between March and May of the second year; Figure 5). Activity levels are decreased, and the period of the circadian cycle exceeds 24 h during most of the remainder of the circannual cycle.

Related seasonal changes also occur in female squirrels entrained to a light–dark photoperiod of 14 hours of light and 10 hours of dark (LD:14:10). The phase angle of the activity onset was advanced during the months of March through June relative to other times of year (Lee, Carmichael and Zucker, 1986). These findings further indicate a circannual influence on the circadian system. We are currently assessing whether circannual variations in hormone secretion (e.g., Licht, et al., 1982; and Zucker and Licht, 1983a) mediate changes in circadian rhythms. An alternative hypothesis is that neural circannual oscillators directly influence circadian pacemakers. In either case, it is now firmly established that endogenous circannual fluctuations affect circadian organization (both period and phase). Such spontaneous changes are of particular interest because they may be related to the apparent circadian rhythm dysfunctions associated with several affective disorders (see review in Rusak, 1984).

HORMONAL INFLUENCES ON CIRCADIAN AND CIRCANNUAL RHYTHMS

Many mammals, including humans, manifest annual rhythms in hormone secretion. Some rhesus monkeys show evidence of circannual rhythms of plasma testosterone (T) levels that persist under constant conditions (Michael and Bonsall, 1977). Licht and co-workers (1982) recently documented similar circannual rhythms in plasma T and luteinizing hormone (LH) levels of male ground squirrels raised from birth in an LD 14:10 photoperiod and maintained at 23°C ± 2°C (Figure 6).

Because of the intrinsic periodicity of homone secretion, we assessed the influence of gonadectomy on the circannual body weight rhythm. Gonadal hormones influence body weight and food intake in several mammalian species (Wade, 1976), and might be

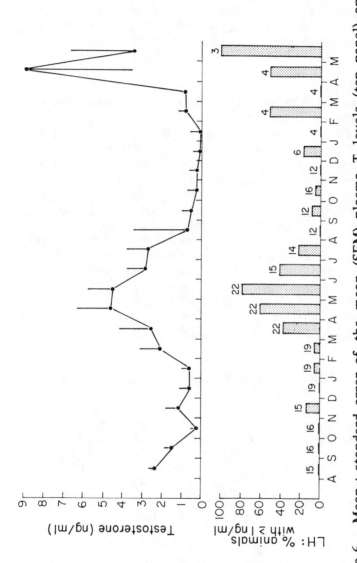

Figure 6 Mean ± standard error of the mean (SEM) plasma T levels (top panel) and percentage of animals with LH levels ≥ 1 ng/mL in laboratory-reared animals. Sample size for each determination is indicated above the bars in the lower panel. All animals contributed to both LH and testosterone determinations, except for March of the first year, where n = 15 for testosterone. Only 6%, 27% and 5% of squirrels had T levels ≥ 0.5 ng/mL during October, November and December, respectively, of the first year. Animals were approximately 70 days old at the time of the bleeding in August of the first year. The abscissa plots months of the year. (From Licht, et al., 1982.)

230

involved in the transduction process by which CNS oscillators impose circannual rhythms in energy balance.

Laboratory-born squirrels were gonadectomized, or sham-operated, at 47 days of age and maintained throughout their lives in an LD 14:10 photoperiod. Intact and gonadectomized animals of both sexes manifested clear circannual body weight cycles (Figure 7); the expression of this rhythm was independent of cyclic secretion of gonadal hormones.

There is a striking sex difference in body weight evident in this data (Figure 8). Of perhaps greater interest is the unexpected discovery that this sex difference waxes and wanes on a circannual basis (Figure 8). Males weigh significantly more than females only during the latter stages of the weight gain phase and the initial portion of the weight-loss phase. Trough weights are similar for both sexes. Most surprising to us was the persistence of this oscillating sex difference in long-term gonadectomized squirrels (Figure 8). Males first weighed more than females long after the gonads were removed; this gender difference disappeared by the end of the weight-loss phase only to reappear during the weight-gain phase of the second cycle. Similar changes were noted for food intake (Figure 9); thus, sex differences in body mass and food consumption appear and disappear on a circannual basis independent of changes in gonadal hormone secretion. We suspect that circannual rhythms in secretion of non-gonadal hormones (e.g., insulin), or rhythms of target tissue responsiveness to such hormones, underlie male-female differences in body weight, but we cannot at present discount intrinsic CNS mediation independent from hormonal cycles.

Several years ago, we reported that hormones of the pituitary-gonadal axis influence the period of circadian rhythms of hamsters (reviewed in Zucker, 1979). Estradiol shortened the period of the circadian activity rhythm of female hamsters (Morin, Fitzgerald and Zucker, 1977) but did not affect the period of this rhythm in males (Zucker, Fitzgerald and Morin, 1980). Removal of the pituitary gland lengthened the circadian period of hamsters of both sexes (Zucker, Cramer and Bittman, 1980). These observations are of interest because there are very few examples of endogenous changes in the internal milieu that affect circadian

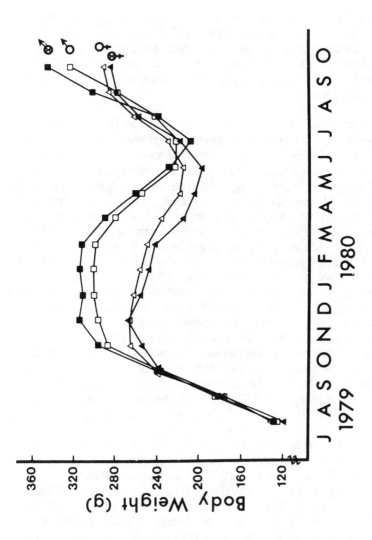

Figure 7 Body weights of intact male (♂; n = 7), intact female (♀; n = 7), gonadectomized male (⊗; n = 12), and gonadectomized female (⊕; n = 8) squirrels. (From Zucker and Boshes, 1982.)

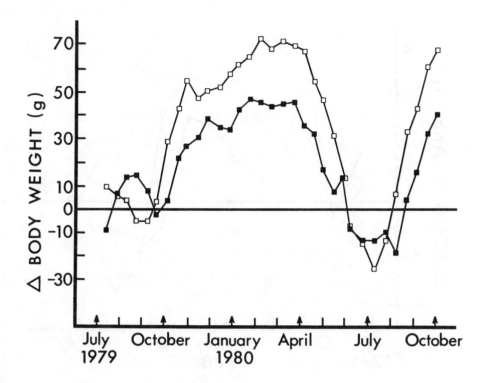

Figure 8   Sex differences in body weight for intact and gonadectomized squirrels. Values were obtained by subtracting mean group body weights of female from male intact squirrels (■) or gonadectomized squirrels (□). (From Zucker and Boshes, 1982.)

organization. We were, therefore, interested in determining whether hormonal fluctuations influenced the period of circannual rhythms. We failed to establish any influence of gonadal hormones on the period of the circannual body weight cycle (Zucker and Boshes, 1982). Intact and gonadectomized animals of both sexes had circannual periods of approximately 300 days (10 months) during maintenance in an unvarying LD 14:10 photoperiod. However, ovariectomized squirrels treated with estradiol benzoate (EB), in

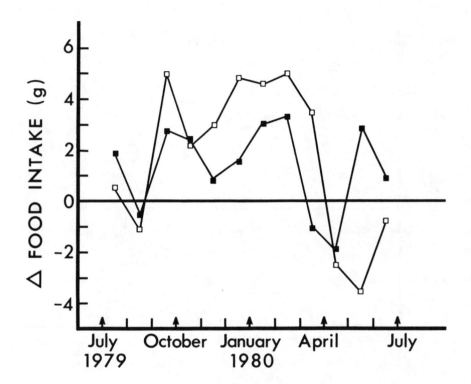

the form of a permanently–implanted Silastic capsule, showed a
substantial change in the wave–form of their circannual body
weight rhythm. Timing of the peak in body weight was delayed by
three months in the hormone–treated animals; squirrels treated
with EB were still in the weight–gain phase at a time when control
animals had made the transition to weight loss (Figure 10). However, both groups of animals achieved trough weights at the same
time; during the ensuing cycle, the phase–delaying actions of

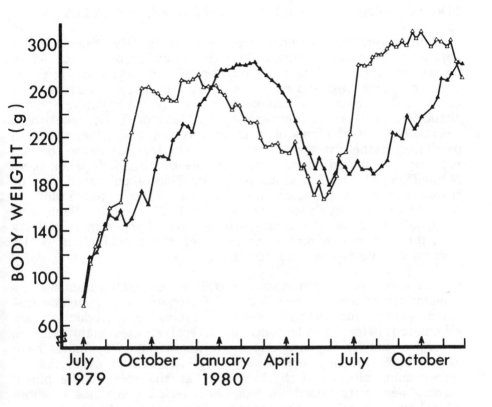

Figure 10   Body weights of individual ovariectomized
squirrels implanted with an empty Silastic capsule (Δ) or
a capsule filled with EB (▲). Ovariectomies and capsule
implantations were performed in July 1979 and capsules
were replaced in February 1980. (From Zucker and
Boshes, 1982.)

EB were repeated. Despite the effect on wave–form, estradiol did
not affect the period of the underlying circannual oscillation. In
addition, the circannual period was unaffected by testosterone
treatment in gonadectomized male squirrels (Zucker and Boshes,
1982).

PINEAL GLAND: INFLUENCE ON CIRCANNUAL CYCLES

In several non-mammalian vertebrates, the pineal gland appears to be a hierarchical or "master" circadian oscillator. After pineal ablation, rhythms in locomotor activity and body temperature of some bird and reptile species are severely disrupted or eliminated; rhythmicity can be restored by transplanting pineal tissue (Gwinner, 1978; Zimmerman and Menaker, 1979; Underwood, 1981). The pineal gland of mammals is not a driving circadian oscillator; rather, it appears to affect rhythm expression through masking effects and not by direct actions on circadian pacemakers (Aschoff, et al., 1982; and Rusak, 1982). Thus, accelerated rates of re-entrainment in pinealectomized rodents after a phase shift in the illumination cycle (e.g., Quay, 1970; Finkelstein, Baum and Campbell, 1978), may reflect postoperative changes in sensitivity to light and not a direct influence of the pineal gland or its hormones on circadian time-keeping.

The pineal gland of mammals is, however, well-established as a major transducer of the effects of photoperiod on the neuroendocrine system; for example, seasonal cycles in reproduction are eliminated after pinealectomy in several species maintained in natural or artificial photoperiods (Reiter, 1980). No studies have assessed pineal involvement in the generation or expression of free-running circannual rhythms; nor has the role of the pineal gland been determined in non-photoperiodic mammals whose annual cycles persist in the absence of fluctuations in photoperiod. We wished to establish whether the pineal gland contributes to the generation or expression of circannual cycles.

Recently-weaned female squirrels were pinealectomized (pinx) or sham-pinx in August 1980, and maintained from September 1980 until January 1983 in an unvarying short-day photoperiod (LD 14:10) at a temperature of $23°C \pm 2°C$. Removal of the pineal gland did not affect the absolute levels of body weight peaks or troughs, but did substantially shorten the period of the circannual body weight rhythm (Zucker, 1985; Figure 11). During the second post-operative cycle, the period of the pinx squirrels was more than 60 days shorter than that of the sham-operated animals. The calendar dates on which animals achieved peak and trough body weights and first came into estrus (Figure 12)

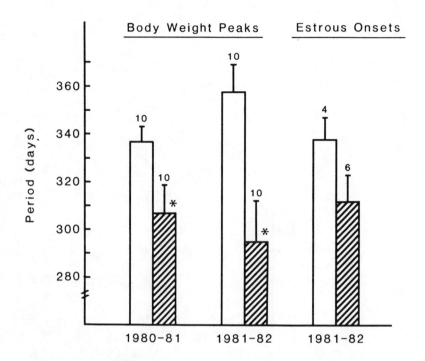

Figure 11   Period of the circannual body weight rhythm
and reproductive cycle of intact (open bars) and pinealectomized (shaded bars) female squirrels maintained in
an LD 10:14 photoperiod. Sample size is indicated
above each bar. The asterisk indicates that intact and
pinealectomized groups differ significantly. (Modified
from Zucker, 1985.)

illustrate the progressively increasing differences between the
groups. In subsequent experiments conducted on these animals,
we failed to detect any effect of pinealectomy on the rate of
re-entrainment of the circadian activity rhythm after a 6-h phase
advance in the LD cycle; nor were the free-running circadian
periods of the two groups different in constant dim illumination
(Martinet and Zucker, 1985). These experiments establish that the
pineal gland exerts a significant effect on circannual but not on

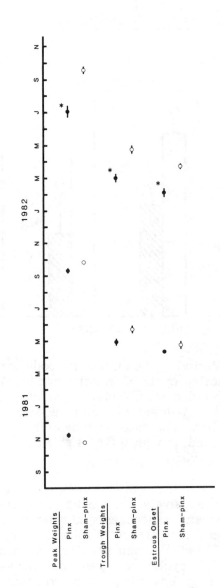

Figure 12 Calendar dates for the occurrence of peak body weights and estrous onsets of intact (–O–) and pinealectomized (–●–) squirrels maintained in an LD 10:14 photoperiod. The asterisks indicate the occasions on which pinealectomized animals achieved peak and trough weights and estrous onsets significantly earlier than did intact animals. (Modified from Zucker, 1985.)

circadian time-keeping. Presumably, pineal hormones lengthen the period of circannual oscillations that time the body weight cycle; in the absence of pineal hormones, the period of this cycle is shortened. There may be substantial hysteresis in the circannual system, since the effects of pinealectomy were more pronounced in the second than in the first postsurgical cycle. Caution must be exercised in interpreting circannual rhythm studies based on one or even two post-treatment cycles.

CIRCANNUAL RHYTHMS IN LUTEINIZING HORMONE LEVELS: INDEPENDENCE FROM STEROID FEEDBACK FROM THE OVARIES

Seasonal ovarian and testicular rhythms of golden-mantled ground squirrels are manifested in gross changes in the reproductive tract of both sexes (Heller and Poulson, 1970; Pengelley and Asmundson, 1974; and Kenagy, 1980) and in plasma LH and T levels of males (Licht, et al., 1982).

Altered sensitivity of the hypothalamic-hypophysial axis to the feedback effects of gonadal steroids has been proposed as one important mechanism for activation and inactivation of the reproductive system. Studies of the role of steroid feedback sensitivity in seasonal timing of mammalian gonadotrophin secretion have heretofore been restricted to species in which the reproductive cycle is synchronized by photoperiod (Turek and Campbell, 1979; Goodman and Karsch, 1981; Legan and Winans, 1981). Experiments were, therefore, undertaken to characterize patterns of gonadotrophin release in a species with a circannual reproductive cycle; in the course of these experiments, we provided information on the role of steroid feedback in reproductive cycles that are not synchronized by photoperiod (Zucker and Licht, 1983a).

Female squirrels born in the laboratory were ovariectomized (ovx) or sham-ovx at approximately 70 days of age. Blood was withdrawn at the time of surgery, 48 h later, and at monthly intervals thereafter. Twenty-two consecutive monthly measurements were available for four ovx squirrels born in June 1979. Consistent LH responses were not observed prior to eight months of age (February 1980, Figure 13). High LH levels (peaks) were recorded between March and July 1980, relatively low or undetectable LH levels were characteristic of the months between August and December 1980, and LH titers were once again elevated between January and March 1981 (Figure 13). Occurrences of LH peaks were observed at intervals of nine or ten months for three of the four squirrels (Figure 13).

In a second experiment, squirrels were ovariectomized on March 25, 1980 at nine and one-half months of age. Levels of LH were undetectable in all animals at the time of ovariectomy. Peaks in LH were attained within two months, in May or June (Figure 14). Levels of LH were undetectable between July and November 1980, at which time the experiment was terminated. Sham-ovx squirrels had undetectable LH levels between March and November.

A similar experiment, performed on squirrels of the same cohort ovariectomized on July 9, 1980 at 13 months of age yielded quite different results. Three of the four ovx animals first manifested elevated plasma LH levels in January or February 1981, six or seven months postoperatively. The fourth squirrel (no. 409) had elevated LH levels one month postoperatively; LH declined to undetectable levels for four of the next five months, and was elevated to high levels beginning in March 1981. Thus, all four squirrels ovariectomized in July failed to sustain high LH levels until the following January through March, or six to eight months after ovariectomy. Plasma LH levels were undetectable for five sham-ovx squirrels between July 1980 and February 1981. Two of these females had detectable LH titers in March and April 1981, respectively.

Female ground squirrels gonadectomized at different times of year thus manifested peak LH values only between February and June. Ovariectomy produced a rise in plasma LH only during the portion of the annual cycle in which intact females were in reproductive condition, independent of when ovariectomy was performed. In long-term ovx squirrels kept under constant environmental conditions of temperature and photoperiod, successive LH peaks occurred at intervals of nine to ten months. Thus, the negative feedback system between ovarian hormones and

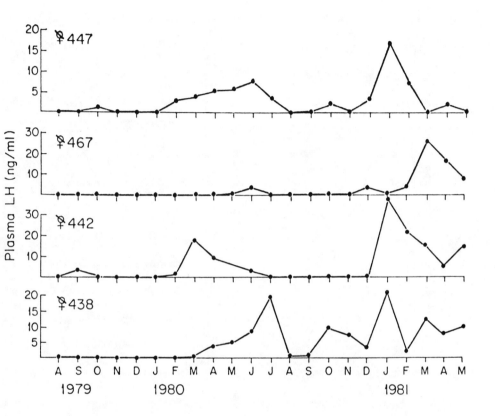

Figure 13   Postoperative plasma LH levels for individual squirrels over the course of 22 consecutive months.
Animals were ovariectomized in August 1979 at 70 days
of age, and maintained throughout the experiment in an
LD 14:10 photoperiod. (From Zucker and Licht, 1983a.)

pituitary LH secretion appears to be operative only during the
breeding season and is controlled by a circannual clock with a
period somewhat shorter than a year. Our studies indicate that the
annual cycle of LH secretion of the female golden-mantled ground
squirrel is almost wholly independent of steroidal feedback from
the gonads. The role of the ovary in the control of gonadotrophin
secretion appears to be confined primarily to modulating the levels

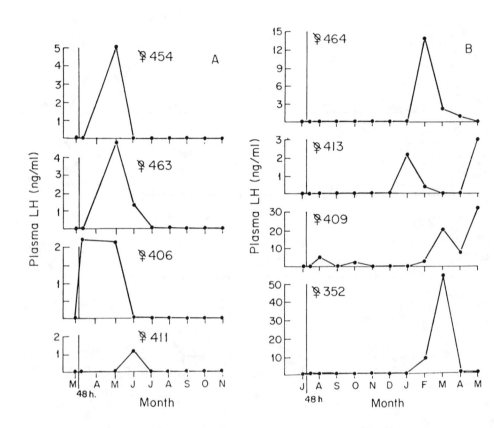

Figure 14 Plasma LH levels for individual squirrels ovariectomized in March, at nine and one-half months of age (A), or in July, at 13 months of age (B). The vertical line separates LH determinations at the time of ovariectomy and 48 h later. Levels of LH were not determined in April. (From Zucker and Licht, 1983a.)

of plasma LH within the breeding season, rather than in controlling the onset or termination of this season. This form of organization of the seasonal gonadal cycle differs markedly from that of photoperiodic rodent species (cf. Turek and Campbell, 1979).

Similar studies conducted concurrently on littermates of the above animals, indicated that levels of plasma LH in male squirrels are subject to negative feedback regulation from the testes during most months of the year (Zucker and Licht, 1983b). The postgonadectomy LH profile was, for the most part, independent of the state of the testis cycle, with similar maximal LH levels attained during all seasons. Not only did mean plasma LH levels increase acutely in all experiments, but LH levels tended to remain chronically elevated in orchidectomized animals (Figure 15).

The persistence of elevated plasma LH levels after orchidectomy contrasts sharply with the brief, seasonally–restricted elevation in plasma LH observed after ovariectomy in the same species; in individual females, LH rarely remained detectably elevated for more than two to three months, and even this transient elevation occurred only during the normal breeding season.

Despite the existence of similar circannual reproductive cycles in male and female ground squirrels, different mechanisms appear to underlie the annual gonadotrophin rhythms in the two sexes. In the female, this cycle appears to be generated primarily by changes in activation of the hypothalamo–hypophysial system that occur independently of influences from the gonads; the negative feedback of gonadal secretions is apparent essentially only during the breeding season. In contrast, gonadal secretions play an integral role in suppressing LH secretion of males during the quiescent phase of the annual reproductive cycle and there is little indication of negative feedback of LH by the gonads during the breeding season (Zucker and Licht, 1983b).

SYNOPSIS AND PROSPECT

Seasonal fluctuations in many human behavioral and cellular activities probably reflect input from CNS circannual oscillators. Practical considerations preclude direct verification of this and other plausible conjectures concerning temporal organization of seasonal cycles in humans. Consequently, the study of animal models remains one of the major routes for gaining insight into the structure and properties of human circannual oscillators.

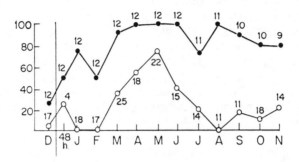

Figure 15 Percentage of squirrels with detectable
plasma LH levels (≥ 1 ng/mL) during different months
of the year. Squirrels were orchidectomized (●) or
sham-operated (O) at six months of age and maintained
throughout in an LD 14:10 photoperiod. Pre- and
postoperative measures are separated by a vertical line
and sample size is indicated above each point.
(Modified from Zucker and Licht, 1983b.)

Although progress has been made toward the creation of a
neurobiology of circannual rhythms, what remains most impressive
is the profound ignorance concerning the location of circannual
oscillators, their neurochemical characteristics and the means by
which they are synchronized to the annual geophysical cycle.
Discouragement must be tempered with the knowledge that this
sub-area of chronobiology has a very short history; the first
publication dealing with mammalian circannual cycles appeared in
1957. Only within the past decade have more than a handful of
individuals devoted serious study to circannual rhythms. Investigation of circannual cycles is destined to lag far behind that of
circadian rhythms. The major stumbling block is the inherent
difficulty in implementing well-designed studies and the patience
required to see them through to their logical conclusion. Clinical
investigators have called attention to phenomena in humans that
invite a circannual perspective, and in so doing, may have provided
the impetus needed to stimulate basic research in more tractable
animal model systems. It is anticipated that the significance of

circannual organization in the genesis and expression of human affective disorders will be established in the near future.

ACKNOWLEDGMENT

The research described in this report was supported by Grant HD-14595 from the National Institute of Child Health and Human Development. I am indebted to many co-workers for their contributions to the conception and execution of the experiments described. Brian Barnes, John Dark and Theresa Lee kindly provided useful comments on the manuscript.

REFERENCES

Aschoff, J., U. Gerecke, C. von Goetz, G.A. Groos and F.W. Turek. 1982. Phase responses and characteristics of free-running activity rhythms in the golden hamster: independence of the pineal gland. In Vertebrate Circadian Systems: Structure and Physiology (Papers Presented at a Meeting Held in October 1980 at Schloss Ringberg), Aschoff, J., S. Daan and G.A. Groos (eds.). Berlin: Springer-Verlag, pp. 29–40.

Bünning, E. 1973. The Physiological Clock (Third Edition). New York: Springer-Verlag.

Carmichael, M.S. and I. Zucker. 1986. Circannual rhythms of ground squirrels: a test of the frequency demultiplication hypothesis. Biol Rhythms 1:277–284.

Dark, J., G.E. Pickard and I. Zucker. 1985. Persistence of circannual rhythms in ground squirrels with lesions of the suprachiasmatic nuclei. Brain Res 332:201–207.

Davis, D.E. 1976. Hibernation and circannual rhythms of food consumption in marmots and ground squirrels. Q Rev Biol 51:477–514.

Ewing, L.L. 1982. Seasonal variation in primate fertility with an emphasis on the male. Am J Primat (Suppl) 1:145–160.

Finkelstein, J.S., F.R. Baum and C.S. Campbell. 1978. Entrainment of the female hamster to reversed photoperiod: role of the pineal. Physiol Behav 21:105–111.

Goodman, R.L. and F.J. Karsch. 1981. A critique of the evidence on the importance of steroid feedback to seasonal changes in gonadotrophin secretion. J Reprod Fert (Suppl) 30:1–13.

Gwinner, E. 1978. Effects of pinealectomy on circadian locomotor activity rhythms in European starlings (Sturnus vulgaris). J Comp Physiol 126:123–129.

Gwinner, E. 1981a. Circannual systems. In Handbook of Behavioral Neurobiology (Volume 4, Biological Rhythms), Aschoff, J. (ed.). New York: Plenum Press, pp. 391–410.

Gwinner, E. 1981b. Circannual rhythms: their dependence on the circadian system. In Biological Clocks in Seasonal Reproductive Cycles, Follett, B.K. and D.E. Follett (eds.). New York: John Wiley & Sons, pp. 153–168.

Hare, E.H. 1980. Seasonal variations in psychiatric illness. Trends Neurosci 12:295–298.

Heller, H.C. and T.L. Poulson. 1970. Circannian rhythms. II. Endogenous and exogenous factors controlling reproduction and hibernation in chipmunks (Eutamias) and ground squirrels (Spermophilus). Comp Biochem Physiol 33:357–383.

Kenagy, G.J. 1980. Interrelation of endogenous annual rhythms of reproduction and hibernation in the golden–mantled ground squirrel. J Comp Physiol 135:333–339.

Lee, T.M., M.S. Carmichael and I. Zucker. 1986. Circannual variations in circadian rhythms of ground squirrels. Am J Physiol 250:R831–R836.

Legan, S.J. and S.S. Winans. 1981. The photoneuroendocrine control of seasonal breeding in the ewe. Gen Comp Endocrinol 45:317–328.

Licht, P., I. Zucker, G. Hubbard and M. Boshes. 1982. Circannual rhythms of plasma testosterone and luteinizing hormone levels in golden–mantled ground squirrels (Spermophilus lateralis). Biol Reprod 27:411–418.

Martinet, L. and I. Zucker. 1985. Role of the pineal gland in circadian organization of diurnal ground squirrels. Physiol Behav 34:799–803.

Michael, R.P. and R.W. Bonsall. 1977. A 3–year study of an annual rhythm in plasma androgen levels in male rhesus monkeys (Macaca mulatta) in a constant laboratory environment. J Reprod Fert 49:129–131.

Morin, L.P., K.M. Fitzgerald and I. Zucker. 1977. Estradiol
shortens the period of hamster circadian rhythms. Science
196:305–307.

Mrosovsky, N. 1975. The amplitude and period of circannual
cycles of body weight in golden–mantled ground squirrels with
medial hypothalamic lesions. Brain Res 99:97–116.

Mrosovsky, N. 1978. Circannual cycles in hibernators. In
Strategies in Cold: Natural Torpidity and Thermogenesis, Wang, L.
and J.W. Hudson (eds.). New York: Academic Press, pp. 21–65.

Mrosovsky, N., M. Boshes, J.D. Hallonquist and K. Lang. 1976.
Circannual cycle of circadian cycles in a golden–mantled ground
squirrel. Naturwissenschaften 63:298–299.

Negus, N.C. and P.J. Berger. 1972. Environmental factors and
reproductive processes in mammalian populations. In Biology of
Reproduction: Basic and Clinical Studies, Velardo, J.T. and
B. Kasprow (eds.). Mexico City: Bay Publishing, pp. 89–98.

Pengelley, E.T. and S.J. Asmundson. 1974. Circannual rhythmicity
in hibernating mammals. In Circannual Clocks, Pengelley, E.T.
(ed.). New York: Academic Press, pp. 95–160.

Pinatel, M.C., J.C. Czyba and C. Souchier. 1982. Seasonal
changes in sexual hormones secretion, sexual behaviour and sperm
production in man. Int J Androl Suppl 5:183–190.

Quay, W.B. 1970. Precocious entrainment and associated
characteristics of activity patterns following pinealectomy and
reversal of photoperiod. Physiol Behav 5:1281–1290.

Reichman, O.J. and K.M. van de Graaf. 1975. Association
between ingestion of green vegetation and desert rodent
reproduction. J Mammal 56:503–506.

Reinberg, A. 1974. Aspects of circannual rhythms in man. In
Circannual Clocks, Pengelley, E.T. (ed.). New York: Academic
Press, pp. 423–505.

Reinberg, A., E. Schuller, J. Clench and M.H. Smolensky. 1980. Circadian and circannual rhythms of leucocyctes, proteins and immunoglobulins. Adv Biosci 28:251–259.

Reiter, R.J. 1980. The pineal and its hormones in the control of reproduction in mammals. Endocrinol Rev 1:109–131.

Rosenthal, N E., D.A. Sack, and T.A. Wehr. 1983. Seasonal variation in affective disorders. In Circadian Rhythms in Psychiatry, Wehr, T.A. and F.K. Goodwin (eds.). Pacific Grove: Boxwood Press, pp. 185–201.

Rusak, B. 1977. The role of the suprachiasmatic nuclei in the generation of circadian rhythms in the golden hamster, Mesocricetus auratus. J Comp Physiol 118:145–164.

Rusak, B. 1982. Circadian organization in mammals and birds: role of the pineal gland. In The Pineal Gland: Reproductive Effects (Volume 3), Reiter, R.J. (ed.). Boca Raton: CRC Press, pp. 29–51.

Rusak, B. 1984. Assessment and significance of rhythm disruptions in affective illness. In Neuroendocrinology and Psychiatric Disorder, Brown, G.M., S.H. Koslow and S. Reichlin (eds.). New York: Raven Press.

Rusak, B. and I. Zucker. 1979. Neural regulation of circadian rhythms. Physiol Rev 59:449–526.

Sadleir, R.M.F.S. 1969. The Ecology of Reproduction in Wild and Domestic Mammals. London: Methuen.

Sasaki, T. and F. Halberg. 1979. Reproducibility during decades and individualization of circannually rhythmic metabolic rate in Japanese men and women. Adv Biosci 19:247–254.

Scragg, R. 1981. Seasonality of cardiovascular disease mortality and the possible protective effect of ultra–violet radiation. Int J Epidemiol 10:337–341.

Speth, J.D. and D.D. Davis. 1976. Seasonal variability in early hominid predation. Science 192:441–445.

Stephan, F.K. and I. Zucker. 1972. Circadian rhythms in drinking behavior and locomotor activity of rats are eliminated by hypothalamic lesions. Proc Nat Acad Sci USA 69:1583-1586.

Turek, F.W. and C.S. Campbell. 1979. Photoperiodic regulation of neuroendocrine-gonadal activity. Biol Reprod 20:32-50.

Underwood, H. 1981. Circadian organization in the lizard Scleroporus occidentalis: the effects of pinealectomy, blinding and melatonin. J Comp Physiol 141:537-547.

von Knorring, L.B., G.L. Almay, F. Johansson, L. Terenius and A. Wahlstrom. 1982. Circannual variation in concentrations of endorphins in cerebrospinal fluid. Pain 12:265-272.

Wade, G.N. 1976. Sex hormones, regulatory behaviors and body weight. In Advances in the Study of Behavior, Hinde, R.A., E. Shaw and C.G. Beer (eds.). New York: Academic Press, Volume 6, pp. 201-279.

Wever, R.A. 1979a. The Circadian System of Man: Results of Experiments Under Temporal Isolation. New York: Springer-Verlag.

Zimmerman, N.H. and M. Menaker. 1979. The pineal: pacemaker within the circadian system of the house sparrow. Proc Nat Acad Sci USA 76:999-1003.

Zucker, I. 1979. Hormones and hamster circadian organization. In Biological Rhythms and Their Central Mechanism, Suda, M., O. Hayaishi and H. Nakagawa (eds.). Amsterdam: Elsevier North-Holland Biomedical Press, pp. 369-381.

Zucker, I. 1983. Motivation, biological clocks, and temporal organization of behavior. In Handbook of Behavioral Neurobiology (Volume 6), Satinoff, E. and P. Teitelbaum (eds.). New York: Plenum Press, pp. 3-21.

Zucker, I. 1985. Pineal gland influences period of circannual rhythms of ground squirrels. Am J Physiol 249:R111-R115.

Zucker, I., C.P. Cramer and E.L. Bittman. 1980. Regulation by the pituitary of circadian rhythms in the hamster. J Endocrinol 85:17–25.

Zucker, I., K.M. Fitzgerald and L.P. Morin. 1980. Sex differentiation of the circadian system in the golden hamster. Am J Physiol 238:R97–R101.

Zucker, I., P.G. Johnston and D. Frost. 1980. Comparative, physiological and biochronometric analyses of rodent seasonal reproductive cycles. Prog Reprod Biol 5:102–133.

Zucker, I. and M. Boshes. 1982. Circannual body weight rhythms of ground squirrels: role of gonadal hormones. Am J Physiol 243:R546–R551.

Zucker, I., M. Boshes and J. Dark. 1983. Suprachiasmatic nuclei influence circannual and circadian rhythms of ground squirrels. Am J Physiol 244:R472–R480.

Zucker, I. and P. Licht. 1983a. Circannual and seasonal variations in plasma luteinizing hormone levels of ovariectomized ground squirrels (Spermophilus lateralis). Biol Reprod 28:178–185.

Zucker, I. and P. Licht. 1983b. Seasonal variations in plasma luteinizing hormone levels of gonadectomized male ground squirrels (Spermophilus lateralis). Biol Reprod 29:278–285.

10

ORDER AND DISORDER IN HUMAN CIRCADIAN RHYTHMICITY: POSSIBLE RELATIONS TO MENTAL DISORDERS

Rütger A. Wever

INTRODUCTION

Circadian rhythmicity is an ubiquitous phenomenon. Nearly all measurable values of nearly all organisms, from unicellular to man, undergo diurnal variations with one maximum and one minimum value within 24 hours (h). In man, this rhythmicity concerns continuous functions, both physiological (e.g., body temperature or hormone secretions) and psychological (e.g., performance or mood scores), and includes the probability of solitary events (e.g., birth or death), as well as sensitivities against external stimuli, like drugs (e.g., cortisol or narcotics), poison (e.g., alcohol) or radiation (e.g., X–rays). The regular functioning of an organism requires the consistent temporal order of all different overt rhythmicities; that is, it requires the phase relationships of every overt rhythm be temporally correct and constant, in both external (i.e., to the external day–night cycle) and internal (i.e., to other internal rhythms) respects. Rhythm disorders lead to disintegrations of the temporal structure of an organism and, hence, can lead to serious malfunctions expressed in somatic or mental diseases. A thorough understanding of such diseases (e.g., depression), therefore, presupposes a thorough knowledge of the basic principles of diurnal or circadian rhythms and, in particular, the mechanisms by which these rhythms become disordered.

Circadian rhythmicity is governed by internal and external impulses which must be separated for the sake of evaluation.

253

External impulses can be eliminated under temporal isolation; that is, after the exclusion of all environmental time cues. Under such "constant" conditions (i.e., under the exclusive internal control of the circadian system), principles of undisturbed and internally disturbed rhythms can be studied, independent of real or imagined social restraints which are unavoidable in the natural environment. Only in a subsequent step should modalities of effective external stimuli be evaluated; those stimuli, when given periodically, can act as "zeitgebers" synchronizing the internally-generated rhythms. Temporal isolation, with the exclusion of all natural time cues, is a necessary prerequisite for the applicability of such artificial zeitgebers, the parameters of which (e.g., the period) can be varied experimentally. Under such "zeitgeber" conditions, the principles of external modifications of the rhythms and, in particular, of externally-induced rhythm disorders can be studied (provided that the principles of internal rhythm control are known). In this paper, special features of internal and, subsequently, external, rhythm control will be summarized. However, it is not the aim of this paper to achieve an exhaustive analysis; it is rather to accentuate such principles which are possibly contingent upon the understanding of mental diseases, with particular emphasis upon the disturbance of the rhythms.

In addition, it may be advantageous to supplement special experimental findings with a simple mathematical model of circadian rhythmicity shown to be in good agreement with various features of disturbed and undisturbed rhythms. In fact, most experimental results to be discussed below have been predicted by corresponding model calculations, and confirmed only subsequently by human experiments. Indeed, several model solutions have not yet been confirmed, because often critical cases concern solutions which may be relevant only to diseased states. The circadian rhythms of patients suffering from these diseases are presently known only in very small part, because the main emphasis has been laid, up to the present, on the evaluation of the principles of circadian rhythms in healthy subjects. It is tempting, however, to speculate about the applicability of such critical solutions of the model.

INTERNAL RHYTHM CONTROL:
INTERNALLY SYNCHRONIZED RHYTHMS

Internal Phase Relationships

In most human subjects studied so far under constant conditions, the rhythms of all measured variables ran in synchrony ("internal synchronization") with periods always close to 25 h. (In 130
subjects examined under such a condition, the mean free–running
period ± standard deviation (SD) was 25.01 h ± 0.51 h.) In the long
run, the individual period maintains a remarkably high stability, but
is not measurable from the beginning of an isolation experiment;
transient behavior during the first cycle is due to a consistent and
considerable change in the internal phase relationships between
different overt rhythms during the transition from 24-h rhythms
(prior to the experiment) to a free–running rhythm with a slightly
lengthened period. For instance, in the 24-h day, the rhythm of
deep body temperature lags behind the sleep–wake rhythm,
whereas it leads the sleep–wake rhythm in the free run. Only in
the final steady state, therefore, do all overt rhythms show the
same period (Wever, 1979a).

Figure 1 exemplifies a special but frequently encountered
type of "initial dissociation"; of the various measured rhythms, only
the rhythms of sleep–wake and rectal temperature are presented.
The left diagram of Figure 1 shows the temporal protocol of the
four-week experiment; the right diagram shows period analyses
calculated separately for every week of the experiment. During
the second to fourth week, both rhythms show an identical and
consistent period of 25.1 h. During the first week, only the rhythm
of sleep–wake exhibits this period, whereas the temperature
rhythm shows a period of 24.0 h. If only the results of the first
week are considered, one will arrive at internally desynchronized
rhythms (see below) where, in fact, the sleep–wake rhythm shows a
typical free–running period, but in which the temperature rhythm
is assumed to be still synchronized by a subtle, and unintentionally
retained, 24-h zeitgeber. The thorough inspection of the total
time series, however, shows that this conclusion is erroneous. The
difference in the periods of the two rhythms during the first week

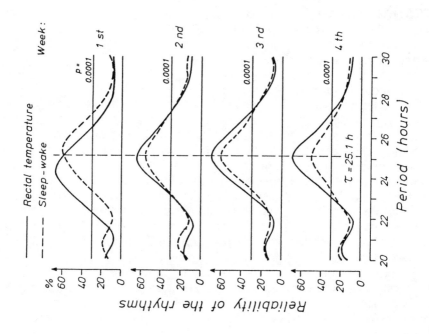

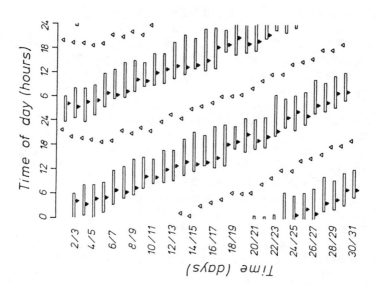

Figure 1

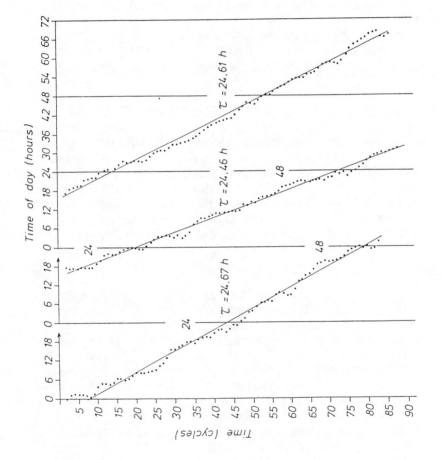

Figure 2

257

Legend for Figure 1 (On Page 256) Free-running circadian rhythms of a subject living under constant environmental conditions without time cues. Left: course of the experiment; presented are the rhythms of sleep/wake (bars: sleep episodes) and rectal temperature (temporal positions of Δ = maxima and ∇ = minima) as functions of local time (abscissa); ordinate: sequence of successive days (for clarity, two successive days are each plotted side by side). Right: period analyses of the two rhythms shown at left, computed separately for every single week of the experiment.

Legend for Figure 2 (On Page 257) Free-running circadian rhythms of three subjects living under constant environmental conditions without time cues (the first and second subject lived for an initial week in an artificial 24-h day). Presented are the acrophases (maximum of the best fitting sine wave) of the rhythm of rectal temperature as functions of local time (abscissa); ordinate: sequence of successive cycles. The computed linear regressions combining the acrophases are drawn as solid lines.

Legend for Figure 3 (On Page 259 following) Computed analyses from free-running circadian rhythms of a subject living under constant environmental conditions (constant bright illumination) without time cues (experiment of four weeks' duration). Presented are results from the rhythms of sleep/wake, continuously recorded rectal temperature, urine volume (from micturitions in self-selected intervals, 6 to 10 micturitions per cycle), and urinary cortisol, melatonin (measured as aMT6s) and potassium. Left: period analyses, right: educed cycles (with standard deviations), computed with the most prominent period of 26.1 h.

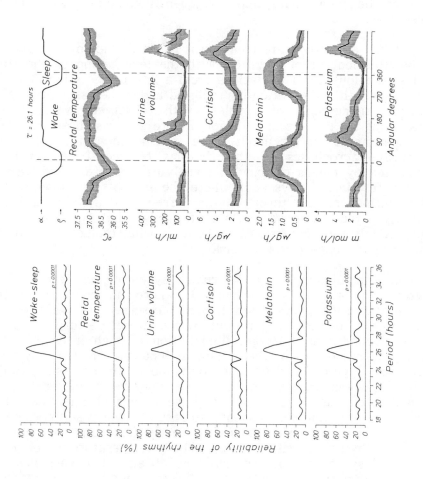

Figure 3

259

is due to transient behavior which cannot be observed in the steady state and which demonstrates that long–term experiments are needed to prevent misleading conclusions. Only after a steady state is guaranteed unambiguously is a final decision concerning the state of the rhythm meaningful. It must be emphasized that transient behavior varies, and is frequently completed after about three days.

When a steady state free–run is reached, the rhythms show a remarkable long–term stability; with the lengthening of the time series, the long–term deviations from a linear regression increase more slowly than theoretically predicted under the assumption of a random succession of cycles with observed variabilities. Illustrating the long–term behavior, Figure 2 shows three examples of experiments lasting about three months each, for which the successive acrophases of the rhythms of rectal temperature, calculated by means of harmonic analyses, are presented. Apart from a few initial days each where the subjects remained under 24–h influence, all three rhythms free ran with remarkable stability: the acrophases fluctuate only slightly around the computed linear regressions, without showing temporal trends or superimposed long–term fluctuations.

A third example of internally synchronized free–running rhythms is presented in Figure 3, where, in contrast to the presentations of Figures 1 and 2, the time series analyses over the four weeks of the experiment which were performed under constant conditions (constant illumination of high intensity), are displayed rather than the temporal courses of the rhythms. Moreover, Figure 3 presents not only the rhythms of sleep–wake and body temperature but also the rhythms of several more variables; on the left, Figure 3 presents period analyses. The analyses of all time series measured result in sharp and consistent peaks at the same period of 26.1 h, clearly demonstrating that, in fact, the rhythms of sleep–wake and body temperature not only ran in mutual synchrony, but the rhythms of all other variables did also, re–emphasizing unambiguously the presence of internal synchronization. The right part of Figure 3 shows reduced cycles of all variables, averaged consistently with the prominent period of 26.1 h. In spite of the high number of 26 successive cycles in every time series, the formally computed standard deviations around the mean cycles are remarkably small, demonstrating in Figure 3 as well the high long-term stability of human circadian rhythms.

Stabilization Mechanism

The intrinsic mechanism responsible for the high long-term stability is evident in negative serial correlations among successive cycles (where a cycle is defined by any consistent phase such as, for instance, the onset of wake or sleep, or minimum of body temperature). With high probability, a cycle that is for any reason longer than average is followed (and preceded) by a cycle of sub-average duration, and vice versa. Any deviation of a cycle length from the long-term mean is corrected to a high degree by the following cycle and, to a lower but still significant degree, by the following but one cycle (Wever, 1979a). The negativity of the first-order serial correlations is significant at a very high level ($p < 10^{-12}$) and that of the second order serial correlation is also significant at a fair level ($p < 10^{-3}$). In addition, the coefficients of the serial correlations of first and second order are negatively correlated among the subjects ($r = 0.673$; $p < 10^{-3}$); i.e., in a subject where the correction of a disturbance by the following cycle is better than average, the correction by the following but one cycle is below average, and vice versa (Wever, 1984b). Consequently, the sum of the serial correlations of the first and second order determines the overall stabilization power of the rhythm.

An intrinsic stabilization mechanism with exactly the same properties as in the human experiments can certainly be established by mathematical equation; the mechanism is bound to a nonlinearity in the "restoring force" (Wever, 1984a). This term had been introduced originally (without any knowledge of the intrinsic stabilization) in order to guarantee the internal coupling between different rhythm parameters such as period, amplitude or mean value, according to contemporary animal experiments (Wever, 1963). Without this term, many features of the rhythm including, for instance, the self-sustainment capacity, remain. Therefore, states of circadian rhythms are conceivable where, specifically, the intrinsic stabilization mechanism is neutralized by some defect; simultaneously, the correlations among the different rhythm parameters mentioned would then be reduced. It may be such a defect that reduces the overall intrinsic stabilization power in old subjects (Wever, 1984b). It is worth investigating whether or not a similar reduction in the stabilization power is manifested in patients with mental diseases.

Apart from the serial correlations among successive cycles within a rhythm, there is always a corresponding negative serial correlation among adjacent sleep and wake episodes. A wake episode that is for any reason longer than average is followed with very high probability ($p < 0.01$) by sleep episodes of sub-average durations, and vice versa (Wever, 1984b). In other and less homogeneous samples, the serial correlation between sleep and following wake may be, on the average, close to zero, while that between wake and following sleep is always negative at a very high level of significance (Wever, 1979a).

The negative serial correlations among adjacent wake and sleep episodes reveal that the intrinsic stabilization mechanism discussed earlier aims only at a stabilization of the full cycles and not at a stabilization of subsections within a cycle. Although these serial correlations had been predicted originally by the mathematical model mentioned above, and hence could be considered to be nothing but mechanical consequences of oscillation laws, they give new insight into the meaning of sleep. A wake episode of an above average duration should be followed by a sleep episode with increased restoring power; the duration of this sleep episode, however will be below average, even if there is no time reference allowing subjective control of the duration of the episodes, indicating that the serial correlations mentioned are related to the control of sleep. Whether or not these types of serial correlations are related to personality data or specific diseases is still unknown but worthy of investigation.

Sex Differences

In free-running and internally synchronized rhythms, there are not only serial correlations within every time series, but also correlations between different parameters of the rhythms. Since the regressions of these correlations are, in part, sex differentiated, previous sex differences of various rhythm parameters require discussion. The first is the period which is identical in all overt rhythms in the experiments considered (with internally synchronized rhythms). Up to now, two different samples of subjects, each in long-term experiments under constant conditions, have been analyzed and will be appraised together as the results obtained in the two samples were similar. Collectively, the free-running period in a total of 23 females was shorter than that in the 37 males, on the average ($\pm$ SD) by 0.37 h $\pm$ 0.58 h, or 22.2 min $\pm$ 34.8 min respectively. This difference is statistically significant (t = 2.403, two-tailed) with p < 0.02 (Wever, 1984c).

In the sleep-wake rhythms, among a great multiplicity of parameters analyzed, only the durations of the wake and sleep episodes are sex differentiated. Both these can be summarized in the fraction of sleep within the total sleep-wake cycle. Joint consideration of the two samples reveals the fraction of sleep in the 23 females was 38.7% $\pm$ 4.3%, and in the 37 males it was 32.2% $\pm$ 4.7%, that is: females slept considerably longer than males. Normalized to a 24-h day, the difference was 1.56 h $\pm$ 1.09 h, or 93.6 min $\pm$ 65.5 min respectively; this difference is statistically significant (t = 5.377, two-tailed) with p < 0.0001 (Wever, 1984b). Since the subjects were naive about the actual lengths of their wake and sleep episodes, the sex difference in the measured sleep durations can be assumed to reflect differential needs for sleep. On the other hand in normal life with ubiquitous time references the duration of sleep is adjusted according to social constraints and, hence, does not necessarily reflect true biological needs.

Other sex differences can be observed in the rhythm of deep body temperature. Certainly additional age dependence must be considered in rhythms of female subjects: rhythm parameters of women with an age between 55 years and 60 years do not differ from those of men, whereas those of younger women do. Temperature rhythms obtained in post-menopausal women differ significantly from those in pre-menopausal women; only those of the younger female subjects can be differentiated from those of male subjects. A similar age dependence in temperature rhythms of male subjects has not been observed. Unfortunately, data from pre-pubescent female subjects are not available since it is not justifiable to test children under age 17 in long-term experiments under temporal isolation. Nevertheless, the available data suggest a hormonal control of the rhythm of deep body temperature, which is the more plausible in light of the fact that steroid hormones are able to modulate circadian rhythms of mammals (Turek and Gwinner, 1982).

The most obvious sex difference regards the amplitude of the temperature rhythm. Out of a homogeneous sample of long-term experiments under constant conditions, the nine younger female subjects (age < 50 y) showed a temperature amplitude (mean ± SD) of 0.296°C ± 0.036°C; the seven older female subjects (age > 60 y) showed the significantly larger amplitude of 0.498°C ± 0.038°C (t = 10.90; p < 10^{-6}), without any overlap in the amplitudes of the younger and older female subjects. In the same sample of experiments, sixteen younger male subjects were included with ages below 50 y demonstrating a mean amplitude of 0.418°C ± 0.073°C which was significantly larger than that of the younger females (t = 4.651; p < 10^{-4}) but could not be differentiated significantly from the amplitudes of the older female subjects. Unfortunately, temperature rhythms from only two older male subjects (age > 60 y) were available rendering a statistical comparison infeasible. These males showed temperature amplitudes of 0.32°C and 0.35°C which were at the lower limit of the temperature amplitudes of younger males (the smallest amplitude in the younger males was 0.33°C) and certainly not higher as was the case with the female subjects. In evaluating these results, it must be emphasized that the data of the volunteering subjects can, on principle, not be generalized, as they are possibly not representative of the two sexes. This is particularly true for the oldest subjects which were probably more active than the general population at this age.

A sex difference in the mean value of body temperature rhythm (and its variability) is rather trivial and already established. Every experiment covers just one menstrual cycle in females thus including a pre-ovulatory section with temperature mean values similar to those in males, and a post-ovulatory section with clearly higher mean values. Only in post-menopausal women do the mean values not show such bimodality, and hence correspond to those in men. Similarly, in the younger females, the joint mean values of the temperature rhythm and also intra-individual variabilities of the mean value are significantly higher than in males (t = 3.812, p < 10^{-3}; and t = 0.898, p < 10^{-6}, respectively), and likewise higher than in older female subjects.

Finally, sex differentiation exists in the reliabilities of the temperature rhythms, or the overall variabilities: this reliability is 74.73% ± 6.85% in the younger females and 84.10% ± 4.55% in the younger males, and is significant statistically at a fair level (t = 4.119, p < 10^{-3}). The overall variability as expressed in the reliability of the rhythm can be thought to be composed of two components which can be calculated separately, i.e., the variability in the time axis and the variability in the temperature axis. Both these partial variabilities are highly correlated inter–individually (r = 0.777, p < 10^{-5}); this result is not trivial and may give insight into the dynamics of the circadian system. The correlation indicates that a relatively large variability in the time axis corresponds to a large variability in the temperature axis, and vice versa.

Correlations with Temperature Rhythm Amplitude

Most of the rhythm parameters discussed above are mutually correlated among the different subjects. Figure 4 shows the fraction of sleep in the upper diagram and, in the lower diagram, the reliability of the temperature rhythm, both drawn as functions of the temperature amplitude. The upper diagram shows strong positive correlations between the amplitude of the temperature rhythm and the fraction of sleep within the sleep–wake cycle, but only when each sex is considered separately. Thus, within each sex, the duration of sleep is longer the larger the temperature amplitude; however, females sleep considerably longer than males although they have considerably smaller temperature amplitudes. As a consequence, there is no correlation between the two variables when the data from both sexes are considered collectively. The data of the two women with ages above 60 y are positioned among the data from the men and far from the data from the younger women. The strong correlations between the two rhythm parameters presented are more remarkable as these parameters originate from different overt rhythms. In a single overt rhythm, this correlation would be in agreement with postulations of the mathematical model. The validity of the correlation among different overt rhythms, therefore, indicates that not only are the periods identical, but also the amplitudes vary proportionally to each other in the two rhythms. In addition, the relation between the two rhythms is different in male and (pre-menopausal) female subjects. The probability of such a displacement in this relation, and the resulting change in the experimental conditions, have been demonstrated previously (Wever, 1981).

The lower diagram of Figure 4 shows a general positive correlation between amplitude and reliability of the temperature rhythm with coinciding regressions in older and younger female and in male subjects. A rhythm is intra-individually more variable the smaller its amplitude; detailed analyses show that this statement is true only with regard to variations in the time axis whereas variations in the temperature axis are independent of the amplitude. The relationship between amplitude and temporal fluctuations, demonstrated in the lower diagram of Figure 4 for random fluctuations, had been shown previously to also be valid with respect to regulator fluctuations: circadian rhythms adapt more quickly to time shifts of a zeitgeber the smaller the amplitude of the rhythm (Wever, 1980a). A rhythm is the more temporally stable the larger its amplitude, while under the influence of randomly and regularly distributed external disturbances.

The diagrams of Figure 4 emphasize the importance of amplitude in circadian rhythms. In most circadian investigations under constant conditions, the only or, at least, the main emphasis is laid on the period, since the period is the rhythm parameter showing the smallest cycle-to-cycle variations. More generally, the aim of the investigations is to determine the properties of the internal pacemaker, or oscillator, measuring the overt rhythms which are coupled to the pacemaker by more or less variable interconnecting processes. The only parameter of the overt rhythms reflecting unambiguously the corresponding parameter of the basic oscillator is the period; amplitude and all other parameters can be changed by the couplings in ambiguous ways. The applicability of model considerations, regarding the amplitude as well as the period, gives us the assurance that the amplitude as measured in the overt rhythms reflects the amplitude of the basic oscillator which is described by the model. Then, the upper diagram of Figure 4 demonstrates that the amplitude of a rhythm

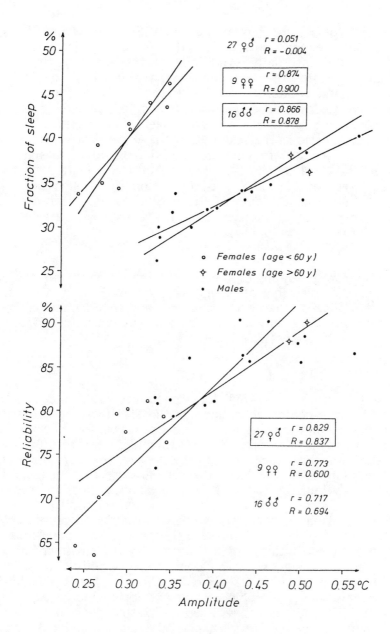

Figure 4

Legend for Figure 4 (On Page 267) Summary from 27 long-term experiments under constant conditions with stable and internally synchronized free-running rhythms. Fraction of sleep within the sleep/wake cycle (above) and reliability of the rhythm of rectal temperature (below) depending on the amplitude of the temperature rhythm. The coefficients of correlation (r: parametric correlation; R: rank-order correlation after Spearman) are each computed from all data and from the data of the (younger) female and male subjects separately. The two regression lines each are computed from the data of the two sexes separately in case of the sleep fraction (above), and from all data in case of reliability (below).

is a marker for the biological need for sleep (it had been deduced above that the fraction of sleep as measured in a time-free environment reflects the need for sleep), and this marker had been shown to be valid not only under constant conditions (cf. Figure 4) but also in the 24-h day (Wever, 1980a).

Other Correlations

Apart from the inter-individual correlations discussed so far, there are further correlations, such as the significant correlations between period and amplitude, on the one hand, and the internal phase relationship between the rhythms of temperature and sleep-wake, on the other. Thus, the longer the period, or the smaller the amplitude, the more the temperature rhythm leads the sleep-wake rhythm, the first correlation with identical regressions, and the latter correlation with different regressions, for the two sexes. In addition, a correlation exists with the intra-individual variability of the internal phase relationship, or the "internal stability" of the rhythms. This variability is smallest, or the internal stability is highest, with values of the period (25 h) and the internal phase relationship itself (+ 1 h) which are just the means of these parameters over all subjects; this variability increases, or the internal stability decreases, with both shortening and lengthening periods and with correspondingly deviating internal phase relationships, respectively. In other words, the free-running rhythms tend to accent parameter values where the internal stability of the system is highest, whereas, with values of the period or the internal phase relationship which deviate considerably from the average, as suggested in patients with depression, the internal stability of the system is significantly reduced.

Further correlations exist between changes in rhythm parameters in individual subjects. In fact, the same correlations can, on principle, also be shown among different subjects; the significance of the intra–individual correlations, however, is frequently much higher than that of the inter–individual correlations because they are not obscured by inter–individual variations. For instance, shortenings of the free–running period as induced by special changes in the environmental conditions are combined, with high probabilities, with increases in both amplitude and mean value, reductions in sleep fractions, changes in wave shape (from skewed to the right to skewed to the left), reductions in the variability of nearly all parameters, but significantly stronger reductions in the variability of wake onset than sleep onset, and several more alterations (Wever, 1968a, 1971). In the mathematical model mentioned above, most of these inter– and intra–individual correlations are consequences of a specific nonlinearity in the restoring force, which is simultaneously responsible for the long–term stability of the rhythms (see above). Possible defects in the physiological correlates to this nonlinearity, therefore, should not only impair the stabilization power but also reduce the correlations mentioned.

The Circadian System as an Amplifier

According to the mathematical model, the steady state amplitude deviates from zero only within a special range of external forces or periods, i.e., the oscillation is self–sustained only within a special "oscillatory range". The amplitude is largest not in the middle of this range but close to its upper limit (i.e., with high external forces, or short periods respectively). Outside this oscillatory range, the feedback mechanism is still in operation but is unable to overcome the increased "friction" of the system completely. It was for this reason that the provocative statement had been made that the circadian system should not be considered as an oscillator but as an (resonance) amplifier – the amplifier can become overmodulated and hence, operate as an oscillator (Wever, 1984a) only under conditions which never occur in nature. Such an unnatural oscillatory state can then be considered as an artifact rather than as the normal state of the circadian system.

In fact, in most animal species tested so far, self-sustained circadian rhythms are present only under special environmental conditions (e.g., frequently only with in a remarkably small range of intensities of constant illumination). Outside of this range, the experiments show dampened circadian oscillations, but with a remarkably small coefficient of dampening indicating unequivocably an intact feedback mechanism. Also, after several internal alterations (e.g., pinealectomy in some avian species, or SCN-lesion in some mammals) such a state can be shown: the animals do not show self-sustained rhythms under constant conditions, but the integrity of the feedback mechanism can be demonstrated under zeitgeber conditions (Wever, 1980b). In healthy human subjects, the absence of any self-sustained circadian rhythmicity had not yet been demonstrated. In patients with special diseases, it is not unlikely that such a state is more frequent than in healthy subjects. If present, or if an amplitude of a free-running rhythm cannot be measured, a weak oscillation strength or a strong "friction" in the concerned rhythms would be indicated.

INTERNAL RHYTHM CONTROL:
INTERNALLY DESYNCHRONIZED RHYTHMS

Heretofore, only properties of free-running rhythms have been discussed where all measured overt rhythms ran, in the steady state, with coinciding periods and, as a result, with temporally constant internal phase relationships; i.e., the rhythms were internally synchronized. Infrequently, in subjects tested under constant conditions, the overt rhythms of different variables run, in the steady state, with different periods, i.e., internally desynchronized (Aschoff, Gereke and Wever, 1967). Character-istically in this rhythm state, the internal phase relationship between different overt rhythms is not temporally constant but varies from cycle to cycle (Wever, 1975a). This state of the rhythm has been observed in 48 subjects, all of which exhibit the overt rhythms of deep body temperature and of most other autonomous functions with the normal circadian period of about 25 h, whereas the sleep–wake rhythm and several more functions showed periods which deviated considerably from 25 h, i.e., by about 5 h or more. In the present series of experiments, sleep–wake periods between 12.5 h and 65 h have been observed.

In about a third of the experiments with internal desynchronization, this state occurred from the beginning of the experiment. In some experiments however, this state occurred spontaneously after one to three weeks of internally synchronized rhythms. Thus we are given the chance to compare the two states, internal synchronization and desynchronization (the reverse spontaneous transition, from internal desynchronization to synchronization, has never been observed). Figure 5 shows two examples of such experiments. The right diagram shows results from a subject whose rhythms initially ran internally synchronized for two weeks, then, the rhythms of sleep–wake and rectal temperature separated spontaneously with immediate alterations in the periods: the period of sleep–wake lengthened considerably while the period of the temperature rhythm shortened slightly. The left diagram shows results from a subject whose rhythms likewise ran internally synchronized initially, then, the sleep–wake period shortened considerably while the temperature period lengthened slightly.

Changes in Period

The right diagram of Figure 5 is characteristic of twenty experiments with internal desynchronization by lengthening. During the initial state of internal synchronization, the joint period is significantly longer than the period of rhythms that do not desynchronize in the long run (25.47 h $\pm$ 0.54 h vs. 25.02 h $\pm$ 0.51 h, t = 2.878, p < 0.01). With the transition to internal desynchronization, the sleep–wake period lengthened by definition; it is, however, meaningful that the temperature period shortened consistently and significantly (by 0.63 h $\pm$ 0.40 h, t = 7.047, p < 10^{-6}). Simultaneously, the fraction of sleep within the sleep–wake cycle decreased from 32.25% $\pm$ 5.72% to 28.36% $\pm$ 6.26%; here too the intra–individual change is fairly significant (t = 3.500, p < 0.001). The left diagram of Figure 4 is characteristic of thirteen experiments with internal desynchronization by shortening. Here, the joint period before the transition to internal desynchronization is, with 24.55 h ± 0.23 h, significantly shorter than the periods of rhythms that do not desynchronize in the long run (t = 2.848, p < 0.01). After the spontaneous separation, the temperature period is significantly lengthened (by 0.35 h ± 0.14 h, t = 9.170, p < 10⁻⁶): the fraction of sleep decreases significantly (by 4.86% ± 2.99%; t = 5.861, p < 0.001). The appraisal of initial period indicates, with high probability, whether or not the rhythms will desynchronize internally later on; and if so, whether they will desynchronize by lengthening or by shortening. Moreover, inspection of the temperature rhythms alone is sufficient to decide about the state of the rhythm; the temperature rhythm is not influenced by naps or by behavioral cues as the sleep–wake rhythm possibly can be (Wever, 1984c).

While the periods of the temperature rhythms before the separation differ from each other at a high level of significance according to the direction of later desynchronization (p < 10⁻⁵) (see above), they cannot be differentiated after the separation: during internal desynchronization by lengthening, the temperature periods have a length of 24.84 h ± 0.23 h; their length during internal desynchronization by shortening is 24.90 h ± 0.16 h. Moreover, while the periods of the temperature rhythms before the separation show significant sex differences as discussed above, they cannot be differentiated by sex after the separation: the temperature periods of the 12 female subjects have a length of 24.85 h ± 0.24 h, and the temperature periods of the 21 male subjects of 24.87 h ± 0.19 h. The distribution of the intrinsic temperature periods is indeed remarkably small; the pooling of all 33 experiments result in a mean intrinsic temperature period (± SD) of 24.86 h ± 0.21 h. Since the intrinsic temperature periods do not show any sex difference; the measured sex differences in internally synchronized rhythms must only be due to an exclusive and considerable sex difference in the intrinsic periods of the sleep–wake rhythm (Wever, 1984c). (As deduced later, the joint period in internally synchronized rhythms is a compromise between the intrinsic periods of the (strong) temperature rhythm and the (weak) sleep–wake rhythm). The additional consideration of the 15

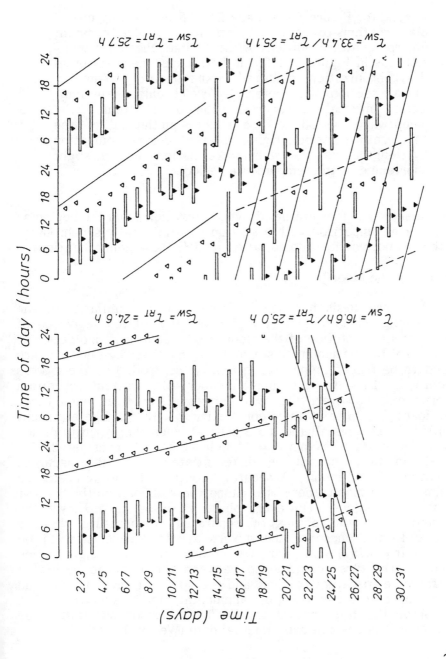

Figure 5

273

Legend for Figure 5 (On Page 273) Free-running circadian rhythms of two subjects living under constant
environmental conditions without time cues. Designations as in Figure 1, left. In both experiments internal
desynchronization occurred spontaneously after an
initial section with internally synchronized rhythms.
Left: internal desynchronization by shortening the
sleep/wake period (and a slight lengthening of the
temperature period); right: internal desynchronization
by lengthening the sleep/wake period (and a slight
shortening of the temperature period).

experiments showing internal desynchronization from the beginning
(i.e., where comparison with a section with internally synchronized
rhythms is not possible) do not at all modify these generalizations.

Control by the Moon?

The hypothesis had been offered that the similarity of the
free-running period of man (τ = 25.01 h $\pm$ 0.51 h) to the period of
the apparent revolution of the moon (Y = 24.83 h) is an indication of
the control by the moon; this would suggest that rhythms that are
stated to be free-running are, in reality, controlled by the moon's
revolution. Due to the high number of constant condition
experiments, however, the two periods differ from each other
significantly in spite of their conformity ($p < 10^{-4}$). The argument
mentioned becomes all the more critical when the intrinsic period
of the temperature rhythm (τ = 24.86 h $\pm$ 0.21 h) is considered; this
period, in fact, cannot be differentiated from the apparent
revolution of the moon. A separate control of the temperature
rhythm by the moon, therefore, cannot be excluded on the basis of
period values alone. However, phase analyses have shown the
distribution of the phases of separated temperature rhythms
relative to the phase of the moon's apparent revolution to be
random ($r = 0.182$) and far from any statistical significance
($p > 0.1$). The close coincidence between the intrinsic period of
separated temperature rhythms and the apparent revolution of the
moon, therefore, can only be accidental; the assumption of a
control of the temperature rhythm by the moon has thus to be
rejected on the basis of experimental data (Wever, 1979a).

Oscillator Interactions

It is of particular importance to the state of internal desynchronization that its investigation gives insights into the dynamics of circadian rhythmicity which cannot be obtained by the inspection of internally synchronized rhythms. Only internally desynchronized rhythms show conclusively that the circadian system relies upon more than one controlling oscillator all of which continually interact. This interaction, in itself, is a contributory determinant of the properties of the system. As long as the interaction between the different oscillators leads to mutual synchronization (i.e., in the state of internal synchronization), the system appears to be controlled by only one oscillator; properties of the interaction, therefore cannot be studied during this state. Properties of the interaction mentioned can be studied only when the interaction is, indeed, present but unable to synchronize the different oscillators mutually (i.e., in the state of internal desynchronization). An intact interaction between the different oscillators within the circadian system is a precondition for the undisturbed functioning of the system; a weakening of this interaction facilitates the occurrence of rhythm disorders which may lead to adverse effects upon the subject concerned. In the context of this paper, therefore, it is of particular interest to evaluate the properties of this interaction.

Naps as an Explanation?

Owing to the practical and theoretical importance of the state of internal desynchronization, it must be determined whether this state really exists, or is simply simulated by an erroneous assessment of naps. It is striking that sleep–wake periods during the state of internal desynchronization by lengthening are, on the average, twice as long as during the state of desynchronization by shortening. This integral relationship could, in fact, arouse suspicion that erroneously classified sleeps, not real differences in the rhythms, form the basis of this differentiation. According to this assumption, every second sleep during desynchronization by shortening should be considered as a nap. This objection, however, can finally be rejected by considering only the rhythms of deep body temperature which are not controlled behaviorally as the sleep episodes can be. As discussed earlier, changes in these rhythms unambiguously indicate internal desynchronization to be a genuine effect. Changes in the period of the temperature rhythm consistently counteract changes in the sleep–wake periods.

The claim that internal desynchronization, in general, is simulated by naps (Zulley and Campbell, 1985) presents a more critical issue. The concept mentioned can be applied, though with some arbitrariness, to a few experiments where sections with internal synchronization alternate with interposed long cycles. Figure 6/III shows an example of such an experiment; the other diagrams of Figure 6 (I and II) show two other typical but differing examples of internal desynchronization by lengthening (of course, there are continuous transitions between the three typical experiments). However, to use such a claim to refute the "desynchronized" classification of all such subjects would involve a pattern of assumptions regarding erroneous sleep and nap classifications which is entirely too arbitrary to be plausible. Even a very rigid application of the concept of erroneously classified naps would only slightly reduce the percentage of experiments showing internal desynchronization and such percentages are anyway dubious as absolute population estimates since the sample is so self–selected. Rather, it is of great interest to show that internal desynchronization is possible, on principle, independent of the frequency of its occurrence. The fundamental possibility of internal desynchronization in human circadian rhythms is not affected by the concept that a few sleep episodes may be classified erroneously as naps. Because of the importance of internal desynchronization, a detailed analysis of the three exemplary cases as presented in Figure 6 will be given later (cf. Figure 8). Before speculating about such details, it would seem to be appropriate to consider the implications of naps.

In several types of experiment subjects were recommended to avoid naps; this was particularly true in experiments with predetermined "day–night" protocols of any mode. In others, the subjects were free to nap at any time but to indicate every sleep, particularly in experiments under constant conditions without any time cues. During initial experiments, in order to avoid possible ambiguities in the results, the subjects had been asked not to nap; subsequently the six preliminary experiments under constant conditions with polygraphic sleep recordings (the preparation of the

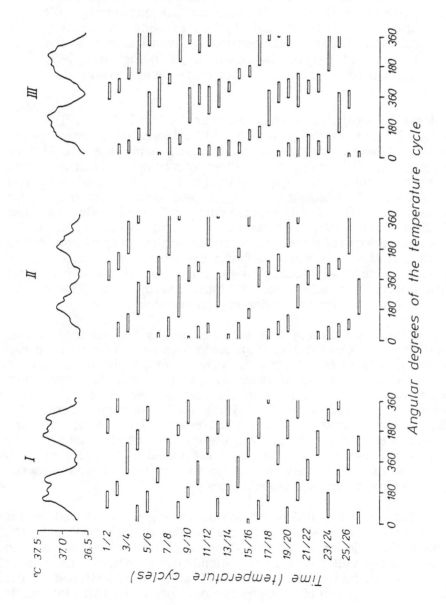

Figure 6

Legend for Figure 6 (On Page 277) Three typical
examples of free–running and internally desynchronized
rhythms, with weak (I), medium (II) and strong (III)
interaction between the rhythms of body temperature
and sleep/wake (with continuous transitions between
the typical cases). Designations as in Figure 1, left;
upper border: educed cycles of rectal temperature.

subjects for sleep lasted about an hour [Zulley, 1976, 1979]) did the
same. In the majority of the hitherto existing experiments
performed under constant conditions, including the majority of
experiments with polygraphic sleep recordings (performed with
advanced techniques, e.g., telemetry), naps were expressly
permitted. Consistently, the experimental strategy was
maintained that in all experiments performed under constant
conditions, the number of meals per cycle and also the types of the
meals were expressly free; no direction for the preparation for the
meals was given. In about half of these experiments, in fact, the
subjects occasionally took naps (in about 40% of the experiments
with internally synchronized rhythms, and in about 55% of the
experiments with internally desynchronized rhythms).

It was remarkable that subjects usually had no doubt about
whether a sleep was a real night sleep or a nap. Frequently a nap
lasted 30 min to 60 min, much shorter than a night sleep while in
several cases naps lasted much longer and, in rare cases, even
longer than the night's sleep of the same subject (one subject took
regularly repeated naps of 15.5 h $\pm$ 0.6 h duration whereas his
night's sleep lasted 10.5 h $\pm$ 1.3 h; Wever, 1979a). Apparently the
subjects were unable to estimate the duration of their naps (in the
case mentioned, the naps had been estimated to last 15 min to 30
min). In extreme cases, the subjective differentiation between
night sleep and naps was unambiguous.

The objective differentiation between night sleep and naps is
unambiguous as well, since the subjects switched off the
illumination during a night sleep but not during a nap; in
experiments under constant illumination where the main
illumination could not be switched off, all subjects switched off the
bed light during the night sleep but not during the nap. Indeed, it

can be argued that the differential control of the illumination in the two types of sleep reflects behavioral conventions rather than biological necessities of different preferential light intensities. However, analogs to such behavior can also be observed in animal circadian experiments (e.g., in finches – Aschoff, Saint Paul and Wever, 1968) where the daily activity patterns frequently showed biomodal patterns.

Another discrimination between night sleep and nap is possible by evaluating the phase position of the sleep relative to the rhythm of deep body temperature. As mentioned above, it is a characteristic of internally desynchronized rhythms that the night sleep can adopt every phase relationship to the temperature rhythm (though mostly with differing frequencies); the naps, on the other hand, are positioned always around a temperature minimum (with only a few exceptions among several hundred naps). This is in contrast to the position of the (less frequent) naps in internally synchronized rhythms which can be only close to a temperature maximum (the minimum positions are held consistently by the night sleeps). From this observation and also from the results of several more experiments, the assumption had arisen that night sleep and naps are controlled (at least in part) by different physiological processes; the incidence of naps is very closely related to the rhythm of deep body temperature but not the incidence of night sleep. Additional evidence for differential coordination of night sleep and naps will be given later in the context of zeitgeber effects (cf. Figure 12). Nevertheless, in order to avoid arbitrary decisions concerning the state of a rhythm, all period analyses are based on a differentiation between wake, on the one hand, and sleep, on the other, independent of whether the sleep is a night sleep or a nap according to the criteria mentioned above.

Finally, a discrimination between internally synchronized and desynchronized rhythms is possible on the basis of another type of analysis, independent of naps: a distinct alteration in the length of the sleep–wake cycle with the occurrence of internal desynchronization is always combined with a similar distinct alteration in the lengths of all subsections within the full cycle. The secondary alteration does not concern only wake and sleep episodes; it also concerns the lengths of the naps and the intervals between wake onset and nap onset; furthermore, it concerns as well the intervals between the meals (all subjects were expressly free to select the number and types of the meals and the intervals between the meals), estimations of the duration of an hour, and various more intervals. All these subsections within a full sleep–wake cycle lengthen or shorten in unison with the full cycle (Wever, 1975a, 1979a; Aschoff, et al., 1984; and Aschoff, 1985). Consequently, even before the onset of a possible nap it can be predicted whether the ongoing wake episode is a part of an internally synchronized or desynchronized cycle (Wever, 1975b). The parallel alterations of the full cycle and its subsections supply us with clear evidence that, in the state of internal desynchronization, the complete sleep–wake rhythm including all its subdivisions runs distinctly slower in the state of internal desynchronization by lengthening and distinctly faster in the state of internal desynchronization by shortening the sleep–wake cycle than in the state of internal synchronization. All these significant results are in clear contradiction to the assumption that internal desynchronization is simulated by erroneously classified naps and, hence, that the sleep–wake rhythms run, on the average, with the same period as the rhythm of deep body temperature (i.e., always with an average period close to 25 h).

That a long wake episode is followed by a normally structurized sleep episode of likewise unusual duration, is another indication of the dramatic retardation of the whole sleep–wake rhythm in the state of internal desynchronization by lengthening. In the present experimental series spontaneous wake episodes up to 45 h without any nap have been observed, without any conscious realization by the subjects. If such a long wake episode were due to an overriding of sleep episode (e.g., because the subject was reading a thrilling book), sleep deprivation would be the necessary consequence. Sleep deprivation, however, is physiologically recognizable in the structure of a sleep which shows the common recovery phenomena (e.g., REM rebound) and lasts longer than a normal sleep episode. Therefore, the polygraphic sleep analyses which display an absence of recovery phenomena in such cases (Wever, 1985b) give further evidence that the length of the wake episode can only be due to a retardation of the whole sleep–wake system (and not to a sleep deprivation per se).

Interactions Between the Controlling Oscillators

After having clarified the existence of internal desynchronization, one can then evaluate the properties of the interaction between the different controlling oscillators. Such an interaction is obvious in the course of the rhythms without any additional analyses. Figure 5 showed that, after the spontaneous occurrence of internal desynchronization, both separated over rhythms run with scalloping phases. As can be seen particularly in the sleep–wake rhythm of the example on the right, the speed of the rhythm fluctuates periodically with a superimposed modulation period of three to four cycles; the indicated period of 33.4 h is only an average (the actual cycle lengths vary between 26.3 h and 41.3 h). The lengths of the wake and sleep episodes vary even more (between 20.0 h and 31.3 h, and between 4.5 h and 17.0 h respectively). The rhythm of deep body temperature shows a similar scalloping of phase (with the same absolute and, according to the shorter temperature period, a larger relative modulation period). Moreover, the temperature rhythms display, analogous to the fluctuations in the wake and sleep episodes, a regular fluctuation in circadian amplitude. The amplitude of the superimposed modulation of the phases and amplitudes is a measure of the strength of the mutual interaction between the two rhythms.

Other indications of the mutual interaction are the products of special analyses. Several parameters of the sleep–wake and the temperature cycle dependent upon the phase relationship between both cycles are, on the one hand, positions and durations of the wake and sleep episodes, and, on the other hand, position, amplitude and waveform of the temperature cycle. If the parameters of the sleep–wake cycle are referred to the temperature cycle, several types of references can be applied, as exemplified in Figure 7; all diagrams of this figure originate from the same data of a typical experiment. In the uppermost diagram wake and sleep onsets are referred to the actual minimum of body temperature that is closest to the episode onset under consideration (Zulley, 1976; Zulley and Schulz, 1980; Zulley, Wever and Aschoff, 1981; and Zulley and Wever, 1982). A disadvantage of this method is that the length of the actual temperature cycle, or the interval between successive temperature minima, is not constant, while the interval between an episode onset and the closest temperature minimum is always related to the constant average period taken to be the 360° of the full cycle. One advantage is that predictions, e.g., concerning the duration of an episode (cf. Figure 8), can be made immediately after the onset of the episode, i.e., during the actual experiment as it runs. In the lower most diagram wake and sleep onsets are referred to the minimum of the educed temperature rhythm; this method having been used elsewhere (Czeisler, 1978; and Czeisler, et al., 1980). An advantage of this method is that the temperature minima are equidistant so that the coordination of an episode onset is unambiguous in all cases, while a disadvantage is that the educing can be calculated only after the complete experiment is terminated, so that possible predictions can be made only after the end of the experiment when the result to be predicted is already known. The calculation of the middle diagram is based on the assumption that the course of body temperature is determined not only by a circadian component but additionally by the "masking effect" (directly evoked alterations in body temperature due to the transitions between wake and sleep; see below).

In internally desynchronized rhythms the masking effect can be evaluated separately and, hence, subtracted from the total temperature fluctuations. The remaining "demasked" temperature rhythm, i.e., the pure circadian component, forms the reference for the episode onsets in the middle diagrams (Wever, 1985a). The three diagrams are similar in general but differ in detail: the reference to the actually measured temperature minima (uppermost diagram) leads to the most highly structured figures, particularly the wake onsets which are more strongly concentrated in the rising part of the temperature cycle than in the other diagrams. Correspondingly, the range of phases in the descending part of the temperature cycle, within which wake onset never occurs, is largest. Furthermore, sleep onset is preferably positioned shortly before an actual temperature minimum but shortly after an educed minimum. All these differences are not peculiarities of a single experiment but characteristic of a great variety of experiments with internally desynchronized rhythms (Zulley, Wever and Aschoff, 1981).

Temperature — Sleep/Wake Interdependence

Figure 7 shows that, independent of the mode of reference, the probability for an episode onset is usually not identical for all phases of the temperature cycle. The interdependence between the rhythms of deep body temperature and sleep–wake as expressed in Figure 7, in fact, is typical of the majority (but not all) of internally desynchronized rhythms; specifically, it characterizes an interaction between the two rhythms of medium strength. More indications of these interactions are presented in Figure 8 for three different intensities of the interaction. For the sake of consistency, Figure 8 includes analyses from the same three exemplary experiments the courses of which have already been presented in Figure 6. Figure 8/II characterizes an interaction of medium strength (as observed in Figure 7); Figure 8/I is typical for internally desynchronized rhythms with a weak interaction (about 15% of the relevant experiments); and Figure 8/III is typical for an interaction between the two rhythms with a particularly strong interaction (measured again in about 15% of the relevant experiments). Again for the sake of consistency, all parameters of the sleep–wake rhythms in Figure 8 are referenced to the educed temperature cycle (cf. lower most diagram of Figure 7). Throughout Figure 8 depending on the phase of the educed temperature cycle (with the mean period taken as 360°) one can observe: (1) the educed cycle of rectal temperature with the formally computed standard deviations among each of about 26 successive temperature cycles; (2) the probability of the subject being awake or asleep; this probability is largest around the temperature maximum and smallest around the temperature minimum; (3) the frequencies of wake and sleep onsets according to Figure 7; the paths of the frequencies correspond most to those as discussed in the context of Figure 7; (4) the duration of the sleep and (5) wake episodes depending on the phase of the midpoint of the respective episode. The measuring points from the 20 episodes each do not cover the full temperature cycle uniformly but show symmetrical courses; when related to onset or end of the respective episodes, the distributions of the episode lengths are asymmetrical; cf. Figure 9. The episodes are longest when their midpoints coincide with the minimum value in rectal temperature and shortest at the phase of the temperature maximum; the distribution of the sleep lengths is occasionally shifted to earlier phases of the temperature cycle.

All parameters of the sleep–wake rhythm presented are independent of the phase of the temperature cycle with a weak, or nearly missing, interaction between the rhythms of rectal temperature and sleep–wake (Figure 8/I). The probability of being asleep fluctuates irregularly and does not depend on the temperature phase at any meaningful level of significance; by chance, the probability of being asleep is smallest around the temperature minimum and not the maximum as in the other cases. As a result, the two rhythms run separated with different periods without showing the regular scalloping commonly characteristic of internally desynchronized rhythms (cf. Figure 6/I). In the two other examples with increasing strength of interaction between the rhythms of rectal temperature and sleep–wake (Figures 8/II and III), all parameters of the sleep–wake rhythm show rhythmic dependencies on the phase of the temperature rhythm, with amplitudes that intensify with increasing interaction strength. The probability of being asleep fluctuates regularly between 56 and 85 in the case of medium interaction (Figure 8/II) and between 38 and 93% in the case of strong interaction (Figure 8/III). Similar relations hold true for the other parameters. In addition, the stronger the interaction between the two rhythms under consideration, the greater the fluctuation of the frequencies of the episode onsets and the durations of the episodes depending on the phase of the temperature cycle; consequently, the separated rhythms run with marked scallopings in phase.

Other differences remain among the three types of internal desynchronization with respect to the variability of the sleep–wake rhythm and the temporal sequences of these variabilities. The variability among successive sleep–wake cycles is about twice as large as in internally synchronized rhythms (cf. Wever, 1984b) in the example with weak interaction (Figure 8/I), about 3.5 times as large in the example with moderate strength of interaction (Figure 8/II), and about 5 times as large in the example with strong interaction. Moreover, the variability of wake onset increases at a greater rate than that of sleep onset. While sleep onset is consistently the most variable phase in internally synchronized rhythms (Wever, 1984b), it shows a similar variability to wake onset in the experiment underlying Figure 8/I but a considerably smaller variability than wake onset in Figure 8/III. In other words, the ratio between the variabilities of sleep and wake onset expressing this asymmetry is 1.447 ± 0.419 in the case of internally synchronized rhythms (Wever, 1984b), but is only 0.95 in the case of Figure 8/I and 0.68 in the other examples. In adherence to this reversed asymmetry in the onset variabilities, the correlations between the lengths of adjacent wake and sleep episodes reverse. In internally synchronized rhythms, a high negative serial correlation exists between wake and following sleep ($r_S = -0.527 \pm 0.221$) but only a low one between wake and preceding sleep ($r_S = -0.119 \pm 0.214$; Wever, 1984b). The latter serial correlation increases characteristically with increasing interaction strength in internally desynchronized rhythms. It is $r_S = -0.26$ in case of Figure 8/I, $r_S = -0.40$ in case of Figure 8/II and $r_S = -0.56$ in case of Figure 8/III. On the other hand, the serial correlation between wake and following sleep diminishes with increasing interaction strength, from $r_S = -0.27$ in case of Figure 8/I down to zero in case of Figure 8/III. The other serial correlation between successive sleep–wake cycles is similar to that in internally synchronized rhythms ($r_S = -0.402 \pm 1.32$; Wever, 1984b) in the case of weak interaction between internally desynchronized rhythms ($r_S = -0.42$ in Figure 8/I), indicating the separate oscillatory origin of the sleep–wake rhythm: it reduces with increasing interaction strength and is close to zero ($r_S = -0.09$) in the case of strong interaction (Figure 8/III).

It may be confusing to learn that the example with the strong interaction (Figure 8/III) is typical only for a minority of experiments, while this state seems to be generally representative of internal desynchronization, or, at least, to dominate, in studies of other authors (Czeisler, et al., 1980; and Zulley, Wever and Aschoff, 1981). The reason for the apparent discrepancy seems to be the differential burdening of the subjects in the different studies. The greater the behavioral stress of the subjects, the more frequently internal desynchronization occurs (see below), and the stronger seems to be the interaction between the rhythms of body temperature and sleep–wake. In fact, the other studies mentioned are each based on small samples consisting mainly of experiments with continuous polygraphic sleep recordings (Zulley, Wever and Aschoff, 1981) or even of experiments where, in addition to the EEG, blood samples have been taken at short intervals (Czeisler, et al., 1980). Both experimental manipulations have been shown to increase the psychological burdening of the subjects. Such a correlation can be confirmed in the much larger sample of about 50 experiments with internal desynchronization upon which the statements of Figure 8 are based. The experiments with strong interaction (Figure 8/III) are only those with complete polygraphic sleep recordings or with subjects with considerably high scores of neuroticism; subjects without sleep recordings and normal or low scores of neuroticism generally show interactions of low or medium strength.

Provided that the correlations just discussed can be confirmed in larger samples of experiments, the closer consideration of internally desynchronized rhythms can help to find a predictor of the subjective burdening of a subject, whether of internal (e.g., neuroticism) or external origin (e.g., stressing experimental conditions). The stronger the internal interaction between the separated rhythms of body temperature and sleep-wake the more the subject is burdened behaviorally. The interaction strength can be measured, for instance, in the amplitude of the fluctuations in the episode lengths, or in the serial correlations between the lengths of sleep and following wake, or in several more parameters of the sleep-wake rhythm which, when measured under standard conditions, may simultaneously serve as measures for the degree of any mental disease.

MASKING EFFECTS

Introduction

Masking effects are the directly evoked alterations of a variable generated by changes of another variable such that the probability of being awake is greater the higher the body temperature, independent of the circadian phase of the sleep-wake cycle, and that the body temperature is generally higher during wake than sleep, again more or less independent of the circadian phase of the temperature cycle. Masking effects can be considered, in a rough approximation, to be superimposed over the corresponding circadian fluctuations and both manifestations of the masking effect will be treated below.

Temperature on Sleep–Wake Cycle

The use of model considerations simplifies the understanding of the masking effects of body temperature on the sleep–wake cycle. The alternation between the two discrete states, wake and sleep, is generated by a continuous oscillation across a threshold; as long as the basic oscillation proceeds above the fixed threshold, it describes "wake" as long as it proceeds below the threshold it describes "sleep". In masking, the basic oscillation is superimposed upon by another oscillation that moves proportional to the temperature rhythm; only the threshold passings of the combined oscillation are considered. In a masking effect of medium strength, such as Figure 9, with a superimposed "masking oscillation" of half the amplitude of the original basic sleep–wake oscillation calculated with the mean temperature cycle taken for 360° and the mean sleep–wake cycle taken for 485.5° (corresponding to, for instance, 25.0 h and 33.8 h), wake and sleep episodes are determined according to passings of the common threshold. The mean value of the masking oscillation is selected so that it does not affect the mean sleep fraction. The diagrams of the middle line where the lengths of wake (left) and sleep (right) are referenced to the midpoints of the respective episode relative to the phase of the temperature cycle are most elucidating. The episodes are longest when their midpoints coincide with the minimum values of the temperature rhythm, and they are shortest when their midpoints coincide with the temperature maxima. In other words, the angular velocity of the sleep–wake rhythm is not constant but alters parallel to the temperature rhythm; it is nothing but a trivial consequence of geometry that the references to onsets or ends of the respective episodes result in asymmetric dependencies of the episode lengths (uppermost and third line of diagrams). It is obvious from Figure 9 that stronger masking effects lead to ambiguities, where particular temperature phases are related to long and to short episodes.

Figure 9 demonstrates that consideration of the masking effect alone is sufficient to produce a dependency of the episode lengths on the phase of the temperature cycle which is similar (but not identical) to that observed in real experiments (cf. Figure 8). The dependency of the probability of being awake (or asleep) Figure 9, second diagrams from bottom) shows only a general path but is rather dissimilar to observed results in detail (cf. Figure 8) when only the masking effect is considered. This is clear evidence that the additional consideration of the other component of interaction, the oscillatory interaction, does not only change the relations quantitatively but also qualitatively such that only the collective consideration of all interaction components leads to a reasonable description of experimental results. Moreover, Figure 9 demonstrates how the changes in the reference phases of the episodes influence the pattern of the dependency of the episode lengths on the temperature phase in a schematic form. Since shifts in the patterns are based on simple geometric laws, equivalents in the schemes and in measurements of real experiments are possible without difficulty.

Sleep–Wake Cycle on Temperature

The masking effect in the other direction, i.e., from sleep–wake to body temperature, had been discussed previously (Wever, 1985a). When continuous temperature measurements (which display a period close to 25 h) are synchronized to the instants of wake and sleep onset (which demonstrate in the internally desynchronized rhythms a period considerably deviating from 25 h), the circadian rhythmicity disappears by desynchronization, and a regular mean course remains that is, on the average, higher by 0.28°C ± 0.06°C during wake than sleep. Immediately following the transitions between wake and sleep, there are overshoots in temperature of about 50% decaying during each one to two hours. Every transition from sleep to wake, therefore, is accompanied by an immediate rise in temperature of about 0.45°C, and every transition from wake to sleep is accompanied by an immediate decline in temperature of about 0.40°C. The masking effect also reduces temperature rhythms within the analyzed period, separately from temperature data obtained exclusively during the wake episodes and from temperature data obtained exclusively during the sleep episodes; again, the differential periods of the rhythms of temperature and sleep–wake makes this possible. The results are two educed temperature cycles, the wake temperature and the sleep temperature cycle, commonly running parallel except for individual details but separated by the mean masking effect of 0.28°C ± 0.06°C. Only a closer inspection shows a small phase dependency of the masking effect which is consistently slightly larger during the descending than ascending section of the

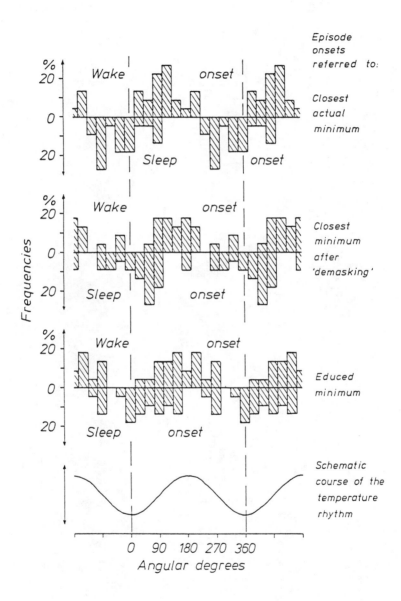

Figure 7

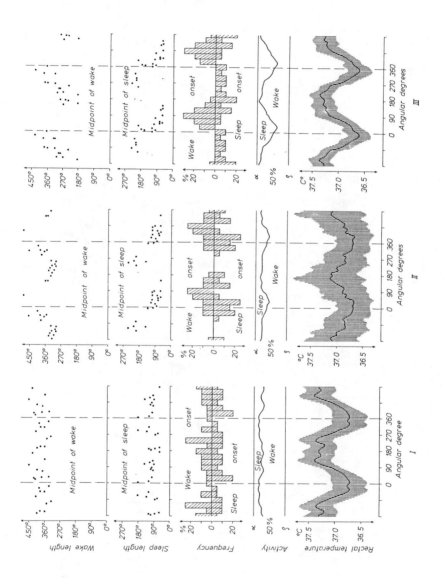

Figure 8

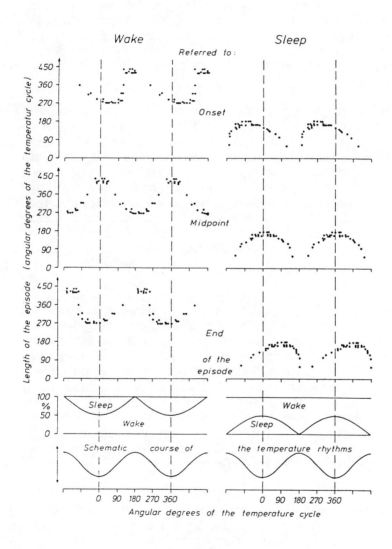

Figure 9

Legend for Figure 7 (On Page 289) Analyses from a typical experiment with free–running and internally desynchronized rhythms (medium strength of the internal interaction). Presented are the frequencies of wake and sleep onsets depending on the phase of the temperature cycle, computed for different phase references. Lowermost diagram: schematic course of rectal temperature (the precise form of the educed cycles would be slightly different for the three diagrams).

Legend for Figure 8 (On Page 290) Analyses from the three typical experiments of Figure 6. Presented are (from top to bottom): durations of the wake and sleep episodes depending on the phases of the midpoints of the respective episode within the educed temperature cycle; frequencies of wake and sleep onsets depending on the phase of the educed temperature cycle, and the probability of finding the subject in a wake or a sleep episode depending on the phase of the educed temperature cycle. Lowermost diagrams: educed temperature cycles (with standard deviations), for reference.

Legend for Figure 9 (On Page 291) Theoretical calculations of the masking effect (of medium strength) from body temperature to sleep–wake (see text for details) in an internally desynchronized rhythm. Presented are (from top to bottom): durations of the wake and sleep episodes depending on the phase of the temperature rhythm, with the onsets, midpoints and ends of the respective episodes for reference; probability of encountering a wake or a sleep episode at each respective phase of the temperature cycle, and the temperature cycles for reference.

temperature cycle. This phase dependency is further expressed in that the sleep temperature cycle is consistently phase advanced relative to the wake temperature cycle, on the average by $13° \pm 4°$ (or, normalized to a 24–h day, by $52 \text{ min} \pm 15 \text{ min}$). Both the masking and the phase advance of the sleep temperature cycle are significant statistically at high levels ($p < 10^{-5}$ each; Wever, 1985a).

Figure 10 presents masking effects obtained as above but not only with respect to body temperature. On the left, Figure 10 shows period analyses from an experiment where a subject was kept for 18 days under constant bright illumination (3,000 lux to 5,000 lux) and subsequently, under constant illumination of normal intensity for 10 more days). The analyses show an internally desynchronized rhythm; sleep–wake shows a dominant period of 31.5 h (as in all other experiments, of course, naps had been classified as sleep) and the autonomous functions show a common, and considerably shorter, period of 25.0 h; all rhythms with the indicated periods are sufficiently reliable. In the second part of this experiment, the rhythm ran internally synchronized with the common period (sleep–wake as well as the autonomous functions) of 24.7 h. In the right part of Figure 10, educed cycles of the few representative rhythms are presented; from the three autonomous functions, the educing had been calculated not only by using all data (solid lines) but also from the wake (broken lines) and the sleep data only (dotted lines). Rectal temperature shows the known masking effect. The sleep temperature cycle has a course similar to the wake temperature cycle but is, on the average, lower by 0.40°C and phase advanced by 1.1 h in comparison to the wake cycle. Urinary cortisol shows a similar masking effect. The wake and sleep curves run with similar paths except for individual details, and the wake curve travels, on the average, 75% higher than the sleep curve and is phase delayed by 2.8 h relative to the sleep curve. Additionally, the urinary electrolytes show, masking effects of the same type as rectal temperature and cortisol, with wake excretions that are, in the rough average, about 100% higher than the sleep excretions.

Melatonin

In the right diagram of Figure 10, furthermore, educed cycles of urinary melatonin (measured as aMT6s; Arendt, et al., 1985) are presented. These melatonin cycles show a completely different pattern. On the average, melatonin excretion is higher during sleep than wake, and the wake and sleep curves are rather dissimilar. Here, however, the differences in the melatonin excretion are due to the suppression of this excretion by bright light (Lewy, et al., 1980) and not to a masking effect in the common sense. On the one hand, under illumination of normal intensity where the melatonin excretion in the pineal should not be suppressed, melatonin does not show any masking effect (see

294

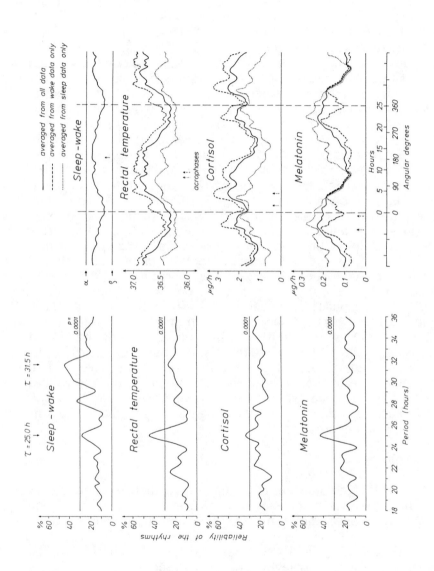

Figure 10

Legend for Figure 10 (On Page 294) Analyses from an experiment with free-running and internally desynchronized rhythms, performed under constant bright illumination. Presented are results from the rhythms of sleep/wake, rectal temperature, urinary cortisol and urinary melatonin (measured as aMT6s). Left: period analyses. Right: educed cycles, computed from all data each, from data obtained exclusively during the wake episodes, and from data obtained exclusively during the sleep episodes. The differences between the wake and sleep cycles in rectal temperature and cortisol constitute the masking effects (they are more or less independent of the intensity of the constant illumination); in melatonin, this difference is due to the suppression of the melatonin excretion by bright light during the wake episodes (with open eyes) but not during the sleep episodes (with closed eyes) (under constant illumination of normal intensity, the wake and sleep cycles of melatonin coincide, hence, there is no masking effect in melatonin).

below). On the other hand, the suppression of melatonin excretion should be effective only during wake when the subject stays active with open eyes, and not during sleep when the subject has consistently closed eyes; i.e., the sleep melatonin curve comes only from periods where the subject was exposed subjectively to only dim illumination in spite of the objectively bright illumination.

In light of these considerations, the sleep melatonin curve must be expected to be higher than the wake curve; it is rather surprising that there is a wake melatonin curve at all, and not a continuous suppression during wake where the subject is fully exposed to the bright illumination. During a quarter of the full cycle (from 50° to 140° in Figure 10), the wake and sleep melatonin cycles coincide; it must be concluded that light is ineffective in suppressing melatonin during this section. During the other parts of the cycle, in fact, melatonin is partially but not fully suppressed during wake in comparison to sleep. It is worth mentioning that the sleep cycle is phase advanced relative to the wake cycle (by three hours). During the second section of the same experiment where the subject was continuously exposed to light of an intensity below the melatonin threshold (and where his rhythm was internally synchronized), the melatonin excretion was generally higher than during the first section under bright light (on the average, by 57%; Wever, 1986). This example demonstrates that a difference in a variable during wake and sleep must not necessarily be due to the common masking effect, i.e., to the difference between wake and sleep in itself; it may rather be due to different light exposures during awake (with open eyes) and sleep (with closed eyes). Discrimination between these two alternatives is possible by performing experiments with internally desynchronized rhythms under different intensities of illumination. Rectal temperature and cortisol (and many other variables) do not show a systematic change in the masking effect with changing light intensity; melatonin, on the other hand, shows a difference between educed wake and sleep cycles only under continuous bright light but not under artificial illumination of normal intensity.

SUSCEPTIBILITY TO INTERNAL DESYNCHRONIZATION

The question remains why internal desynchronization occurs spontaneously under constant conditions only in a small proportion of the subjects, while this state does not occur in the majority of subjects tested so far under identical conditions. Among the many personality data obtained from the (healthy) subjects, only two have been shown to be related to internal desynchronization. The first is the score of neuroticism (Lund, 1974). Subjects whose rhythms desynchronize internally show a significantly higher score of neuroticism (though consistently within the physiological range) than subjects whose rhythms stay internally synchronized in the long run; this is true according to two different tests which correlated highly. The second relevant item is the age of the subjects. Unfortunately, there is not a steady age distribution among our subjects, but there are, rather, two groups. The majority of subjects includes young persons with a mean age ($\pm$ SD) of 25.1 y $\pm$ 3.1 y; the other group includes older subjects with ages between 50 y and 80 y. Within both younger and older groups, there is no age dependency in the incidence of internal desynchronization. Between the two groups, however, there is a considerable difference. While only 20% of the younger subjects show internal desynchronization (and those are only those with higher scores of neuroticism), about 80% of the older subjects show this state (through the older subjects are not more frequently neurotic than the younger). There appears to be a threshold age anywhere between 35 y and 50 y (in this range, unfortunately, only a very few subjects were available); below this age, internal desynchronization is a rare phenomenon, and above this threshold age, it is almost the rule rather than the exception. The high tendency towards the spontaneous occurrence of internal desynchronization in older subjects, of course, cannot be in contradiction to the assumption of an evolutionary pressure to avoid this state (Wever, 1975c, 1979a).

INTERNAL RHYTHM CONTROL:
EXTERNAL MODIFICATIONS OF FREE-RUNNING RHYTHMS

Introduction

The parameters of free-running rhythms, internally synchronized or desynchronized, are not fixed quantities but depend on experimental conditions. When an experiment with one particular subject is repeated under identical conditions, as has been done with intervals between two months and six years, the results are remarkably similar. This statement does not only concern the period and other parameters, but also, for instance, the wave shape including individual details. When the conditions are varied, however, the parameters of the free-running rhythms may vary, including the tendency toward the spontaneous occurrence of internal desynchronization. Many experiments have been performed in which two to four successive sections of 10 cycles to 15 cycles duration each followed each other, where the experimental conditions (e.g., the intensity of constant illumination) were varied from one section to another.

Lumination Intensity

The first external stimulus to be tested was the intensity of illumination, since light had been shown in most animal species to be the most important stimulus in the control of circadian rhythms. Twenty experiments have been performed where the subjects were exposed to different intensities of illumination during the different sections of an experiment; the different light intensities followed each other in irregular sequences. The intensities ranged from total darkness up to 1,500 lux, because this range had been considered originally to cover all meaningful intensities of artificial illumination. As to the result of these experiments, neither the period nor any other rhythm parameter varied systematically with light intensity; to be sure, in several of these experiments, the period changed at the day when the intensity of illumination changed, but with inconsistent direction of correlation (Wever, 1969, 1973). This result holds true even for total darkness; also the rhythms of several totally blind subjects did not differ from rhythms of sighted subjects (Lund, 1974). In addition, the tendency towards the spontaneous occurrence of internal desynchronization was independent of the intensity of illumination (Wever, 1979a).

In another series of experiments, the illumination was not continuously in operation but switched on by the subjects when getting up and off by the subjects when going to sleep. In this type of experiment, the subjects were exposed to a light–dark (LD) alternation which was not controlled externally, but by the subject's own sleep–wake cycle. Such a "self-controlled" LD alternation does not break the autonomy of the system; however, such a self–control mode does affect the circadian system. Under self–controlled illumination (n = 29) the period is significantly longer (by 20 min ± 30 min; t = 3.10; p < 0.005) and the tendency toward the spontaneous occurrence of internal desynchronization significantly greater (13/29 vs. 24/103; p = 0.015) than under constant illumination (n = 103). Hence, the experiments under self controlled illumination demonstrate a marginal but significant effect of light on human circadian rhythms (Wever, 1969, 1973, 1979a).

With joint consideration of the experiments under self–controlled illumination, and under objectively constant illumination, the subjects are exposed subjectively to a self-controlled LD alternation, constituted by the opening and closing of the eyes. Such subjective self–control should lengthen the period with increasing light intensity. On the other hand, the continuous action of light should theoretically shorten the period, the brighter the light. Both effects operate in opposite directions; on the average but not in every individual subject, both effects are of equal strength, so that they compensate for each other. This hypothesis has been tested, and confirmed, in subtle experiments with singly and collectively isolated subjects which were exposed to constant and self-controlled illumination (Wever, 1979a).

Very recently a considerable effect of the intensity of illumination on free-running circadian rhythms of man was observed, provided that this intensity exceeded a threshold at about 2,500 lux. In several experiments where the intensity of illumination was continuously 3,000 lux to 5,000 lux in one section and 300 lux or zero lux in another section, the period was considerably and significantly longer, and the tendency toward a spontaneous occurrence of internal desynchronization was considerably and significantly greater under brighter than normal illumination (or total darkness; Wever, 1985c, 1986). In reference to the hypothesis just mentioned, the self-control effect increases with the increasing intensity of illumination whereas the effect of continuous action reaches a saturation value. Considering the results of these bright light experiments, the previously deduced statement must be revised: it is only light below an intensity of about 2,500 lux that has a marginal influence on free-running circadian rhythms of man; light with intensities above this threshold has a clear influence on these rhythms which is comparable with that of light of any intensity in most animal circadian experiments.

Ambient Temperature

The next stimulus to be investigated is ambient temperature; ambient temperature does not even affect the free-running circadian rhythms of most mammals which are sensitive to changes in the intensity of illumination. After human rhythms have been shown to react only marginally to changes in the intensity of illumination, a consequence of changes in ambient temperature is scarcely to be expected. For this reason effects of ambient temperature on free-running rhythms have been tested only in a self-control mode which is obviously more sensitive to external stimuli than a continuous action. In eight experiments, healthy human subjects have been exposed, under constantly maintained illumination, to constant ambient temperature during one section and to a self-controlled alternation in ambient temperature (6°C higher during wake than sleep; same average temperature as in the section first mentioned) in another part of the same experiment (with an alternating temporal sequence in the two sections). The consistent and significant result (t = 6.09; p < 0.001) was a longer free-running period (by 22 min ± 10 min) under self-control than under constant conditions (Wever, 1974a). consequently, ambient temperature is a stimulus that affects free-running circadian rhythms of man, though only marginally.

Electric Fields

Another environmental stimulus of physical nature which exerts a considerably stronger influence on the free-running circadian rhythms of man than light (in the normal intensity range) and ambient temperature, is a weak electric AC field (10 Hz square wave; field strength 2.5 V/m). When given continuously, such a field shortens the period by 1.21 h ± 0.81 h (n = 12); such a difference between sections with the field continuously in operation, and sections with the absence of artificial fields and shielding from natural electric and magnetic fields, is significant statistically at a fair level (t = 5.18; p < 0.001; Wever, 1967, 1979a, 1985e). In addition, this difference has been shown to be independent of sex and age of the subjects, and independent of mode and intensity of illumination. Moreover, as a determinant of the period, this field alters all measurable rhythm parameters according to previously predicted rules (Wever, 1968a). And finally, this subtle stimulus prevents the rhythm from internal desynchronization which had never been observed when the field was in continuous operation; the effect of the field is significant statistically at a high level (p < 0.001). The field mentioned cannot be perceived consciously by the subjects in any way; for this reason, the field cannot operate via any behavioral influences as light can (a subject may exert different types of activity in bright and dim illumination, and particularly in total darkness). The main reason for the fact that the subtle and imperceivable field has a much greater effect on circadian rhythms than will perceivable illumination (as long in the intensity range of normal artificial illumination), may be the neglect of a subjective self-control effect: in contrast to light, the electric field affects the subjects equally during wake and sleep.

In several more experiments, the 10 Hz field was not in operation continuously but only during the wake episodes of the subjects; it was switched on and off automatically without being perceived by the subjects. In contrast to the shortening effect of the continuously operating field, such a self-controlled field alternation lengthened the period systematically ($p < 0.01$); the lengthening effect of self-control is thus independent of the stimulus, whether the stimuli under consideration are perceptible or not, and whether the stimuli, when given continuously, shorten or lengthen the period.

Social Contacts

All experiments discussed so far were performed with singly isolated subjects. It could be protested, therefore, that the deviation of the free-running from 24 h may be due to the social deprivation of the subjects. To evaluate the influence of social contacts, groups of two and four collectively isolated subjects had been tested under conditions identical with those of the singly isolated subjects. Initially, all subjects within the groups showed mutually synchronized rhythms, even after the spontaneous occurrence of internal desynchronization where not only the rhythms of deep body temperature but also the sleep-wake rhythms each ran in synchrony; i.e., after the separation of the rhythms, both rhythm components (with different periods) were mutually synchronized among the subjects independent of each other. Secondly, the twelve groups showed significantly longer periods (25.08 h $\pm$ 0.21 h) than the 37 subjects who were singly isolated under otherwise identical conditions (24.79 h $\pm$ 0.41 h; $t = 2.34$; $p < 0.0125$). The tendency toward the spontaneous occurrence of internal desynchronization was greater in the groups than in the single subjects (4/12 vs. 4/37), though this difference failed to be statistically significant ($p = 0.072$), indicating that social contacts within the groups of collectively living subjects, but not in the singly isolated subjects, exert a clear influence on human circadian rhythms (Wever, 1975b, 1979a). The objection mentioned concerning the effect of social deprivation must be rejected; in groups where the social deprivation is, at least, much more weakly pronounced than in singly isolated subjects, the deviation of the free-running period from 24 h is significantly larger rather than smaller than that observed in the single subjects.

Physical Work

Another objection concerns the exemption of the subjects during the temporal isolation from hard physical work load. To evaluate the influence of physical work load on human circadian rhythms, nine experiments have been performed where subjects had to exercise a hard physical work load (mostly seven times per wake episode a load of 100 W on a bicycle ergometer) which resulted in increases in deep body temperature of 0.5°C to 1.0°C each time. Whereas the subjects had to perform this work load in one section, they had to refrain from any physical exercise in another section of the same experiment (again, of course, with alternating temporal sequence of the two sections). The result was that neither the period or any other parameter of free-running rhythms, nor the tendency to the spontaneous occurrence of internal desynchronization, was affected by the work load; thus, objections concerning the deprivation of the subjects from physical work load must be rejected. Physical work load appears to have no influence on human circadian rhythms (Wever, 1979b).

Psychological Stress

In contrast to physical work load, psychological or behavioral burdening of the subjects does seem to have an influence on human circadian rhythms, by lengthening the period and increasing the tendency toward internal desynchronization. The difficulty in establishing significant results issues from the difficulty of quantifying behavioral stress; there are, however, different types of experiments which all give, independently, the same suggestion, such as six early experiments with complete polygraphic sleep recordings which could be recorded, at that time, only by connecting the electrodes with the recording equipment outside the experimental unit by wires. During the four-week experiments the subjects had to attach the electrodes, every time before going to rest, to control the contact resistances, and to connect the wires to a terminal near their bed. During the sleep, the subjects felt "chained up", according to their own statements, at least initially, and perceived it as an unusual "stress". Perhaps as a result, four out of the six experiments showed internal desynchronization, whereas only six out of 46 experiments under identical conditions but without sleep recordings showed this state; this difference is significant statistically with p = 0.002 (Wever, 1979a).

Later experiments with polygraphic sleep recordings, performed with improved technique (e.g., telemetry) did not show a difference from the other experiments without sleep recordings; and the subjects in these more recent experiments were not found to be stressed in any way. In addition, contributing to the difference in the burdens of the different experiments, only in the earlier sample of EEG experiments were naps not allowed, because of the protracted procedure of attaching the electrodes; in all other experiments, including the later sample of EEG experiments, naps were expressively permitted. Another suggestion regarding the effect of behavioral stress comes from the summarizing inspection of rhythm data from different years where the amounts of tests to be performed by the subjects were different. To be sure, the same test may be an arduous burden for one subject while a stimulating diversion for another subject, so that only the consideration of averages can be meaningful. In years with an increase of burdening tests, in fact, the periods were significantly longer and the tendency toward internal desynchronization was significantly greater than in years with fewer burdening tests (p < 0.005; Wever, 1979a, 1982b). In conclusion, psychological burdening or behavioral stress affects human circadian rhythms in the same manner as social contacts do.

Conclusions

In summary, several generalizations can be deduced from the various external and internal conditions which influence the period and other parameters of free-running circadian rhythms in man and, in addition, the tendency toward the spontaneous occurrence of internal desynchronization. Changes in the experimental conditions which lengthen the free-running period simultaneously increase the tendency toward internal desynchronization, and increase the inter-individual variability among different subjects under the same condition. Consequently the shortening effect of a certain change in the experimental conditions is greater the longer the period in the section with the longer periods. The magnitude of the effect thus depends on the initial conditions (Wever, 1979a).

EXTERNAL RHYTHM CONTROL

Introduction

In nature, organisms, including all human subjects, do not live under temporally constant conditions, but under the influence of day/night alternations with a period of precisely 24.0 h. Consequently, circadian rhythms of all organisms including those of man have, under natural conditions, periods of precisely 24.0 h and are, thus, always synchronized to the external day/night rhythm. Fortunately, under laboratory conditions artificial zeitgebers are also effective in synchronizing circadian rhythms, not only to periods of 24 h but also to periods deviating with a limited range of entrainment, which gives us an opportunity to evaluate the properties of entrainment, in general, and to evaluate modes of external stimuli which exhibit the capability of acting as zeitgebers, in particular. A relative measure of the strength of a zeitgeber is the width of the range of entrainment, the precise estimation of which enables us to compare different zeitgeber modes quantitatively.

LD Alternation

For the great majority of biological species so far tested, a LD alternation is the most effective and, under natural conditions, the most important external zeitgeber. For this reason, investigations of effective zeitgeber modes in humans commenced with LD zeitgebers. In a series of eight experiments, human subjects were exposed to artificial 24–h LD alternations (with about 300 lux in L and about 0.01 lux in D) with L:D ratios of 12:12 and 15:9 h (with twilight transitions of 40 min each); during the dark phase the subjects had the opportunity to switch on small auxiliary lamps making reading possible. Hence, the artificial LD alternation corresponded to a natural one where sunset is nowadays not a compelling reason to go to bed but rather an indication that it is evening and that artificial lamps should be switched on. In summary, none of the eight subjects was fully synchronized to the 24–h day (Wever, 1970b). Figure 11 details the courses of two exemplary experiments; on the left, the subject showed a free–running rhythm during the entire experiment, in spite of the presence of a 24–h zeitgeber; i.e., the rhythm behaved as under constant conditions. Only a closer inspection reveals that the zeitgeber was not completely ineffective but caused relative coordination; i.e., during those days when the phase relationship to the zeitgeber corresponded to the common one (days 1 to 8, and 22 to 26), the rhythm shifted more slowly against the zeitgeber than at other days. Similar results have been obtained in four more experiments; on the right of Figure 11, the first ten days show a result similar to that at the other example: the rhythm free-ran in spite of the presence of the 24-h zeitgeber. At day 10, spontaneous internal desynchronization occurred as in several experiments under constant conditions (cf. Figure 5). However, while the separated sleep-wake rhythm free-ran with a considerably lengthened period, the separated temperature rhythm shortened slightly as expected, but showed a clear 24.0-h period; closer inspection of this experiment (and of two more experiments with similar results) revealed synchronization to the 24-h zeitgeber excluding the possibility of a free-running rhythm with a period which was, by chance, very close to 24.0 h (Wever, 1978). Summarizing all eight experiments of this type, the range of entrainment of the LD zeitgeber is about ± 0.5 h since this zeitgeber is too weak to synchronize a common free-running rhythm with a period close to 15 h with the 24-h day.

In addition to the eight experiments mentioned, a ninth experiment with a pure LD zeitgeber but a period of 25.25 h can be included. Apart from the period, the ninth experiment differed from the others in two respects: the (female) subject was encouraged to follow the LD protocol with her sleep-wake behavior, whenever possible; and the subject fell ill on the fifth day of the running experiment (German measles, with fever up to 39.6°C) but insisted upon continuing the experiment (she was restored to health by the eleventh day of the experiment). The (unusual) course of this experiment is shown in Figure 12 (left diagram): the subject followed the zeitgeber with her sleep-wake alternations, though with large fluctuations, indicating good motivation to follow instructions; the temperature rhythm showed, on the average, a shorter and free-running period of 24.5 h, indicating internal desynchronization. However, the separation of the two rhythms commenced only during the illness of the subject (around days 9 and 10). In any case, it was a unique observation among more than 100 experiments with spontaneous (see above) and forced (see below) internal desynchronization that the separated rhythms showed periods which were so close together and were separated only by 45 min while the difference in the periods of separated rhythms was, at least, several hours in all other cases (Wever, 1978). It is plausible that this unusual rhythm disorder was only triggered by the subject's illness. Of course, it would be a very interesting question whether or not such a correlation between health disorder and rhythm disorder is significantly more prevalent; unfortunately, however, such experiments can be performed unintentionally but not by design.

Moreover, Figure 12 (left) shows that the subject frequently took naps though she stated that it was in strict contrast to her habit to do so. The naps were positioned exclusively around minimum values in body temperature and, hence, had a period coinciding with that of the temperature rhythm and deviating from that of the sleep–wake rhythm; consequently, the naps shifted consistently relative to the sleep–wake cycle. To elucidate such shifts, the left diagram of Figure 12 also includes the meals; the subject took three meals per cycle, and analyses of the meals revealing a "feeding period" of 25.25 h. During the first part of the experiment, the naps were positioned in the late subjective afternoon, i.e., several hours after lunch and frequently shortly before dinner; in a later part of the experiment the naps were positioned immediately after lunch, and at the end of the experiment they were positioned between breakfast and lunch. The naps can be designated only rarely as "post–lunch dips"; the subject had not realized consciously such a consistent shift of her naps. Confirmed by computed period analyses, night sleeps (with $\tau = 25.25$ h) and naps (with $\tau = 24.5$ h) followed different rhythms, or basic oscillators; the rhythm of the night sleeps was clearly synchronized to the zeitgeber, while the rhythm of the naps was just clearly free–running together with the rhythm of body temperature. An analysis of the locomotor activity of the subject (number of steps per unit time) as presented in the right part of Figure 12, shows unambiguously two highly reliable rhythms with periods of 24.5 h (corresponding to the rhythm of the night sleeps). For comparison, the lower diagram shows the period analysis of the rhythm of rectal temperature: there is only one reliable rhythmicity with the period of 24.5 h.

"Gong" Signals

The nearly ineffective pure LD zeitgeber gained an adequate efficiency when supplemented by regular signals (gongs) requesting the subjects for micturitions and tests (in the hitherto discussed experiments the subjects had to select the intervals between the micturitions themselves). Figure 13 shows an example of an experiment where a subject was exposed to such a combined zeitgeber, with three alterations of the zeitgeber period, and demonstrates that the subject was synchronized to the zeitgeber, not only to the period of 24.0 h but also to the period of 26.67 h. The educed cycles in the right diagram show that the phase relationship changed considerably with the zeitgeber period, not only between the rhythms and the zeitgeber (external) but also between the rhythms of body temperature and sleep/wake (internal phase relationship). The subject reacted as an extreme "morning type" in the 24-h day, but as a clear "evening type" in the 26.67-h day. After a third experimental section with a 24-h zeitgeber, the period was shortened to 22.67 h; this period was obviously too short for the rhythm to become synchronized, and the result was a typical free-running rhythm. In other words, the period of 22.67 h was outside of the range of entrainment (Aschoff, Saint Paul and Wever, 1968).

In total, 15 experiments have been performed with the type of zeitgeber under discussion, and with at least one alternation of the zeitgeber period. In summary, all 15 subjects were synchronized to the zeitgeber within a range of entrainment of between about 23 h and 27 h, and showed free-running rhythms in spite of the presence of the zeitgeber (but with relative coordination; cf. Figure 11) outside of this range. Inside the range of entrainment, not only did the external phase relationships alter depending on the period consistently in the same direction as in Figure 13, but also the internal phase relationships between the different overt rhythms changed (Wever, 1974b).

Consequently, there is a clear difference between zeitgeber experiments with and without the regular requesting signals (or gongs). Interviews with the subjects revealed that the LD alternations were attributed consistently to an automatic switch clock, whereas the gong signals were considered as directly operated by the experimenter, i.e., as social contacts. The second estimation, of course, was wrong, but it suggests that social contacts, even when only imagined, can act as potential zeitgebers. In the meantime, the greater effectiveness of social contacts as a zeitgeber in comparison to the lesser effectiveness of LD alternations has been shown in various types of experiments.

The difference between experiments with and without the regular gong signals is more relevant since it was discovered by accident. Originally, the requesting signals had been considered to be ineffective as a zeitgeber, and had been introduced only to obtain the urine samples and tests in equidistant intervals. Only after a technical breakdown of the gong system immediately following the beginning of an experiment, resulting in failing synchronization to the remaining 24–h LD zeitgeber, was the relevance of the signals discovered; only subsequently, were experiments without the requesting signals performed systema- tically. In another experiment where the illumination remained in operation due to another technical mistake, the experiment was continued for a while under constant illumination but with the regular requesting signals in a 26–h sequence. The result was clear synchronization to mere signals as the zeitgeber (the free–running period of the respective subject was shown in the later course of this experiment to be 24.9 h).

Absolute LD Alternation

The effectiveness of the zeitgeber can be enhanced further by removing the auxiliary lamps. In such an absolute LD alternation (in contrast to a relative LD with access to auxiliary lamps during the dark phase), the subjects follow the zeitgeber with the sleep/wake rhythm within a wide range, whereas most of the physiological rhythms including the rhythm of deep body temperature can be synchronized to such a zeitgeber only within the same limits as the relative LD zeitgeber with requesting signals. The ranges of entrainment of different overt rhythms have different widths (Wever, 1974b). Of particular interest are the ranges of zeitgeber periods that are outside the range of entrainment of the physiological rhythms but inside the range of entrainment of the sleep/wake rhythm; i.e., ranges within which several rhythms are free-running whereas others are synchronized to the zeitgeber. Within these ranges, the rhythms are partially synchronized to the zeitgeber, and are internally desynchronized. One of the advantages of such an experimental protocol is the capability of forcing internal desynchronization in every subject, independent of his age and personality data. Certainly, the term "forced" does not mean that the subjects have any perception of their state of internal desynchronization; rather, they experience a minimal sensation as during spontaneously occurring internal desynchronization under constant conditions. Another advantage of this experimental protocol is that it enables us to investigate properties of free-running rhythms but with regular signals (including signals during the sleep episodes) requesting the subjects for testing. By these means, psychological data, both objectively measured performance tests and subjectively scored mood data, can be obtained without having consistent night gaps in the data. Such night gaps are unavoidable in experiments under constant conditions, however, they prevent the thorough evaluation of parameters from psychological rhythms (Wever, 1982b).

Psychological Rhythms

Surprisingly, psychological data form performance tests and self-rate mood scales result in reliable rhythms with a period deviating from sleep/wake when data obtained after awakenings from sleep are included; clearly these "sleep data" show impaired values. However, reductions in performance and mood induced by masking are mostly distinctly smaller than the circadian variations in these; consequently, significant free-running rhythms have been established under the influence of a zeitgeber with a period outside of the range of entrainment of the respective rhythms (Wever, 1982b). a separation of wake and sleep data (or, more accurately, data obtained shortly after awakening from sleep) show mean "wake" and "sleep" cycles running parallel up to individual details in the same way as body temperature and many other physiological rhythms (cf. Figure 10); even the "post-lunch dip" in performance or the dip in performance around the temperature maximum, appears consistently not only in the wake data but also in the sleep data. The interval between wake and sleep cycle constituting the masking effect is distinctly smaller than the amplitude of either cycle; the sleep cycle is consistently phase-advanced relative to the wake cycle (Wever, 1985a).

310

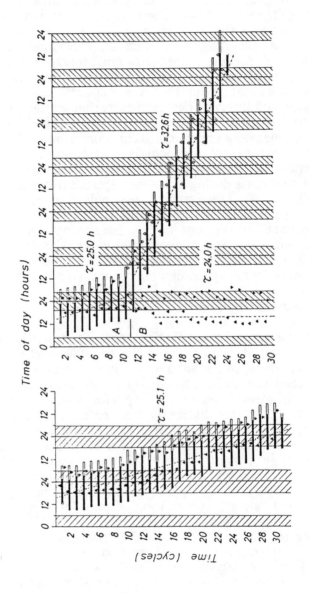

Figure 11

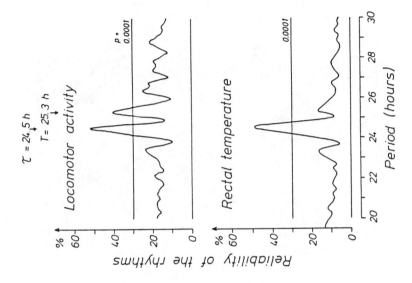

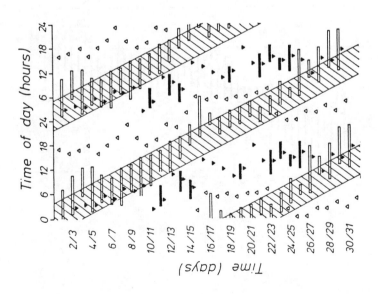

Figure 12

311

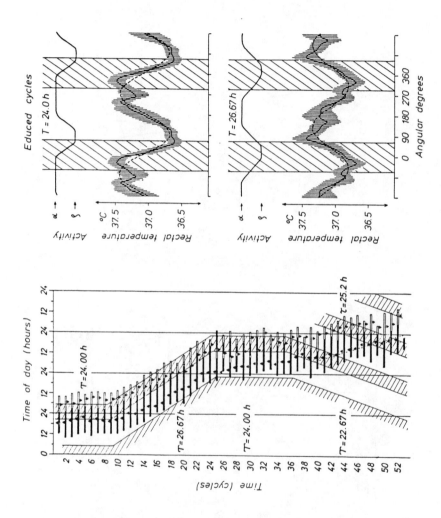

Figure 13

312

Legend for Figure 11 (On Page 310) Circadian rhythms of two subjects living without natural time cues but under the influence of artificial 24-h zeitgebers (relative LD alternations). Presented are the rhythms of sleep/wake (bars; black: wake episodes; white: sleep episodes) and of rectal temperature (temporal positions of Δ = maxima and ∇ = minima, open triangles: temporal correct redrawings of corresponding black triangles). Successive cycles are drawn, one beneath the other, as functions of local time (abscissa); ordinate: sequence of successive cycles: shaded areas: dark time of the zeitgeber. Right: undisturbed free-running rhythm during the entire experiment. Left, A and B: sections before and after the spontaneous occurrence of internal desynchronization; the internally synchronized rhythms in section A and the separated rhythm of sleep/wake in section B free-ran, but the separated rhythm of rectal temperature was synchronized to the LD zeitgeber.

Legend for Figure 12 (On Page 311) Circadian rhythm of a subject living without natural time cues but under the influence of an artificial zeitgeber (relative LD alternations) with a period of 25.3 h; in contrast to Figure 11, the subject had strict instructions to follow the zeitgeber. Left: course of the experiment; designations as in Figure 1; left; black bars: naps; shaded areas: dark time of the zeitgeber. Right: period analyses of the rhythms of locomotor activity (number of steps per unit time) and rectal temperature.

Legend for Figure 13 (On Page 312) Circadian rhythm of a subject living without natural time cues but under the influence of an artificial zeitgeber (relative LD alternations and regular requesting signals or "gongs"), with four different zeitgeber periods successively. Left: course of the experiment; designations as in Figure 11. Right: educed cycles of the rhythms of sleep/wake and rectal temperature (with standard deviations, dotted lines: best fitting sine waves), computed separately from the first and second experimental sections.

When comparing parameters of rhythms established in the manner above, consistent results of many experiments of differing types indicate that the mean levels of psychological rhythms are higher in internally desynchronized than synchronized rhythms; this unexpected development during the unphysiological state of internal desynchronization is valid in objectively measured performance (e.g., computation speed or error frequency) and in subjectively rated mood data (e.g., alertness or contentment; Wever, 1979a, 1982b). In order to verify this result and to exclude the influence of a temporal trend, the temporal sequences of experimental sections with internal synchronization and desynchronization had been commuted repeatedly from experiment to experiment; nevertheless, the results mentioned were consistent. Surely as this result was obtained in experiments of four to six weeks' duration, it would be unreasonable to assume that it would be valid in the very long run. On the other hand, such results assure us that the state of internal desynchronization may be forced in every healthy subject without running the risk of harmful consequences. Forced internal desynchronization may be applied as a kind of stimulation therapy in special types of mentally injured patients; a precondition for a positive effect of internal desynchronization upon the subject appears to be a steady–state where the temperature rhythm runs steadily with its intrinsic period. Mood and performance are reduced, even when measured with the same equipment in the same manner (Wever, 1980a), during the apparently similar state of internal dissociation after a phase shift of the zeitgeber ("jet lag") when rhythms are not in a steady state but a transient state, i.e., when all rhythms are constrained by a zeitgeber but are not free to run with their intrinsic periods.

Entrainment Limits: Fractional Desynchronization

In total, 44 experiments have been performed where subjects have been exposed to absolute LD zeitgebers with periods remaining constant for at least 12 days; these experiments had been performed to answer various questions. As a result, it can only be stated that the lower entrainment limit of the physiological rhythms is anywhere between 22 h and 23 h, and that the upper entrainment limit is at a period shorter than 28 h. In order to estimate the entrainment limits more precisely, experiments have been performed where the zeitgeber period was not altered step-wise in intervals of about two weeks but steadily (Wever, 1983b). Figure 14 shows two examples of such experiments; in the upper example, the first zeitgeber cycle was 24:00 h long, and every subsequent cycle was 5 min shorter than the preceding cycle. While sleep/wake was synchronized to the zeitgeber during the entire experiment, the rhythm of rectal temperature was synchronized to a period of 22:30 h; at or about the period of 22:25 h, it broke free from the zeitgeber and started to free-run with a period of 24.8 h. In the lower example the initial five zeitgeber cycles were 26:00 h long, and subsequently, every cycle was 10 min longer than the preceding cycle. Again, sleep/wake ran in synchrony with the zeitgeber during the entire experiment; however, the rhythm of rectal temperature displayed an upper entrainment limit of 26:50 h, free-running thereafter. The analysis of 12 experiments with a shortening protocol results in a mean ($\pm$ SD) lower entrainment limit of the temperature rhythm of 22.41 h $\pm$ 0.17 h, and that of nine experiments with a lengthening protocol results in an upper entrainment limit of 26.95 h $\pm$ 0.23 h. After the separation in all 21 experiments the mean free-running period of the temperature rhythm was 24.67 h $\pm$ 0.21 h. Consequently, the range of entrainment is positioned symmetrically around the free-running period, with a width of $\pm$ 2.27 h. Moreover, a closer inspection reveals that this width is not identical in all rhythms but is very significantly correlated with the free-running period. (Lengthening the free-running period by one hour not only shifts the center of the range of entrainment by one hour to longer periods but also enlarges it by 0.60 h; Wever, 1983b).

As regards body temperature, the free-run subsequent to the separation of the rhythms can be determined mostly but not with confidence. In several cases, rather, the masking effect is so strong that the masking component which runs always parallel to sleep/wake dominates the free-running component. A period estimation based on the estimation of successive acrophases cannot be applied at all in these cases, and a period analysis of the experimental section after the separation of the rhythms, based on a Fourier or a periodogram algorithm, results in two rhythmicities: rhythm separation, therefore, is obscured. A variable that does not show any masking effect, as exemplified in Figure 15, melatonin (measured as aMT6s; Arendt, et al., 1985) is considered in an experiment analogous to that of Figure 14, lower diagram. With the zeitgeber cycle as the abscissa, successive zeitgeber cycles are drawn one beneath the other (and, for clarity, each two cycles side by side). Until cycle 12, or a period of 27:10 h, the melatonin rhythm was in synchrony with the zeitgeber though with advanced phase position. From cycle 13 on, the melatonin rhythm clearly broke free from the zeitgeber and began to free–run, with a period of 24.9 h; this separation, or the subsequent free–run, was not obscured by any masking effect. Remarkably, the mean level of the melatonin excretion, and hence the melatonin production, decreased in the course of the synchronization toward the limit of entrainment, to a third of its original value. Immediately after the start of the free–run, the melatonin excretion again increased back up to its original value (i.e., a threefold increase). The suppression of melatonin during the synchronization close to the entrainment limit corresponds in its amount to the suppression of melatonin by bright light (Lewy, et al., 1980; see also Figure 10), but is certainly independent of light. In fact, during the final stage of synchronization (cycles 7 to 12), the melatonin excretion shifted into the light phase of the zeitgeber, according to the lengthened period; the illumination during the light phase, however, was too weak ($\approx$ 300 lux) to suppress melatonin, and particularly, during the later course of the free–run, melatonin excretion took place frequently, as during the light phase (cycles 13 to 15 and 17 to 21), but was by no means suppressed. Melatonin suppression, not by light but by a zeitgeber, should be taken into account whenever the physiological pathways of melatonin suppression are discussed (Wever, 1986).

The experimental design of the steadily varying zeitgeber period was originally introduced in order to look for functional interdependencies between different variables; if the rhythms of different variables can run internally desynchronized from each other, they cannot be casually related. Overt rhythms that split off from the zeitgeber at different days, and thus at different periods, run mutually desynchronized, at least for several days; such successive splittings initiated the name "fractional desynchronization" for this design. Apart from desynchronization between sleep/wake and body temperature, such desynchronizations between several overt rhythms have been shown, e.g., between urinary sodium and potassium excretion, between these excretions and body temperature, and between body temperature and psychomotor performance (Wever, 1983a). When both rhythms under consideration show strong masking effects, the evidence of a rhythm separation is more difficult to establish. As mentioned above, the acrophase estimation then becomes ambiguous because two rhythm components are included in every time series and, hence, cannot be applied. The periodogram analyses, on the other hand, allows a separation of the components only when a sufficient number of cycles is included in the computation; however, the estimation of the separation day may then become difficult.

Figure 16 shows, as an example, the separation of the rhythms of rectal temperature and cortisol excretion (and, hence, cortisol production), again from an experiment of the type shown in Figure 14, lower diagram. Special analyses are necessary since both variables, rectal temperature and urinary cortisol, are strongly masked by sleep/wake. To obtain a sufficient resolution power, periodogram analyses over 10 cycles each have been computed in overlapping intervals; up to cycle 11 both variables showed monomodal rhythmicities, with periods close to 26 h according to the mean zeitgeber period during these cycles. Beginning with the third interval (cycles 3 to 12), in the cortisol analysis (but not yet in the temperature analysis) another rhythm appeared, with a period of 24.5 h; this rhythm corresponded to the typical free–running period until the end of the experiment, whereas according to the lengthening zeitgeber period the secondary peak shifted slowly from interval to interval to longer periods. The same picture was present in the temperature analysis but with the free–running rhythm appearing later, in the fourth or fifth interval. Consequently, a free–running rhythm component of cortisol split off from the zeitgeber at cycle 12 (this component was not recognizable until cycle 11) while a masking component remained synchronized to the zeitgeber.

A free–running component of the body temperature rhythm split off from the zeitgeber between cycles 13 and 14. Until the second interval, and from the fifth interval on, the analyses from both variables showed nearly identical spectra; only the third and fourth intervals resulted in different spectra. These differences, however, are clear evidence that the rhythms of the two variables ran mutually desynchronized during these cycles, suggesting that rectal temperature and urinary cortisol are, on principle, separable. This result, of course, does not mean that the rhythms of body temperature and urinary cortisol can run internally desynchronized in every subject; it does mean, however, that there is a fundamental possibility of separating these rhythms, and that there cannot be a causal relationship between the two variables under consideration. Another important question is whether the strength of the interaction between the two variables (as expressed in the probability of separating these variables in time) is correlated to any personality data or to specific mental diseases.

It may be argued that experiments with absolute LD alternation give evidence for an effective influence of light (in contrast to the poor effectiveness of a relative LD alternation) (Czeisler, et al., 1981), particularly since the regular signals do not seem to play an important role (preliminary experiments with an absolute LD alternation but without the regular signals showed similar results). Such an argument, however, neglects the twofold effectiveness of light: a direct physiological effect and an indirect effect via the influences of light on behavior. With regard to sleep/wake, an absolute LD alternation is less of a zeitgeber (as the relative LD alternation is) but is still a phase determinant, because there is no opportunity to elude the zeitgeber, this being an inherent precondition of the zeitgeber definition. The difference between a zeitgeber and a phase determinant can be seen clearly in Figure 15, where the melatonin rhythm, but not the sleep/wake cycle, shifts its phase relationship to the zeitgeber depending upon the zeitgeber period. If it is completely dark during the dark phase of an LD, light off and light on act as strong cues for rest and for getting up; certainly an indirect component of light effectiveness supplements the possible direct effect. The relative weights of the two components can be tested by exchanging the light-induced requests for acoustical requests during constant illumination or continuous darkness.

Information Zeitgeber

Two series of experiments have been performed in which the subjects were exposed to constant illumination (or darkness in one experiment) but received two acoustically transmitted requests per cycle: to go to bed and to get up (Wever, 1983a), examples of which are presented in Figure 17. In the left example, the requests followed a 23.5-h schedule consistently. The period of 23.5 h is outside of the range within which free-running periods have been observed, but close enough to the mean free-running period that synchronization could be expected. As the result of this experiment (and of two more experiments of this type), sleep/wake followed the imposed schedule indicating good motivation in the subjects; in addition, however, the rhythms of rectal temperature and other measured variables were unambiguously synchronized to the "information zeitgeber". In the example on the right, the experimental protocol with the steadily lengthening zeitgeber period was applied; the first cycle of the "information zeitgeber" was 24.00 h long, and every subsequent cycle was 10 min longer than the preceding cycle. In this experiment and two more experiments of this type, one of which was under continuous darkness, sleep/wake followed the imposed schedule during the entire experiment, indicating again good motivation of the subjects to follow instructions. On the other hand, the rhythm of rectal temperature (and the rhythms of several more variables) followed this schedule only up to a period of about 27 h; i.e., the entrainment limit of these rhythms coincided with that under the influence of an absolute LD zeitgeber (see above).

The zeitgeber constituted by a behavioral component and without any participation of light (Figure 17, right) has about the same strength as the combined zeitgeber consisting of a similar behavioral component and, in addition, a physiological component using the light directly. The additional physiological component has a negligible strength in comparison to the strength of the behavioral component (the only alternative, i.e., the assumption of an absolute entrainment limit at about 27 h independent of the zeitgeber strength, can be rejected; cf. Figure 18). In summary, therefore, these experiments confirm the poor zeitgeber effectiveness of a LD alternation; in addition, the similarity of the discussed experiments with only two requests per cycle (Figure 17) to the experiments with 7 signals in addition to two light-induced requests (Figure 14) proves that the regular requesting of signals does not play a relevant role in structuring the "day".

Bright Light Zeitgeber

In all hitherto discussed experiments with LD alternation of any type, the intensity of illumination during the light phase was about 300 lux, and only in special cases 1,000 lux. The zeitgeber strength of a LD alternation increases many times over when the intensity of illumination during the light phase reaches values above the threshold for melatonin suppression (see above). The strength of a "bright light zeitgeber" (with about 3,000 lux during the light phase) was tested in the same way, i.e., with steadily varying zeitgeber periods. Figure 18 shows two examples of such experiments; in comparison to the examples with the normal light zeitgeber (Figure 14), the rates of the shortening or lengthening of the period are increased to 10 min/cycle (above) and + 15 min/ cycle (below), in order to enlarge the ranges of periods to be covered within an experiment of reasonable duration. As a result, not only sleep/wake (as also in Figure 14), but also the rhythm of rectal temperature followed the zeitgeber down to the final period of 18:30 h, and up to 31:30 h, respectively, without reaching an entrainment limit.

From these experiments (and from those of four more experiments with similar results), it is still unclear whether or not there is an entrainment limit at all. The latter assumption would mean that the bright light zeitgeber is so strong that it completely overrides the self-sustainment capacity of the rhythms. In any case, the range of entrainment with the bright light zeitgeber is at least three times wider than that with normal light (see above). Consequently, the bright light zeitgeber is three times stronger than the normal LD zeitgeber. The behavioral component of the LD alternation (see above) cannot be responsible for this strengthening, because it can only be either present or absent but not vary in its effectiveness. Only the component of a direct physiological effect of light remains which had been found to be nearly negligible in the case of normal LD alternation; such a direct component, therefore, must increase in its strength tremendously. The direct physiological effect of light must acquire another quality when the intensity of illumination increases to values above the threshold for melatonin suppression (Wever, Polasek and Wildgruber, 1983). Such a result as this supplements and confirms the effect of light when operating continuously under constant conditions.

In subjective perception, very little difference between light intensities of about 1,000 lux and about 3,000 lux exists, and even

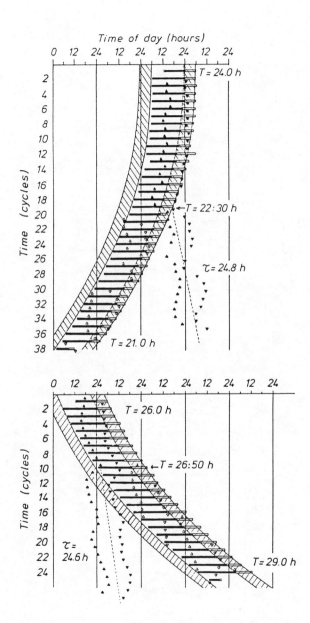

Figure 14

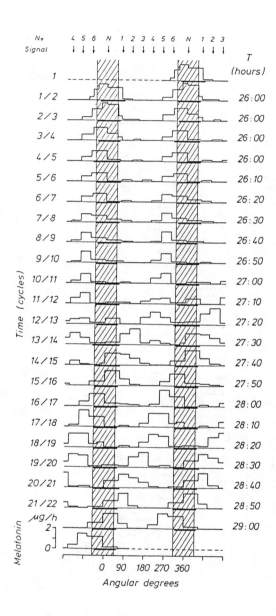

Figure 15

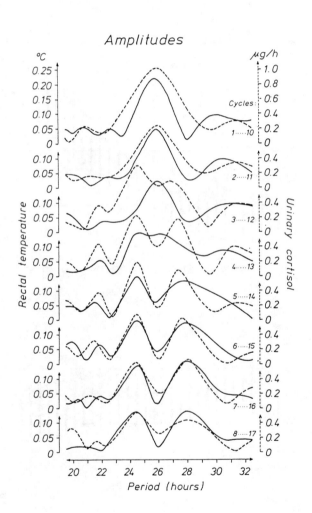

Figure 16

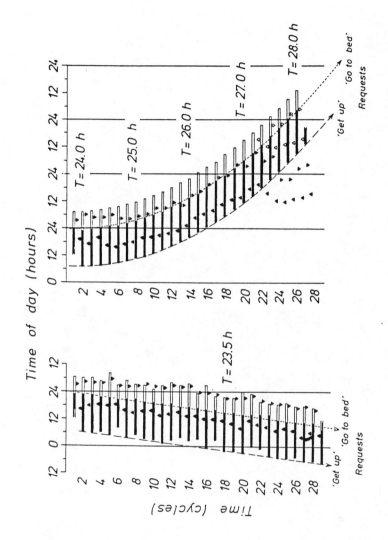

Figure 17

324

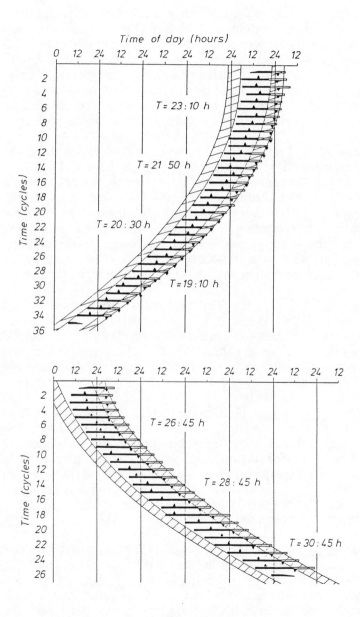

Figure 18

Legend for Figure 14 (On Page 321) Circadian rhythms of two subjects living without natural time cues but under the influence of artificial zeitgebers (absolute LD alternations and regular requesting signals) with steadily changing zeitgeber periods. Designations as in Figure 11; arrows indicate the limit periods down to which (above) and up to which (below) the rhythm of rectal temperature was synchronized to the zeitgeber.

Legend for Figure 15 (On Page 322) Results from an experiment of the same type as in Figure 14, lower diagram. Presented are, relative to the zeitgeber cycle (abscissa), the courses of sleep/wake (black bars: sleep episodes) and urinary melatonin (measured as aMT6s); successive zeitgeber cycles are drawn one beneath the other, for clarity, two cycles each are drawn side by side (i.e., the data is double plotted). The durations of the zeitgeber cycles are indicated at the right border.

Legend for Figure 16 (On Page 323) Analyses from an experiment of the same type as in Figure 14, lower diagram. Presented are the results from period analyses of the rhythms of rectal temperature and urinary cortisol, computed each over ten successive zeitgeber cycles.

Legend for Figure 17 (On Page 324) Circadian rhythms of two subjects living under constant illumination without natural time cues but under the influence of artificial "information zeitgebers" (two acoustically transmitted requests per cycle). Designations as in Figure 11. Left: information zeitgeber with a constant period; right: information zeitgeber with a steadily lengthening zeitgeber period.

Legend for Figure 18 (On Page 325) Circadian rhythms of two subjects living without natural time cues but under the influence of artificial bright light zeitgebers (absolute LD alternations and regular requesting signals) with steadily changing zeitgeber periods. Designations as in Figure 11.

this small difference disappears after sufficient adaptation. With respect to the circadian system, however, there is a fundamental difference between these light intensities which obviously cannot be reduced by adaptation: only the higher intensity of illumination exerts a direct effect upon the circadian system comparable to the effect of light on most animal circadian systems, whereas the slightly lower intensity is nearly ineffective in the direct operation, but is effective only indirectly by behavioral impulses (in the same way as the higher intensity). Differential effects of light must be considered in the search for physiological pathways in the control of the circadian system.

The great widening of the range of entrainment of the temperature rhythm under the bright light zeitgeber does not pertain to the rhythms of all variables; rather, under this zeitgeber, the rhythms of special variables break away from the zeitgeber and run desynchronized from other rhythms within the duration of the experiments, as exemplified by urinary excretions of certain electrolytes in several experiments. Separation of different psychological variables are of special interest in the context of this paper. For example, Figure 19 presents the results of an experiment under the bright light zeitgeber where the rhythm of rectal temperature is synchronized externally throughout the entire experiment. In addition, results of two apparently similar performance tests are included (Search And Memory test; Folkard, Wever and Wildgruber, 1983); in SAM1, one letter is given for every line which has to be cancelled out in the subsequent line of random letters; and in SAM5, five different letters have to be stored in the memory and then cancelled out in the following line. While SAM1 tests perceptual performance, SAM5 is memory-loaded and, hence, tests cognitive performance. As the result of the experiment underlying Figure 19 (and of several more experiments of similar types), SAM1 always ran in synchrony to body temperature and, hence, to sleep/wake and the zeitgeber, while SAM5 broke away from the zeitgeber (and, thus, also from the temperature rhythm) at a period of about 27 h, and started to free-run. The period of the free-running and separated rhythm of this variable (both here and, in all similar experiments) was, unusually short (21.5 h), and not comparable to any known physiological rhythm.

The search for a physiological correlate to the rhythm of memory-loaded performance must be continued. Thus, internal

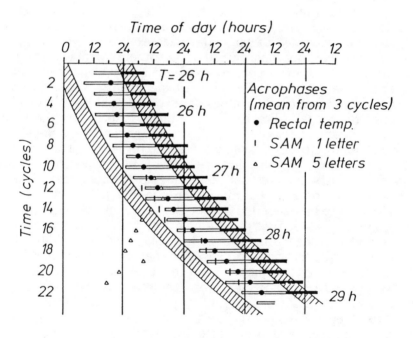

Figure 19

Legend for Figure 19 (On Page 328) Circadian rhythm of a subject living without natural time cues but under the influence of an artificial bright light zeitgeber (absolute LD alternation and regular requesting signals) with steadily lengthening zeitgeber period. Indicated are the acrophases (maximum of the best fitting sine wave) of rectal temperature and two different performance tasks, without (SAM 1) and with (SAM 5) a memory load.

desynchronization between different performance rhythms was shown indicating that the multi-oscillatory character of the human circadian system must be extended from physiological to psychological functions (Folkard, Wever and Wildgruber, 1983). In addition, there cannot be a functional interdependence between the different types of performance, with and without participation of the memory. And finally, if the two performances could be separated from each other, it is possible that two other pairs of psychological items such as differing types of subjective rating (e.g., mood and impulse) might be separated from each other in time, and their mutual functional independence be shown. It is still an open question whether or not the tendency towards such a separation is correlated to any personality data, or even to specific diseases.

Weak Electric Field

Finally, another type of zeitgeber should be mentioned briefly: a periodically switched weak electric AC field (10 Hz square wave, 2.5 V/m). Such a field has been shown previously to be effective when operating continuously. If such a field is switched on and off alternatingly with periods between 23.5 and 26.0 h, it has the capacity of synchronizing human circadian rhythms, at least temporarily. Proper analyses of 10 experiments result in a range of entrainment of about ± 1 h (Wever, 1979a, 1985); i.e., the strength of this zeitgeber is just at the limit where human rhythms with intrinsic periods close to 25 h can be synchronized to the natural 24-h day. On the other hand, it is remarkable that such an imperceptible zeitgeber is almost twice as strong as an easily perceptible LD zeitgeber (as long as the intensity of illumination during the light phase does not exceed the normal range of artificial illumination at about 1,000 lux). It is not very likely (but not out of the question) that such a field zeitgeber will have as practical an importance as bright light or social contacts; the discovery of the effectiveness of such a field zeitgeber, however, will certainly have an important theoretical value.

Conclusions

In summarizing the inspection of all those periodically operating stimuli having the capability to act as zeitgebers, it can be deduced that all those stimuli which can modify free–running rhythms when operating continuously under constant conditions can act as zeitgebers when operating periodically and vice versa. This experimental result is not a theoretical necessity. Rather, models are under discussion where stimuli having the capability of acting as zeitgebers are unable to modify free–running rhythms (and where stimuli having the capability of modifying parameters of free running rhythms are unable to act as zeitgebers). Such concepts, however, are not in agreement with the experimental results discussed in this paper (Wever, 1982a). The discovery of the identity of stimuli releasing the two different effects gives relevant insight into the dynamics of the human circadian system. It is a logical necessity of every model that every stimulus that can act as a zeitgeber, when given periodically, releases a phase shift of the rhythm when given solitarily, and that the direction and amount of the phase shift depends on the phase of the rhythm affected by the stimulus. A "phase response curve", therefore, may very well supplement other findings, but it cannot give independent insight, as it is only a trivial consequence of zeitgeber effectiveness.

Endogenously generated circadian rhythmicity can be controlled externally by stimuli as various as bright light, social contacts, and very weak and imperceptible electromagnetic fields, and in identical manner. Currently, no stimulus is known which controls different overt rhythms within the human multi–oscillator system in another manner (Wever, 1975a); apparent differences could be shown to be due to the varying oscillatory strengths of underlying oscillators (and hence, ranges of entrainment of different widths) or to accidentally different states of the different rhythms. Merely the diversity in the stimuli releasing the same reactions suggests a joint direct influence upon the circadian system, e.g., via an unspecific stimulation. This would mean that all different types of effective stimuli give rise to an identical stimulation of the organism, and that the level of stimulation influences the circadian system directly. Such an unspecific stimulation can be realized in the circadian system; there should be a "missing link" that is produced by all effective external stimuli equivalently, and that should release the unspecific stimulation, or the "activation" (possibly of the cell membranes), directly. Very speculatively one may identify this missing link as hydrogen peroxide; very small doses of H_2O_2 produced by the input of any form of energy (e.g., electromagnetic fields) into water containing oxygen have been shown to affect the circadian systems of several animal species in the same way as weak electromagnetic fields or light do (Wever, 1985e). Surely, the hypothesis of the possible existence of a missing link summarizing all effective stimuli of natural origin, cannot exclude a separate effectiveness of stimuli of unnatural origin like drugs or poison (e.g., lithium as effective in one direction, and rubidium as effective in the other direction) on the pacemaker. If the hypothesis can be confirmed and H_2O_2 really is the missing link with regard to the circadian pacemaker, it should be able to substitute for the external stimuli mentioned with regard to other effects upon the activation of the organism. Moreover, in this case an opposite effect to that of H_2O_2 (i.e., a deactivation of the organism) should be caused by the well known enzymes deforming H_2O_2 (e.g., peroxidase or catalase).

GENERAL CONCLUSIONS

From the discussed results, several generalizations concerning human circadian rhythms can be deduced:

Multi–Oscillatory Rhythm Generation

Circadian rhythms are generated endogenously. Most of the natural and experimental observations can be defined by one single rhythmicity. In a considerable number of experiments, however, the assumption of one single circadian oscillator is insufficient to characterize the observations and, hence, must be expanded to a system of several mutually interacting oscillators; in several cases, these different oscillators can be seen to lose their synchrony. Consequently, a more general concept is a multi-oscillator system governing the circadian variations of a great multiplicity of physiological and psychological variables. Every basic oscillator controls a variety of overt rhythms, possibly all rhythms, though with very different weights. In return, every overt rhythm is controlled by several, possibly by all, different basic oscillators simultaneously, but again in very different proportions. The degree to which different basic oscillators contribute control of an overt rhythm varies considerably from variable to variable, and differs slightly from subject to subject, even from one experimental condition to the next.

The number of basic oscillators which are actually in operation, and the relations between these oscillators, are not fixed quantities. As mentioned above, in the majority of observations the assumption of a one-oscillator system is sufficient. In most of the remaining cases, a two-oscillator system with defined mutual relations leads to an appropriate description of various experimental findings; the strengths of the two involved basic oscillators are in a ratio which is often close to 1:12. The stronger oscillator (type I; Wever, 1975a, 1979a) is characterized by its dominant control of the overt rhythm of body temperature, and the weaker oscillator (type II) is characterized by its dominant control of the sleep/wake rhythm. Finally, several experimental findings compel the assumption of three or even four basic oscillators participating in the control of the circadian system (Wever, 1979a); consistent findings show the dominant control of special psychological rhythms (controlling memory-loaded performances; cf. Figure 19) by a basic oscillator which is different from type I and type II (Folkard, Wever and Wildgruber, 1983). It is unreasonable to assume a number of participating basic oscillators considerably larger than four, because basic oscillators can exist concurrently only if there are intervals of a few hours between their intrinsic periods (otherwise they would synchronize each other), so that a limited number of separated oscillators can be present within the circadian range simultaneously.

The abstract multi-oscillator model can be transferred hypothetically into a structural model (Wever, 1979a). Virtually, every single cell has the capacity to operate as an oscillator, or pacemaker, via an internal feedback mechanism, though with tremendously differing strengths in different types of cells. Adjacent cells tend to synchronize each other mutually. If a cluster of mutually synchronized cells is large enough, it constitutes an oscillatory center; the number of cells combined in such a center determines the oscillatory strength of that center. Such an oscillatory center will synchronize more distant cells or organs via neuronal and/or humoral pathways. In a specified organ like the hypothalamus, several oscillatory centers can compete with each other and, hence, constitute a multi-oscillator system. The boundaries between the different oscillatory centers may fluctuate, and adjoining centers may fuse; the oscillatory centers with different intrinsic periods may be conceived as analogous to regions in a solid body with different magnetic orientations. Consequently, a fluctuating equilibrium will develop with the number of oscillators actually present varying from subject to subject and from one experimental condition to another.

Modes of External Rhythm Control

Endogenously generated circadian rhythms are exogenously modified, becoming synchronized to the 24-h day by external zeitgebers. Since the mean value of the intrinsic periods of human circadian rhythms is about 25 h, a steady acceleration of one hour per day is necessary to guarantee this synchronization. In contrast to frequently formulated views, there exists an evolutionary pressure to hold a difference of about an hour between the earth's rotation and the intrinsic circadian period (Wever, 1982b). The biological advantage is an external stability (i.e., a stability in the phase relationship to a zeitgeber) which is greater when there is a difference between zeitgeber period and intrinsic period, than there is when the two exactly coincide. This theoretical prediction had been confirmed experimentally. Although the intrinsic period cannot be changed, the period of an artificial zeitgeber can. The phase of the temperature rhythm (with an intrinsic period of about 25 h) relative to a synchronizing zeitgeber is less stable in an artificial 25-h day than in a 24-h or 26-h day, at least concerning the temperature minimum during sleep (Wever, 1981). It is remarkable that this maximum in external stability coincides with the maximum in internal stability (see above). In other words, a 24-h rhythm is most stable externally relative to the zeitgeber as well as internally concerning the phase relationships among different overt rhythms, when its intrinsic period is close to 25 h; and both stabilities are reduced the more the intrinsic period deviates in either direction from 25 h.

Another expression of the common deviation of the intrinsic period from 24 h states that the phase control of circadian rhythms by the natural 24-h zeitgeber operates with bias tension, as all biological control systems do. With such a bias tension, any disturbances are restored more quickly than when the system rests in an indifferent equilibrium. Whether the continuous tension of the circadian system, which is certainly advantageous in the rhythm control of healthy subjects, is still advantageous in patients who are disordered in any way remains a question. The continuous pressure of about one hour per day may be overstressing in such patients and, hence, it may be helpful to expose them to conditions where the intrinsic and the zeitgeber period are closer together or even coinciding. The disadvantage of a less stable phase position, then, may be overridden by the advantage gained from the loss of continuous pressure.

The zeitgeber action causing the steady phase shift of an hour per day (on average) is mediated by periodic stimuli of various modalities, i.e., by zeitgebers. It is of theoretical interest that so diverse stimuli (for instance, bright light, social contacts and very weak electromagnetic fields) are effective. As has been mentioned previously, it is just this diversity which may open a view to the physiological pathways in the control of circadian rhythmicity, possibly assuming that these pathways are valid, not only in the control but also in the generation of circadian rhythms. The modalities of effective zeitgebers and their relations are of practical importance, particularly in the consideration of rhythm disorders: several rhythm disorders are based on zeitgebers which are too weak for a complete synchronization of rhythms, the correction of which is possible only by strengthening the overall zeitgeber effectiveness.

The only zeitgebers which are relevant in controlling circadian rhythms under normal conditions are social contacts and bright light. The effects of bright light have been discovered only recently (Wever, Polasek and Wildgruber, 1983) since they can now be attained with artificial illumination. An exposure of at least three hours' duration per day in light of an intensity of at least 3,000 lux appears to be necessary to muster the zeitgeber effects. Indoors, the intensity of illumination commonly remains far below this value. Consequently, the bright light zeitgeber remains irrelevant for a considerable segment of the population in modern industrial societies.

In healthy subjects with appropriate social contacts, the social zeitgeber is always sufficiently effective. Patients with various disorders, particularly with those of mental origin, however, may suffer from a want of social associations. In old age, the deprivation from social contacts is the most serious psychological problem; the internal stability of the rhythms is reduced, as expressed in a considerable increase in the tendency toward internal desynchronization (see above). In these cases the effectiveness of the social zeitgebers becomes reduced, and eventually becomes ineffective for complete external synchronization of the circadian system. Thus, the psychological problem of social impoverishment acquires a physiological dimension. According to several animal experiments, the danger of this occurring in old age increases because the rhythm disorders which may be consequences of aging problems themselves accelerate the aging process, so that a vicious circle arises (Wever, 1979a).

If the strengthening of social zeitgebers is not practicable, the bright light zeitgeber must be activated. As far as can be determined from preliminary experiments, its effectiveness is independent of the age of the subjects. Problematically, those patients who suffer from a lack of social contacts are frequently restricted to bedrest or, at least, must usually remain indoors. Rhythm therapy would then attempt to bring these patients outdoors into bright sunshine, if at all practicable. If outdoor activities are not practicable, bright indoor illumination should be arranged, either by light from large windows, or by extensive artificial illumination; modern techniques enable daylight-like illumination within whole rooms.

     As a stimulus controlling human circadian rhythms light is
effective only when its intensity is above a threshold at about
2,000 lux to 3,000 lux. Such a threshold in light intensity was first
discovered in the suppression of melatonin secretion (Lewy, et al.,
1980). It is not yet known with certainty but it is very likely that
both these thresholds have the same meaning for rhythm control
and melatonin suppression. Suppression of melatonin secretion also
occurs under specific zeitgeber conditions (synchronization close to
the limit of entrainment; cf. Figure 15) without any participation
of light. Finally, the application of bright light has been shown to
be an effective therapy for certain types of depression [seasonal
affective disorders (Lewy, et al., 1982; Rosenthal, et al., 1984)];
the existence or even the position of an intensity threshold for this
effect has not yet been systematically investigated. Consequently,
it is still unclear whether or not the antidepressive effect of bright
light is related to the effectiveness of bright light in circadian
rhythmicity; however, it cannot be ruled out that the antidepressive effect is directly caused by zeitgeber effect.

The Meaning of the Rhythm's Amplitude

     The amplitude of circadian rhythms has been shown to be the
most relevant parameter of these rhythms. The period is in the
foreground of discussions in most circadian investigations,
particularly in animal experiments. Firstly, the period is more
precisely measurable; all other parameters, including the
amplitude, show much larger intra- and inter-individual variations. Secondly and most importantly, if it is accepted that only
observable overt rhythms are coupled to the hypothetically
underlying oscillators to which oscillation laws are applicable, and
that, by intermediated delaying processes, the period is the only
parameter of the overt rhythm which reflects unambiguously the
corresponding parameter of the basic oscillator, then amplitude
and all other parameters are likely to be changed by the coupling
processes.

     However, the applicability of various oscillation laws to
parameters of overt rhythms beyond the period, and particularly to
the amplitude (see above), shows that the participation of the
intermediated coupling processes mentioned are unlikely to cause

false conclusions to be drawn when parameters of the overt rhythms are used to infer corresponding parameters of the basic oscillators; the coupling processes are either negligible, or they are, indeed, of a pronounced quality but only slightly variable and independent of the environmental conditions. The observation that the amplitude of the temperature rhythm is highly correlated to the sleep fraction within the sleep/wake rhythm (cf. Figure 4, left) is an indicator that the amplitude of the underlying sleep/wake oscillator, establishes equivalent alterations in the amplitudes of different oscillators within the multi–oscillator system. In summary, the measured amplitude of an overt rhythm is related to the amplitude of the underlying basic oscillator by processes which are, on principle, not exactly known, but our absence of knowledge regarding these processes no longer supplies a hindrance to applying this amplitude measure in theory development.

The amplitude of a rhythm determines its internal stability. The larger the amplitude the smaller is the cycle–to–cycle variability of the rhythm (cf. Figure 4, right), and also, the more rigid is the rhythm against external, irregular or even regular disorders (e.g., phase shifts of the zeitgeber; Wever, 1980a). Moreover, the amplitude determines the internal stability of the multi–oscillator system. The larger the amplitude the stronger is the internal interaction between different oscillators within the system and, hence, the smaller is the tendency toward the spontaneous occurrence of internal desynchronization. Consequently, the internal rhythm stability is larger in male than in (younger) female subjects (post–menopausal females show the same higher internal stability as males).

There are various indications that depressives display reduced body temperature rhythm amplitude (Lund, Kammersloher and Dirlich, 1983; Figure 20). It is likely, therefore, that the higher incidence of depression in women is related to the sex difference in amplitude; also the lower incidence of depression in post– than in pre–menopausal women, with the incidence in post–menopausal women corresponding to that in men, supports the idea. Moreover, behavioral stress seems to reduce the rhythm's amplitude, concurrently with the lengthening of the period (Wever, 1979a).

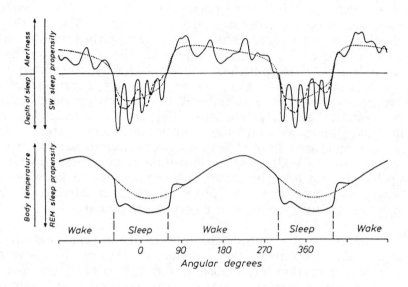

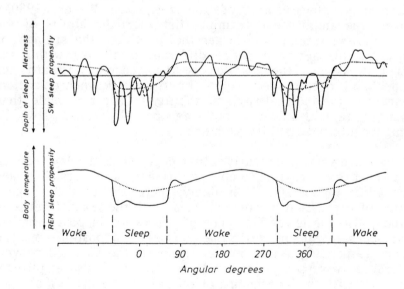

Figure 20

<u>Legend for Figure 20</u> (On Page 338) Computer simulations applying an established mathematical model (Wever, 1964, 1984a, 1985d), demonstrating the interaction between circadian and ultradian systems. The upper diagram of every part shows the "sleep-wake oscillation" which is divided by a threshold in "wake" (above the threshold) and "sleep" (below the threshold). Dotted line: undisturbed circadian sleep-wake oscillation; solid line: sleep-wake oscillation with superimposed random noise and a self-sustained ultradian oscillation; broken line: sleep-wake oscillation with superimposed random noise only (during wake identical with the solid line). The lower diagram of every part shows the circadian "body temperature oscillation" with (solid line) and without (dotted line) consideration of the masking effect (from sleep-wake to body temperature). The upper part may serve as a model of healthy subjects. The lower part shows the model after halving the circadian amplitudes of both oscillations but superimposing the same random noise and the same contribution of the ultradian system as above (upper diagram) and considering the same masking effect as above (lower diagram); this modification may serve as a model of disordered patients.

REFERENCES

Arendt, J., C. Bojkowski, C. Franey, J. Wright and V. Marks. 1985. Immunoassay of 6-hydroxymelatonin sulphate in human plasma and urine: abolition of the urinary rhythm with atenolol. J Clin Endocrin Metab 60:1166–1172.

Aschoff, J. 1985. On the perception of time during prolonged temporal isolation. Hum Neurobiol 4:41–52.

Aschoff, J., U. Gerecke and R. Wever. 1967. Desynchronization of human circadian rhythms. Jpn J Physiol 17:450–457.

Aschoff, J., U.V. Saint Paul and R. Wever. 1968. Circadiane Periodik von Finkenvogeln unter dem Einfluß eines selbst-gewahlten Licht–Dunkel–Wechsels. Z Vgl Physiol 58:304–321.

Aschoff, J., R. Wever, C. Wildgruber and A. Wirz–Justice. 1984. Circadian control of meal timing during temporal isolation. Naturwissenschaften 71:534–535.

Borbély, A.A. 1984. Sleep regulation: outline of a model and its implications for depression. In Sleep Mechanisms (Experimental Brain Research, Supplementum 8), Borbély, A.A. and J.-L. Valatx (eds.). Berlin: Springer–Verlag, pp. 272–284.

Czeisler, C.A. 1978. Human circadian physiology: internal organization of temperature, sleep–wake and neuroendocrine rhythms monitored in an environment free of time cues. (Doctoral dissertation, Stanford University.) Palo Alto: University Microfilms (No. 79–05, 838).

Czeisler, C.A., J.C. Zimmerman, J.M. Ronda, M.C. Moore–Ede and E.D. Weitzman. 1980. Timing of REM sleep is coupled to the circadian rhythm of body temperature in man. Sleep 2:329–346.

Czeisler, C.A., G.S. Richardson, J.C. Zimmerman, M.C. Moore–Ede and E.D. Weitzman. 1981. Entrainment of human circadian rhythms by light–dark cycles: a reassessment. Photochem Photobio 134:239–247.

Folkard, S., R.A. Wever and C.M. Wildgruber. 1983. Multioscillatory control of circadian rhythms in human performance. Nature 305:223–225.

Lewy, A.J., T.A. Wehr, F.K. Goodwin, D.A. Newsome and S.P. Markey. 1980. Light suppresses melatonin secretion in humans. Science 210:1267–1269.

Lewy, A.J., H.E. Kern, N.E. Rosenthal and T.A. Wehr. 1982. Bright artificial light treatment of a manic–depressive patient with a seasonal mood cycle. Am J Psychiatr 139:1496–1498.

Lund, R. 1974. Personality factors and desynchronization of circadian rhythms. Psychosom Med 36:224–228.

Lund, R., A. Kammersloher and G. Dirlich. 1983. Body temperature in endogenously depressed patients during depression and remission. In Circadian Rhythms in Psychiatry, Wehr, T.A. and F.K. Goodwin (eds.). Pacific Grove: Boxwood Press, pp. 77–88.

Rosenthal, N.E., D.A. Sack, J.C. Gillin, A.J. Lewy, F.K. Goodwin, Y. Davenport, P.S. Mueller, D.A. Newsome and T.A. Wehr. 1984. Seasonal affective disorder: a description of a syndrome and preliminary findings with light therapy. Arch Gen Psychiatr 41:72–80.

Turek, F.W. and E. Gwinner. 1982. Role of hormones in the circadian organization of vertebrates. In Vertebrate Circadian Systems: Structure and Physiology (Papers Presented at a Meeting Held in October 1980 at Schloss Ringberg), Aschoff, J., S. Daan and G.A. Groos (eds.). Berlin: Springer–Verlag, pp. 173–182.

Wever, R. 1963. Zum Mechanismus der biologischen 24–Stunden–Periodik. II. Mitteilung: Der Einfluß des Gleichwertes auf die Eigenschaften selbsterregter Schwingungen. Kybernetik 1:213–231.

Wever, R. 1967. Uber die Beeinflußung der circadianen Periodik des Menschen durch schwache elektromagnetische Felder. Z Vgl Physiol 56:111–128.

Wever, R. 1968a. Gesetzmäßigkeiten der circadianen Periodik des Menschen, gepruft an der Wirkung eines schwachen elektrischen Wechselfelds. Pflugers Arch 302:97–112.

Wever, R. 1969. Autonome circadiane Periodik des Menschen unter dem Einfluß verschiedener Beleuchtungs–Bedingungen. Pflugers Arch 306:71–91.

Wever, R. 1970a. Die gegenseitige Kopplung zwischen den circadianen Periodizitaten verschiedener vegetative Funktionen beim Menschen. Pflugers Arch 319:122.

Wever, R. 1970b. Zur Zeitgeber–Starke eines Licht–Dunkel– Wechsels fur die circadiane Periodik des Menschen. Pflugers Arch 321:133–142.

Wever, R. 1971. Influence of electric fields on some parameters of circadian rhythms in man. In Biochronometry: Proceedings of a Symposium (Friday Harbor, Washington; 1969), Menaker, M. (ed.). Washington, D.C.: National Academy of Sciences, pp. 117–133.

Wever, R. 1973. Der Einfluß des Lichtes auf die circadiane Periodik des Menschen. I. Einfluß auf die autonome Periodik. Z Phys Med 3:121–134.

Wever, R. 1974a. The influence of self–controlled changes in ambient temperature on autonomous circadian rhythms in man. Pflugers Arch 352:257–266.

Wever, R. 1974b. Der Einfluß des Lichtes auf die circadiane Periodik des Menschen. II. Zeitgeber–Einfluß. Z Phys Med 3:137–150.

Wever, R. 1975a. The circadian multi–oscillator system of man. Int J Chronobiol 3:19–55.

Wever, R. 1975b. Autonomous circadian rhythms in man: singly versus collectively isolated subjects. Naturwissenschaften 62:443–444.

Wever, R. 1975c. Die Bedeutung der circadianen Periodik fur den alternden Menschen. Verh Dtsch Ges Pathol 59:160–180.

Wever, R. 1978. Grundlagen der Tagesperiodik beim Menschen. In Rhythmusprobleme in der Psychiatrie (Aktuelle Psychiatrie, Bd. 1), Engelmann, von W., Heimann, von H. Heimann and B. Pflug (eds.). Stuttgart: Fischer, pp. 1–23.

Wever, R.A. 1979a. The Circadian System of Man: Results of Experiments Under Temporal Isolation. New York: Springer-Verlag.

Wever, R.A. 1979b. Influence of physical workload on free-running circadian rhythms in man. Pflugers Arch 381:119–126.

Wever, R.A. 1980a. Phase shifts of human circadian rhythms due to shifts of artificial zeitgebers. Chronobiologia 7:303–327.

Wever, R.A. 1980b. Circadian-rhythms of finches under bright light: is self-sustainment a pre-condition for circadian rhythmicity? J Comp Physiol 139:48–58.

Wever, R.A. 1981. On varying work-sleep schedules: the biological rhythm perspective. In Biological Rhythms, Sleep and Shift Work, Johnson, L.C., D.I. Tepas, W.P. Colquhoun and M.C. Colligan (eds.). New York: Spectrum Publications, pp. 35–60.

Wever, R.A. 1982a. Commentary on the mathematical model of the human circadian system by Kronauer, et al. Am J Physiol 242:R17–R21.

Wever, R.A. 1982b. Behavioral aspects of circadian rhythmicity. In Rhythmic Aspects of Behavior. Brown, F.M. and R.C. Graeber (eds.). Hillsdale: L. Erlbaum Associates, Inc., pp. 105–171.

Wever, R.A. 1983a. Organization of the human circadian system: internal interactions. In Circadian Rhythms in Psychiatry, Wehr, T.A. and F.K. Goodwin (eds.). Pacific Grove: Boxwood Press, pp. 17–32.

Wever, R.A. 1983b. Fractional desynchronization of human circadian rhythms: a method for evaluating entrainment limits and functional interdependencies. Pflugers Arch 396:128–137.

Wever, R.A. 1984a. Toward a mathematical model of circadian rhythmicity. In Mathematical Models of the Circadian Sleep–Wake Cycle. Moore–Ede, M.C. and C.A. Czeisler (eds.). New York: Raven Press, pp. 17–79.

Wever, R.A. 1984b. Properties of human sleep–wake cycles: Parameters of internally synchronized free–running rhythms. Sleep 7:27–51.

Wever, R.A. 1984c. Sex differences in human circadian rhythms: intrinsic periods and sleep fractions. Experientia 40:1226–1234.

Wever, R.A. 1985a. Internal interactions within the human circadian system: the masking effect. Experientia 41:332–342.

Wever, R.A. 1985b. Circadian aspects of sleep. In Methods of Sleep Research. Kubicki, S. and W.M. Herrmann (eds.). Stuttgart: Fischer–Verlag, pp. 119–151.

Wever, R.A. 1985c. Use of light to treat jet–lag: differential effects of normal and bright artificial light on human circadian rhythms. In The Medical and Biological Effects of Light [Based on the Conference of the Medical and Biological Effects of Light, New York City, October–November 1984 (Annals of the New York Academy of Sciences, Volume 453)], Wurtman, R.J., M.J. Baum and J.T. Potts, Jr. (eds.). New York City: New York Academy of Sciences Press, pp. 282–304.

Wever, R.A. 1985d. Modes of interaction between ultradian and circadian rhythms: toward a mathematical model of sleep. In Ultradian Rhythms in Physiology and Behavior (Experimental Brain Research, Supplementum 12), Schulz, H. and P. Lavie (eds.). Berlin: Springer–Verlag, pp. 309–317.

Wever, R.A. 1985e. The electromagnetic environment and the circadian rhythms of human subjects. In Biological Effects and Dosimetry of Static and ELF Electromagnetic Fields. Grandolfo, M., S.M. Michaelson and A. Rindi. New York: Plenum Press, pp. 477–523.

Wever, R.A. 1986. Characteristics of circadian rhythms in human functions. In Melatonin in Humans: Proceedings of the First International Conference on Melatonin in Humans (Vienna, November 1985), Wurtman, R.J. and F. Waldhauser (eds.). Vienna: Springer–Verlag.

Wever, R.A., J. Polasek and C.M. Wildgruber. 1983. Bright light affects human circadian rhythms. Pflugers Arch 396:85–87.

Wirz–Justice, A., R.A. Wever and J. Aschoff. 1984. Seasonality in free–running circadian rhythms in man. Naturwissenschaften 71:316–319.

Zulley, J. 1976. Schlaf und Temperatur unter freilaufenden Bedingungen. Ber Dtsch Ges Psychol 30:398–399.

Zulley, J. 1979. Der Einfluß von Zeitgebern auf den Schlaf des Menschen. (Doctoral dissertation, Universitat Tübingen.) Frankfurt am Main: Rita Fischer–Verlag.

Zulley, J. and H. Schulz. 1980. Sleep and body temperature in free–running sleep–wake cycles. In Sleep 1978: Sleep Onset, Pathology of Child, Sleep and Coma, Hypophyseal Secretions and Sleep, Idiopathic Hypersomnia, Neurophysiology, Pharmacology, Methodology, Psychology and Psychiatry (Proceedings of the Fourth European Congress on Sleep Research; Tîrgu–Mures, Romania; September 1978), Popoviciu, L., B. Asgian and G. Badiu (eds.). Basel: S. Karger, A.G., pp. 341–344.

Zulley, J., R. Wever and J. Aschoff. 1981. The dependence of onset and duration of sleep on the circadian rhythm of rectal temperature. Pflugers Arch 391:314–318.

Zulley, J. and R.A. Wever. 1982. Interaction between the sleep–awake cycle and the rhythm of rectal temperature. In Vertebrate Circadian Systems: Structure and Physiology (Papers Presented at a Meeting Held in October 1980 at Schloss Ringberg), Aschoff, J., S. Daan and G.A. Groos (eds.). Berlin: Springer–Verlag, pp. 253–261.

Zulley, J. and S.S. Campbell. 1985. Napping behavior during "spontaneous internal desynchronization": sleep remains in synchrony with body temperature. Hum Neurobiol 4:123–126.

INDEX